DIGNITY MATTERS

DIGNITY MATTERS
Psychoanalytic and Psychosocial Perspectives

Edited by
Susan S. Levine

Routledge
Taylor & Francis Group

LONDON AND NEW YORK

First published 2016 by
Karnac Books Ltd.

Published 2018 by Routledge
2 Park Square, Milton Park, Abingdon, Oxon OX14 4RN
711 Third Avenue, New York, NY 10017, USA

Routledge is an imprint of the Taylor & Francis Group, an informa business

British Library Cataloguing in Publication Data

A C.I.P. for this book is available from the British Library

ISBN-13: 9781782202158 (pbk)

Typeset by Medlar Publishing Solutions Pvt Ltd, India

CONTENTS

ACKNOWLEDGEMENTS

I would like to express gratitude to the *International Journal of Psychoanalysis* for permission to use my paper originally published there as "Means and ends in Hitchcock's *Vertigo*, or Kant you see?" (*96*: 225–237 (2015)).

My thanks, too, to the *American Journal of Psychoanalysis* and Palgrave Macmillan for kind permission to reprint Salman Akhtar's "Some psychoanalytic reflections on the concept of dignity" (*75*: 244–266 (2015)).

"In Memory of Sigmund Freud", copyright © 1940 and renewed 1968 by W. H. Auden; from *W. H. Auden Collected Poems* by W. H. Auden is used by permission of Random House, an imprint and division of Penguin Random House LLC. All rights reserved. Copyright © 1940 by W. H. Auden, renewed. It is reprinted by permission of Curtis Brown, Ltd.

I would also like to express my appreciation to the Psychoanalytic Center of Philadelphia for allowing the reprinting of "Dignity" by Eli Marcovitz; my sincere thanks, too, to Robert Marcovitz, PsyD, for kindly providing me with biographical information about his late father.

Finally, I would like to express my appreciation to the Bryn Mawr College Library Special Collections for their gracious permission to use the cover image of the figure of Dignity. This emblem, taken from the

1779 book collected by George Richardson, reproduces the original by Cesare Ripa (c. 1600). The description of the figure: "[Dignity] is allegorically characterized by the figure of a woman richly dressed, with a golden chain about her neck. With both hands she supports a stone of an enormous size upon her shoulders, which is adorned with a crown, sceptre, and other valuable ornaments. By her side is placed a chair on the summit of a few steps, as a mark of distinction. The rich dress and golden chain, allude to honours by birth, or those attained by persons in high offices. The enormous stone which this figure is supporting, is allusive to the weight of the important affairs of those persons invested with dignified employments, and the trouble of discharging the duties of their office with honour and decorum."

ABOUT THE CONTRIBUTORS

Salman Akhtar, MD, is Professor of Psychiatry at Jefferson Medical College and a Training and Supervising Analyst at the Psychoanalytic Center of Philadelphia. He has served on the editorial boards of the *International Journal of Psychoanalysis* and the *Journal of the American Psychoanalytic Association*. His more than 300 publications include fifteen books—*Broken Structures (1992)*, *Quest for Answers (1995)*, *Inner Torment* (1999), *Immigration and Identity* (1999), *New Clinical Realms* (2003), *Objects of Our Desire* (2005), *Regarding Others* (2007), *Turning Points in Dynamic Psychotherapy* (2009), *The Damaged Core* (2009), *Comprehensive Dictionary of Psychoanalysis* (2009), *Immigration and Acculturation* (2011), *Matters of Life and Death* (2011), *Psychoanalytic Listening* (2013), *Good Stuff* (2013) and *Sources of Suffering* (2014),—as well as forty-three edited or co-edited volumes in psychiatry and psychoanalysis. Dr. Akhtar is the recipient of the Journal of the American Psychoanalytic Association's Best Paper of the Year Award (1995), the Margaret Mahler Literature Prize (1996), the American Society of Psychoanalytic Physicians' Sigmund Freud Award (2000), the American College of Psychoanalysts' Laughlin Award (2003), the American Psychoanalytic Association's Edith Sabshin Award (2000), Columbia University's Robert Liebert Award for Distinguished Contributions to Applied Psychoanalysis

(2004), the American Psychiatric Association's Kun Po Soo Award (2004), the Irma Bland Award for being the Outstanding Teacher of Psychiatric Residents in the country (2005), and the Nancy Roeske Award (2012). Most recently, he received the Sigourney Award (2013), which is the most prestigious honour in the field of psychoanalysis. Dr. Akhtar has served as the Film Review Editor for the *International Journal of Psychoanalysis*, and is currently serving as the Book Review Editor for the *International Journal of Applied Psychoanalytic Studies*. He has published eight collections of poetry and serves as a Scholar-in-Residence at the Inter-Act Theatre Company in Philadelphia.

Stanley Coen, MD, is a Training and Supervising Analyst and Senior Associate Director for Academic Affairs at the Columbia University Center for Psychoanalytic Training and Research, Clinical Professor of Psychiatry at the Columbia University College of Physicians & Surgeons, and a member of the editorial boards of the *Journal of the American Psychoanalytic Association*, *Journal of Clinical Psychoanalysis*, and the *International Journal of Applied Psychoanalytic Studies*. He chairs the subcommittee on University Forum of the APsaA Program Committee. He is the author of *The Misuse of Persons: Analyzing Pathological Dependency* (1992, The Analytic Press); *Between Author and Reader: A Psychoanalytic Approach to Writing and Reading* (1994, Columbia University Press); and *Affect Intolerance in Patient and Analyst* (2002, Aronson). He has published extensively on problems in clinical psychoanalysis and psychoanalytic literary criticism.

M. Gerard Fromm, PhD, is currently Senior Consultant to the Erikson Institute of the Austen Riggs Center and Assistant Clinical Professor, Yale Child Study Center. He was the first Evelyn Stefansson Nef Director of the Erikson Institute from 2002–2013, and directed the therapeutic community programme at Riggs for many years. Dr. Fromm is certified in psychoanalysis by the American Board of Professional Psychology, is on the faculty of the Massachusetts Institute for Psychoanalysis, and has taught at a number of psychoanalytic institutes, including the Berkshire Psychoanalytic Institute, the Emory Psychoanalytic Institute, and the Chicago Center for Psychoanalysis and the Psychoanalytic Institute of Northern California. He is also Past President of the International Society for the Psychoanalytic Study of Organizations and a past President of the Center for the Study of Groups and Social Systems in Boston, where he served for three years as Director of CSGSS's residential group relations conferences. He has also served on the staff of group relations conferences in the United States, Europe, and Israel, and is a member of the International Dialogue Initiative, which works on the psychodynamics of societal conflict. Dr. Fromm has presented and published widely, including the edited volume, with Bruce L. Smith, PhD, *The Facilitating Environment: Clinical Applications of Winnicott's Theory; Lost in Transmission: Studies of Trauma Across Generations; Taking the Transference, Reaching toward Dreams: Clinical Studies in the Intermediate Area*; and *A Spirit That Impels: Play, Creativity and Psychoanalysis.*

Donna Hicks, PhD, is an Associate at the Weatherhead Center for International Affairs, Harvard University. Dr. Hicks was Deputy Director of the Program on International Conflict Analysis and Resolution (PICAR) at the Weatherhead Center for International Affairs at Harvard University for nine years. She worked extensively on the Israeli/Palestinian conflict and as a member of the third party in numerous unofficial diplomatic efforts. In addition to her work in the Middle East, Dr. Hicks founded and co-directed a ten-year project in Sri Lanka, which brought the Tamil, Sinhalese, and Muslim communities together for dialogue. She has been actively involved with the conflict in Colombia, where she was invited to give workshops and lectures in conflict resolution. For several years, she was involved in a project designed to improve relations between the U.S. and Cuba. Dr. Hicks was a consultant to the British Broadcasting Company where she co-facilitated encounters between victims and perpetrators of the Northern Ireland conflict with Archbishop Desmond Tutu. The encounters were made into three television programmes that were aired throughout the United Kingdom and on BBC World. Dr. Hicks has taught courses in conflict resolution at Harvard, Clark, and Columbia Universities and conducts trainings and educational seminars in the U.S. and abroad on the role dignity plays in healing and reconciling relationships in conflict. She consults to corporations, schools, churches, and non-governmental organisations. She is the author of the book *Dignity: The Essential Role It Plays in Resolving Conflict* (2011, Yale University Press).

Dorothy Evans Holmes, PhD, is Professor Emeritus of Clinical Psychology at The George Washington University where she directed the Professional Psychology Program and Clinic (2005–2011). She is also a

Teaching, Training, and Supervising Analyst emeritus at the Baltimore Washington Institute for Psychoanalysis. She has written extensively on intrapsychic influences of race, gender, and class on the psychoanalytic treatment process. Currently, she serves on the Board of Directors of the National Register of Health Service Psychologists, the Ethics Committee of the American Psychological Association, and the Program Committee of the American Psychoanalytic Association. She has served on the editorial boards of the *International Journal of Psychoanalysis* and the *Journal of the American Psychoanalytic Association*. Dr. Holmes was the 2012 recipient of a Division 39 Career Achievement Award for outstanding contributions to the advancement of women's and racial issues in psychoanalysis, and she was the 2014 Helen Meyers Traveling Psychoanalytic Scholar. Presently, she is in private practice in Bluffton, SC.

Robert Kravis, PsyD, earned his BS in psychology from University of Pennsylvania and his PsyD from Hahnemann Medical University. He is a graduate of the Philadelphia Association of Psychoanalysis in child, adolescent and adult psychoanalysis. He serves as adjunct faculty in the Widener University Graduate Program in Clinical Psychology. Dr. Kravis is on the faculty of the Institute of the Psychoanalytic Center of Philadelphia where he is Co-Director of the Training Program in Child and Adolescent Psychotherapy. He is a consultant to Access Services, Inc. He is in private practice of psychoanalysis, psychotherapy, and supervision of children, adolescents, and adults in Elkins Park, Pennsylvania.

Richard P. Kluft, MD, PhD, practices psychiatry, psychoanalysis, and medical hypnosis in Bala Cynwyd, PA. Clinical Professor of Psychiatry at Temple University School of Medicine, he also serves on the faculties of the Psychoanalytic Center of Philadelphia and the China America Psychoanalytic Association. Dr. Kluft has authored over 250 scientific papers and book chapters. He edited *Childhood Antecedents of Multiple Personality*, *Treating Victims of Sexual Abuse*, and *Incest-Related Syndromes of Adult Psychopathology*. He and Catherine G. Fine, PhD, co-edited *Clinical Perspectives on Multiple Personality Disorder*. His book, *Shelter from the Storm* (2013), won the 2013 Written Media Award of the International Society for the Study of Trauma and Dissociation. Former Editor-in-Chief of the journal *DISSOCIATION*, he currently serves on the editorial staff of the *International Journal of Clinical & Experimental Hypnosis* and the *American Journal of Clinical Hypnosis*. Dr. Kluft has presented and taught in thirteen nations. He was co-founder and an early President of the International Society for the Study of Trauma and Dissociation. He also served as President of the American Society of Clinical Hypnosis and the Society for Clinical and Experimental Hypnosis. Recognitions include four Erickson Awards for the best paper of the year from the *American Journal of Clinical Hypnosis*. He directed the Dissociative Disorders Program at The Institute of the Pennsylvania Hospital for eight years. Dr. Kluft served as a consultant to Showtime's series, "The United States of Tara", and was featured in the Showtime documentary, "What Is DID? With Richard P. Kluft, MD", which won the 2009 Media Award of the International Society for the Study of Trauma and Dissociation. His novel, *Good Shrink/Bad Shrink*, and his novella, *How Fievel Stole the Moon: A Tale for Sweet Children and Sour Scholars*, were published in 2014.

Susan S. Levine, LCSW, BCD, is in the private practice of psychoanalysis, psychotherapy, and clinical supervision in Ardmore, Pennsylvania; she also offers writing consultations for clinicians. She is on the faculty of the Institute of the Psychoanalytic Center of Philadelphia and of the Center for Psychoanalysis in the Department of Psychiatry at Albert Einstein Medical Center. She earned her graduate degree from the Bryn Mawr College Graduate School of Social Work and Social Research, studied psychoanalytic psychotherapy at the Philadelphia Psychoanalytic Institute, and completed psychoanalytic training at the Institute of the Psychoanalytic Center of Philadelphia. She has been a faculty member in the graduate programs at Bryn Mawr College and Widener University. A former editorial associate and a current editorial reader at the *International Journal of Psychoanalysis*, she is on the editorial board of the *Clinical Social Work Journal*. She has published *Useful Servants: Psychodynamic Approaches to Clinical Practice* (Aronson, 1996) and *Loving Psychoanalysis: Technique and Theory in the Therapeutic Relationship* (Aronson, 2009), which was a finalist for the Gradiva Award for best clinical book.

Eli Marcovitz, MD, was born and raised in Boston and attended high school in Montreal. He graduated from University of Pennsylvania and then attended Tufts Medical School. He did two residencies, at the Institute of Pennsylvania Hospital in neuro-pathology and then at the New York Neurological Institute. After practicing psychiatry and neurology in several Philadelphia Hospitals, he enlisted in the Air Force in 1942, going in as a captain. He served mainly in March Field CA where his interest in psychoanalysis may have begun. He became friendly there with Otto Fenichel and his wife (also a psychoanalyst). After leaving the Air Force as a major, he returned to Philadelphia and completed psychoanalytic training. Robert Waelder was one of his teachers. By the mid-fifties he was a training analyst, having served for some years as chief of the outpatient department at the Philadelphia Psychiatric Center (now Belmont). He was Clinical Professor at Thomas Jefferson University Department of Psychiatry and later a Clinical Professor Emeritus there, where he supervised many psychiatry residents and many local mental health professionals. He was a respected Training and Supervising Analyst at the Philadelphia Association for Psychoanalysis until his death in 1982.

Kenneth A. Richman, PhD, is Professor of Philosophy and Health Care Ethics at MCPHS University (formerly the Massachusetts College of Pharmacy and Health Sciences), Boston. His published work explores the philosophy of medicine and bioethics, including research ethics, as well as early modern philosophy and the philosophy of education; he is the author of *Ethics and the Metaphysics of Medicine* (2004, MIT Press). He chairs the Institutional Review Board for protection of human subjects of research at MCPHS, and has worked with social scientists for over ten years to examine ethics in the practice of community-based research. He earned a B.A. in philosophy from Haverford College and a PhD in philosophy from Rutgers University.

Susan C. Vaughan, MD, was born and raised in Houston, Texas. She is a graduate of Harvard College and Columbia College of Physicians and Surgeons. She remained at Columbia for her psychiatric residency, chief residency, psychoanalytic training, and a research fellowship in affective and anxiety disorders and is now an Assistant Professor of Psychiatry and on the faculty of Columbia Center for Psychoanalytic Training and Research. She has written two books, *The Talking Cure: The Science Behind Psychotherapy* (1998) and *Half Empty, Half Full: Understanding the Psychological Roots of Optimism* (2000). She is the Past Chair of the Committee on Sexuality and Gender of the American Psychoanalytic Association. She is the recipient of the John J. Weber prize for research, the Alexander Beller Award for writing, and the Howard Klan teaching award for teaching at Columbia. She is especially interested in gender and sexuality, work with dreams, and the psychoanalytic process. She lives with her wife Deborah and her two daughters Savannah and Whittier in New York City where she maintains a private practice in psychiatry and psychoanalysis.

INTRODUCTION

Susan S. Levine

Dignity matters.

As Justice Potter Stewart famously said of hard core pornography, "I shall not today attempt further to define the kinds of material I understand to be embraced within that shorthand description; and perhaps I could never succeed in intelligibly doing so. But I know it when I see it ..." Likewise with dignity—we know it when we see it, or we think that we do. A search of the thesaurus yields the following list of synonyms for dignity: self-respect, self-regard, self-worth, self-esteem, pride, formality, gravitas, bearing, mien, comportment, elegance, poise, status, nobility, prestige, lordliness. This is quite a range. The shift from one sort of meaning to another is striking. But how many sets of meanings are there? What *is* it that we see when we believe we observe dignity? Psychoanalysts and other mental health professionals have indeed rarely spoken or written about dignity. This book advocates making dignity a standard, routine, and consciously considered factor in our professional interventions with patients and our approaches to our colleagues and our communities.

Before the panel that Kimberlyn Leary and I organised and that I chaired at the January 2014 meetings of the American Psychoanalytic Association, there had been virtually no psychoanalytic consideration of the subject of dignity. The papers by Salman Akhtar and M. Gerard Fromm, as well as an oral version of the essay by Donna Hicks, were presented on that occasion. As of that date, there had been fewer than ten articles with dignity in their title in the PEP database; indeed, Freud himself uses the word just twenty-three times in the *Standard Edition*. Yet professional codes of ethics often cite dignity as an organising principle. The code of ethics of the American Psychoanalytic Association proclaims in its second sentence that "the psychoanalytic relationship is predicated on respecting human dignity".

Our lack of attention to the concept of dignity is rather curious—and potentially dangerous. It appears that the American Psychological Association condoned and even furthered psychologists' involvement in aspects of the torture of terrorism suspects. This would have been in direct violation of APA's ethical principles "A: Beneficence and Nonmaleficence", and "E: Respect for People's Rights and Dignity": "[p]sychologists respect the dignity and worth of all people, and the rights of individuals to privacy, confidentiality, and self-determination" (American Psychological Association, 2010).

When I set out to survey the literature on dignity, I expected a leisurely trip in a glass-bottomed boat on a clear, calm lake; instead, I found myself looking into a murky, turbulent ocean. I learned a great deal from two excellent books on the term "dignity," one by the political philosopher Michael Rosen (2012) and the other by the legal scholar Jeremy Waldron (2012). Just to give a taste of how complex the subject is, these two dignity experts disagree about whether dignity is, or should be, primarily a legal or a moral term. Two other prominent scholars, the bioethicist Ruth Macklin and the psychologist Steven Pinker, have even questioned whether dignity is a useful term at all. Macklin argues that dignity adds nothing to the concept of autonomy, and Pinker calls it a "squishy, subjective notion" (Pinker, cited in Rosen, p. 120).

"When someone's dignity shatters in front of you, it leaves a hole that any feeling heart naturally wants to fill, if only with its own sadness." So writes Supreme Court Justice Sonia Sotomayor in *My Beloved World* as she describes catching shoplifters as a teenage clerk in a Bronx store (2013, p. 95). Clearly, Sotomayor had a highly developed empathy and sensitivity to dignity at a very tender age; indeed, it is not a stretch to say that dignity is a leitmotif of her autobiography. In truth, I cannot think of a more evocative statement of what I feel as I listen to patients tell of the dignity violations they have endured. Listening to reports of dignity violations against (or by) one's patients contributes to the vicarious traumatisation from which clinicians may suffer; we may also be the objects of dignity violations by our patients or colleagues.

To say that empathy is a required capacity for clinicians is nothing new. But I have never heard a colleague or any of my instructors in all my years of graduate and postgraduate training say that a sensitivity to dignity is also essential for the clinician. This volume demonstrates that dignity is a highly salient theoretical and experiential concept. I hope that a consideration of dignity, developmentally and in the contemporaneous functioning of the patient, will become a standard element in our assessment. If we do not do so, we are handicapped in helping patients to understand another dimension of intrapsychic, interpersonal, and moral life in experience-near language. And we need to attend carefully to protecting and enhancing every patient's dignity in each encounter; this is our ethical charge. Clinicians are certainly well aware that our interpretations or confrontations may be narcissistically injurious, and it is commonplace for us to choose our words and our timing with this in mind. However, honouring a patient's dignity provides a less pathological orientation, and does not carry the implication that a patient may be too vulnerable to be able to hear something. We need, too, to consider the dimension of dignity when we write about patients and discuss them with colleagues, supervisors, supervisees, and students.

Just as the world was discomfited by Freud's demonstration that sexuality began rather earlier than anyone had comfortably considered, we may be surprised to discover that a working concept of dignity may exist from quite early in life. A colleague of mine reported on a treatment of a precocious two-year-old who had been brought to her essentially as the result of a dignity violation and its traumatic sequelae. This child, left in the care of a loving and devoted nanny, became ill, and the nanny took his temperature rectally, despite the child's (accurate) protestations that his mother always used an oral thermometer. The child then developed symptoms requiring psychological attention. In the course of the therapy, the child reported having warned the nanny that what she was doing would hurt him for a long time. The child relinquished the worrisome symptom after the nanny apologised for her action; in a joint session she had respectfully listened to the boy describe the traumatic and undignified experience.

This anthology begins with Donna Hicks whose concept of the dignity violation is essential—simple, powerful, evocative. Her essay will serve to introduce and argue for the centrality of dignity in individual and social experience. As Hicks emphasises, dignity is a fundamental and irreducible human need and striving. The achievement and maintenance of dignity spans the human experience. Her contribution, as well as that of Robert Kravis, which addresses dignity in child development, raises the question as to whether dignity might be appropriately considered as a motivational force.

Following the overture that Hicks furnishes, I have arranged the chapters, roughly speaking, from the theoretical to the practical to the applied. Salman Akhtar and Kenneth Richman confront the complexity of the term and offer their own creative and original taxonomies of dignity. Akhtar suggests a categorisation based on his careful reading of the historical and philosophical literature, and then moves on to outline its relevance to the analytic attitude and situation. He brings to bear on this subject his characteristic perspective—comprehensive, poetic, and practical—and Richman brings a philosopher's and medical ethicist's perspective to our subject, offering a creative and original reorganising of the many usages and meanings of the term dignity. He proposes that we regard all forms of dignity as either emanating from the source (*arche*) of being human or as a reflection of our aim (*telos*) in striving for dignified mien or conduct. Richman uses the fictional Sara Crewe (*A Little Princess*), as an exemplar of extraordinary dignity in a child.

In sharp contrast to Sara's dignity even while dressed in rags, the real child described by Robert Kravis had little opportunity to develop a sense of dignity; clothing and modesty practice were central problems in the family. Kravis discusses dignity as linked to but distinct from the concepts of self-esteem and narcissism. If dignity may have its own developmental line, as Kravis suggests, would it not also be appropriate to expect that a successful psychoanalytic treatment ought to repair or restore the development process? In other words, should we add to the assessment of the readiness to terminate treatment the evaluation of whether the patient, child, or adult, is more sensitive to his or her own dignity and to the dignity of others? Should we want and expect to see that the patient treats the analyst or therapist, himself or herself, and others with greater dignity? Richman, in fact, argues this point persuasively. Perhaps this is already part and parcel of the way we understand growth in psychoanalysis, even if we have not articulated it as such.

I am delighted to be able to include Eli Marcovitz's (1966) paper for both its content and its historical status. The first psychoanalytic paper on dignity, it existed in obscurity for several decades. It is both remarkable and also an artifact of its time, showing attitudes and assumptions that are now anathema to the consensus about women's rights. But in this, it serves as an apt lesson that dignity is a moving target, the definition altering as our conception of human rights expands. Although there is far to go, we have come a very long way since Marcovitz wrote in 1966; in that era, it would not have been considered essential to include in a book such as this a chapter addressing the dignity of LGBT persons. We cannot know what human or animal rights we will discover in the future that we are unaware of violating today.

M. Gerard Fromm uses his experience working with individuals, within a therapeutic community, and in the international arena, to call our attention to the importance of dignifying the negative, that is to say, what the individual and society refuse to acknowledge. There is a fundamental moral goodness to psychoanalytic listening and its promotion of a search for truth. Fromm argues that psychoanalytic listening dignifies every aspect of the human mind and the human experience, the ugly as well as the beautiful, and in individuals, families, and groups. As Richman also points out, citing Jonathan Lear, if we do not know ourselves, we cannot live up to the fundamental responsibility of striving for a moral existence.

Susan Vaughan addresses dignity, indignity, and the LGBT experience at a particularly remarkable moment. The U.S. Supreme Court gay marriage decision both mandates and reflects a sea change in the U.S. While there is far to go in according full legal rights to gays, lesbians, and transgender persons, it would have been unimaginable just a few short decades ago for Vaughan to write this essay to a public and professional audience that officially, at least, regarded homosexuality as a diagnosable mental disorder. Both Vaughan and Richard Kluft outline the terrible damage that can occur when significant others or communities deny the reality of an individual's experience. Children whose subjective experience of gender and sexuality falls outside the expectations of their families will not have a language with which to begin to articulate their feelings and thoughts. They are then at risk of having the essential dignity and integrity of their lived experience foreclosed or invalidated. Andrew Solomon, in *Far From the Tree* (2012), has written with great empathy and sympathy about how difficult it can be for parents to acknowledge and support children that they experience as radically different from themselves. But to do so is an essential responsibility of parenthood.

Dorothy Holmes joins Vaughan in urging us to seek the humanity we all share rather than participating in the "othering" that characterises both homophobia and racial prejudice. Holmes analyses the intersection between the social and the intrapsychic through her close parsing of Freud's description of the Acropolis. She demonstrates the unique power of psychoanalysis in its theoretical understanding of how social biases and prejudices and dignity violations become part and parcel of the self. And why clinical psychoanalysis can and should help individuals recognise how they have objectified and othered themselves as well as the objects of their bias. To the extent that we participate in the conscious or unconscious dignity violations of others, we corrode our own dignity and humanity.

The essays by Holmes and Vaughan challenge us to reflect on how rigorous our theories and treatments can possibly be if we do not address the "isms". It is vital to use any aspects of difference between therapist and patient as an entrée into consideration of larger questions of difference in the patient's mind. Just as we do not generally include in our evaluation an assessment of the patient's relationship with money—a crucial matter in our culture and for every individual—so, too, must we encompass the fact that racism, sexism, and other "isms" are part of the texture of every patient's existence. It is especially relevant for patients who may have benefitted from the "isms" in an invisible or passive manner. And we clinicians have the responsibility to understand ourselves thoroughly in regard to these issues.

Richard Kluft expands upon Holmes and Vaughan in arguing that some psychoanalysts and other clinicians do not live up to their own codes of ethics in the way they treat each other and the degree of dignity we accord each other as individuals and as groups. Kluft has found on numerous occasions that colleagues do not respect what could be termed the dignity of facts or the dignity of reality in their rigid adherence to theory. Kravis wonders (personal communication) whether some of the disturbing experiences Kluft reports might be related to the troubling nature of a particular patient population. In other words, the trauma histories can be so disturbing even to other clinicians that there may be an unconscious need to discount not only the message but also the messenger.

My own contribution to this volume offers an example of how a psychoanalyst might apply the idea of dignity to a work of art. I use the Kantian categorical imperative as a lens through which to view one of the greatest films ever made, Alfred Hitchcock's *Vertigo*; I propose that the story of *Vertigo* can be understood as an exchange of dignity violations. Since publishing the paper in the *International Journal of Psychoanalysis* (2015), I have had the benefit of several conversations with colleagues following presentations of the paper, and am pleased to have been able to add some further thoughts in the version that appears here. I hope that the other scholars will see fit to use the concept of dignity in the psychoanalytic exploration of other films and works of art.

Stanley Coen's epilogue provides a rousing coda. He argues passionately for the importance of considering dignity in every aspect of a clinician's work and, indeed, in every aspect of the work of being a human being. He demonstrates in his trademarked manner that both intellect and introspection, erudition and emotion, are indispensible elements of the self-actualised and dignified citizen-psychoanalyst. Coen offers us his self-analysis about writing this essay in his further reflections about the pride, pleasure, shame, and humility of writing and professional achievement. To cite him, that's dignity—the unique dignity of the psychoanalyst.

I hope that *Dignity Matters* will set in motion an unearthing of the subject of dignity in psychoanalytic thinking. There remain unexplored theoretical, clinical, and philosophical debates. For instance, the relationship between dignity and aggression and masochism calls for our attention. So, too, does the curious fact that our notion of dignified behaviour has to do with keeping our human bodies and bodily functions relatively hidden from view; sometimes it involves managing our feelings to keep them far from the surface, too. In other words, what we think of as human dignity relies to a great extent on our regulation of what is most human about us—our instincts and affects. Finally, of course, there remain diverse clinical areas and populations to study. We could all benefit from considerations of dignity as it relates to the elderly and dying, the incarcerated, immigrants, the developmentally challenged, the poor, and to many religious and ethnic minorities. (Solomon's *Far*

From the Tree, while not intended as a study of dignity, nonetheless serves well as an introduction to dignity concerns in the various groups he examines.) Fruitful work could also be done on dignity in teaching, in the workplace, in organisations (especially psychoanalytic ones) and in the political world. Whether we are listening to individuals, families, groups, communities, or nations, dignity must be an essential component of the analytic attitude.

On a personal note, I have found my immersion in what I have come to call "the dignity project" to be uplifting and full of an unusual number of serendipitous events. I keep returning to the phrase "that dignity karma" each time an author has thanked me for the invitation to participate in the original panel presentation or in this book. I do not think it coincidence that the collaboration with each author has been deeply rewarding and pleasurable, co-operative and mutually respectful. Most of all, these discussions were educational, at least for me. I am grateful to each of the contributors—true dignitaries—and to Kimberlyn Leary for the extraordinary conversation from which my interest in dignity emerged. I can only hope that we have been able to convey some of this to you through our words, and that these words will have enhanced your experience of yourself and your compassion for others. Dignity brings good things.

I would like to extend appreciation to Oliver Rathbone, Rod Tweedy, Cecily Blench, and the entire team at Karnac Books. And I will conclude with a note on style—or, really, on the question of enacting dignity in editing at the micro level of letters. Karnac has graciously allowed some inconsistencies of usage. First, with regard to the use of initial capitals in designations of race, I have respected authorial dignity by retaining each contributor's style. Second, I have used the American spellings and initial capitals only for names of certain formal programmes and for the titles of individuals or organisations. Again, I am grateful to Karnac for this courtesy.

References

American Psychological Association (2010). General principles section. In: Ethical Principles of Psychologists and Code of Conduct. http://www.apa.org/ethics/code/index.aspx. Date accessed: 2 May 2015.

Levine, S. S. (2015). Means and ends in Hitchcock's *Vertigo*, or Kant you see? *International Journal of Psychoanalysis, 96*: 225–237.

Marcovitz, E. (1970). Dignity. *The Bulletin of the Philadelphia Association for Psychoanalysis, 20*: 105–116. Reprinted in: M. S. Temeles (Ed.), *Bemoaning the Lost Dream: Collected Papers of Eli Marcovitz, M.D.* Philadelphia: The Philadelphia Association for Psychoanalysis, 1982–1983.

Rosen, M. (2012). *Dignity: Its History and Meaning*. Cambridge: Harvard University Press.

Solomon, A. (2012). *Far From the Tree: Parents, Children, and the Search for Identity.* New York: Scribner.

Sotomayor, S. (2013). *My Beloved World.* New York: Knopf.

Waldron, J. (2012). *Dignity, Rank, and Rights.* Oxford: Oxford University Press.

CHAPTER ONE

A matter of dignity: building human relationships

Donna Hicks

"Treat people as they want to be and you help them become what they are capable of being."

Johann Wolfgang von Goethe

Everyone desires dignity. I believe that along with our survival instincts, it is the single most powerful human force motivating our behaviour. In some cases, I think it is even stronger than our desire for survival. People risk their lives to protect their honour and dignity all the time. You violate people's dignity and you get an instinctive reaction—people feel humiliated and get upset and angry. You violate people's dignity repeatedly and you'll get a divorce or a war or a revolution.

My awareness of the power of dignity came during the last twenty-five years of working as an international conflict resolution professional. I could see a yearning for dignity at the core of all the conflicts I had worked on over the years—Israel/Palestine, Sri Lanka, Colombia,

Cambodia, the Balkans, U.S./Cuba, Northern Ireland, among others. When the political issues were stripped away, and the *human* experience of conflict was laid bare, what remained was a common yearning for dignity—to feel free from harm and worthy of being treated well.

The desire for dignity is a powerful force and the time has come to recognise it and understand it. No amount of external power, including military force, can overcome it. I will never forget a conversation I had with a member of the Tamil Tigers, a guerilla organisation that was fighting the Sri Lankan government for autonomy for the minority Tamil people in the north of Sri Lanka. I asked him how he could explain the fact that while the Tigers were outnumbered by the government forces, they still managed to keep control of a strategic area in the north.

"It is easily explained," he said. "The government soldiers are not fighting for the liberation of their people. For them it's a job. For us, our dignity is on the line."

Understanding these longstanding conflicts, such as in Sri Lanka, becomes a tangled mess because parties that hold the power are also motivated by the desire to be treated with dignity. You may have to look into the past to see the roots of their violations, but it does not take long to find them. Most likely, they, too, were once oppressed and violated. In the case of Sri Lanka, the majority Sinhalese population were treated as second-class citizens by the British during the colonial period while the minority Tamils were privileged, giving them unequal access to education, jobs, and other social advantages.

Which brings me to an important point: the experience of humiliation, resentment, and anger that these dignity violations instinctively create do not go away on their own. The injuries are as serious as a gunshot wound, but no one is rushed into an emergency room when they happen. They leave a vengeful and often crippling mark on peoples' souls and without attention paid to these injuries, they can linger on in perpetuity, dominating one's personal and group consciousness.

We have to take dignity seriously. How we treat one another *matters*. And it is as true at the international level of human interaction as it is in our daily interchanges with our loved ones and colleagues. When we violate each other's dignity, there are consequences because human beings are hardwired to react—often violently—to them.

Even though the refinement of my thinking about dignity came through my work in international conflict, it was only one of many possible routes one could take to figure out something universal about the human experience. We do not like to be harmed or treated badly, and especially do not like being humiliated by others. We'd rather drink vinegar than face public humiliation. And our desire for revenge—an instinctive reaction to a dignity violation—only creates and perpetuates a cycle of injuries that keeps conflicts alive. The problem is how do we get the cycle to stop? What do we have to do to address the dignity violations?

Using dignity as a lens for understanding conflict and the breakdown in relationships, no matter what level you wish to apply it to, requires some background knowledge. Having the insight that we all desire to be treated with dignity is not enough, but it is the starting point. Whenever I tell people that I am writing about dignity, there appears to be an instant recognition that creates a pause in the conversation. They look at me and shake their heads and say: "Yes. That is so important." We all have an intuitive understanding of what dignity means. That's good because then we are all at the starting point together. But to describe specifically what would look like—to put dignity into practice and make it a *way of life*—that's a different story.

I have a lot of faith in human beings. That probably sounds strange coming from someone who has worked on some of the most brutal conflicts in the world, having witnessed some of the worst of what we humans are capable of. But the truth is that given a choice, given a dignified way out of these conflicts, most people want and are yearning for that option.

I remember a story that a colleague from Colombia told of a conversation he had had with an injured, young guerilla member, whose organisation was fighting for political autonomy from the Colombian government. He told my friend that he was tired of fighting, that he wanted a different life. He was haunted by the number of people he had killed and did not want to do it anymore. He wanted to have a family and grow to be old. He wept with my friend. He wanted a way out but did not know how to go about it.

Although the predicament this young guerilla was in is an extreme example, I think the essence of it rings true for many of us. If only we had a dignified way out of our conflicts with others. If only we knew how to save face and avoid the embarrassment of appearing "wrong" or having made a mistake.

Our self-preservation instincts, which are very strong, tell us that it is better to cover up the truth than to reveal it; we may look bad. And looking bad in the eyes of others is one of the most painful human experiences. The dreaded feeling of being publicly exposed before we are ready is as powerful a human force as any other. In this chapter, I'll explore the scientific explanation for why we resist this kind of humiliation.

Evolutionary biologists know a lot about these deep drives that run so much of our behaviours—survival behaviours that we inherited from our early ancestors. They also know that we are not doomed to be a slave to them. Fortunately, evolution has given us the power to find our way out of this predicament. Finding the way out requires some focused attention on our part. It does not come to us in the form of a knee-jerk response. In fact, the answer is to hold that knee-jerk response (self-preservation) in abeyance so that another part of us can take over the decision-making; so that we can make a *choice* about how to respond to a threatening situation.

While our self-preservation instincts are very strong—and if left to their own devices produce rage, revenge, and righteous justification of the use of violence—we also have the power within us to make different choices about how we treat ourselves and one another. We have evolved a "new brain" (neocortex) that enables us to transcend our instincts (the old brain) and discover the magical power of believing in our own worthiness and the worthiness of others. I have faith that if given the option to make dignity a way of life, we will take it.

The purpose of this chapter is to share the "dignity model": what I have learned through my research and personal experiences in my work with people around the world struggling to find the dignity that we all yearn for and deserve. Using evolutionary biology, I will describe why dignity matters to us. I will then introduce a framework for self-understanding that helps explain why we react so strongly to a dignity violation. Here I will rely on Williams James's distinction between the "I" and the "Me". Finally, I will present the essential elements of dignity—concrete ways in which dignity can be honoured or violated. I believe it is critical for anyone interested in leadership to learn and live by the power of dignity.

Probably the biggest obstacle in understanding dignity is the misguided belief that it comes from outside ourselves, from the way others treat us. And by holding fast to this belief, we give others the power to determine our worthiness.

It is important to understand where that belief comes from. There are two sources. First: if, as children, we were not treated with dignity by our caregivers (parent, teachers, siblings, clergy, etc.), we learn early on—before we have the capacity to know better—that we are not worthy. Children have primitive ways of making meaning and when someone treats them badly, they believe they are bad. They have yet to develop the cognitive sophistication to understand that the problem is most likely with the caregiver, not them. No child deserves to be harmed or treated badly. The legacy of early violations of their dignity lives on until they realise, as adults, the truth about their worthiness. This is not to say that we never make mistakes or do things wrong. We all do. My point is that our dignity—the core essence of our humanity—is never up for question. On the other hand, because we are an evolving species that learns from our mistakes, our behaviour, is open for discussion. We need feedback from others in order to help us see what we cannot see—to illuminate our blind spots. As long as the feedback is given in a way that promotes learning we don't usually have trouble with it. The problem is, feedback is often used as a weapon, especially in the heat of the conflict. Learning how to give feedback in a way that still honours a person's dignity is an essential part of resolving conflict.

Second, our cultures are filled with distorted beliefs about the superiority of some peoples and groups over others. It is in the air we breathe, penetrating us, consciously and unconsciously, like poison gas. Until we understand the falsity of these lethal beliefs, they will continue to undermine our social relationships. We will continue to live in a state of inner turmoil, searching for the recognition of our dignity that we will never find exclusively outside of ourselves. The time has come to reclaim our birthright and to locate dignity where it belongs: deep within each and every one of us.

Why dignity matters

Why is it that when we are treated in an undignified way by others it feels so bad? I have yet to meet anyone who has never experienced the shame of feeling unworthy. The circumstances leading up to it are always different, but the feeling is the same: we all dread it. And it is not something we talk about very often, because it's embarrassing even to admit feeling unworthy or that we have been treated in an undignified way. The truth is, the feeling of shame and unworthiness are reactions that are hardwired within us all by virtue of our shared evolutionary history and our common identity as Homo sapiens (Pinker, 2001).

As humans we have developed all kinds of strategies to mask our inner feelings of unworthiness, from medicating ourselves with drugs and alcohol to self-deception, to starting wars in order to reclaim lost dignity. As Desmond Tutu said to me after co-facilitating ten days of encounters between victims and perpetrators of the Northern Ireland conflict, "Aren't human beings funny creatures. We all do the same thing—we just hate to admit we've done something wrong."

We are all part of the same human family, and like all families, we have the capacity for harming as well as loving one another. Thinking of ourselves as members of the human family helps us understand that we are related by what has been passed down to us by our evolutionary history. This "evolutionary legacy" is better known as our "human nature" or the part of us that evolved over 100,000 years ago when our early ancestors roamed the savannah looking for food and a safe haven from the unrelenting threats to their existence. Because we share their genetic material—ninety-eight per cent of it, to be precise—we come into the world equipped with some fairly automatic reactions to being threatened—we either fight, freeze, or flee. Evolutionary biologists know a great deal about what makes us humans tick and they have known it for a long time. It will give us some insight into why dignity matters so much to us.

Evolutionary legacy

Evolutionary biologists know that we do not come into the world a blank slate and that we have a powerful evolutionary legacy encoded in our genes, predisposing us to a wide range of behaviours (Barkow, 2006). They tell us that we have a "human nature" that was inherited from our early ancestors and their quest to survive. They tell us that this human nature propels us throughout our lives. Some call these aspects of our human nature *instincts*, as they seem to automatically and unconsciously guide us towards what to seek out and what to avoid. On one hand, these instincts get called up like 911 when there is danger and possible threat. On the other hand, they have the power to turn us into kittens when there is an opportunity to be cared for and loved.

Biologists know that one of the things that makes us uniquely human is that we have a highly evolved part of our brain (called the neocortex) that enables us to perform sophisticated intellectual feats. They also know that we have embedded within our brains a more primitive component, commonly called the "old brain", which we inherited as a consequence of evolution and still remains with us today (Restak, 2003). This ancient part of our brain controls our emotional life and most of our instinctive reactions. When we perceive a threat, the old brain is activated, ready to protect us from predators. All of this we have inherited from our early ancestors from the Pleistocene era, 100,000 years ago. The problem is, the environment in which we live today is very different from the "survival" mode of existence that our ancestors lived in 100,000 years ago, when threats were defined in life-or-death terms. Our ancestors' environment was filled with danger, from wild animals swooping up their children to the day-to-day threats that nature's harsh reality presented.

Because it takes so long for genes to evolve and change, the instinctive self-protective behaviours we inherited, the ones ideally suited to promote survival in a hunter-gatherer environment, are still with us today. This is true even though they are not at all suited for the complex, interdependent world we currently live in. What this means is that in the present, when we feel something is a threat to our well-being, our "default" reaction—reactions that are unconsciously triggered and usually feel out of our control—are often "overkill" reactions.

Daniel Goleman, in his bestselling book *Emotional Intelligence*, describes this experience of being captured by our default reactions as being "emotionally hijacked" (Goleman, 1995). The old brain is so "at the ready" to protect us during threatening situations that it feels like we have been taken over by it. This happens to us all. How many times have we told ourselves that we would not let someone get the best of us, then, when we meet up with that person, in spite of our best intentions, we get into a heated argument? This is what Goleman means when he says the old brain has the power to "hijack" our best selves—the part of us that wants to work things out rationally.

In fact, after considering the above-cited research, I have concluded that today most perceived threats to our well-being are not physical and life-endangering at all. Rather, what triggers our self-protective instincts today is more psychological in nature. They are, by and large, threats to our *dignity*. We have the power, with our negative judgements and demeaning criticisms, to propel each other's old brains into action.

Dignity threats call up our old brain as if our lives were on the line, even when they are not. When our old brain is activated, it does not know the difference between a physical threat (such as a tiger at our heels) and

a psychological threat to our dignity. All it knows is that we have experienced an assault and it is ready for action—reactive, self-protective,
defensive, maybe even violent action. One example of this today is road
rage. When someone cuts in front of us on the highway, many of us find
ourselves screaming obscenities at the person—a reaction that is much
bigger than the situation calls for. All we are thinking (if we are thinking
at all) is that the guy violated us and deserved our abusive reaction; that
is the old brain in its full glory.

Key to understanding both the role dignity violations plays in our
lives and the premise of this chapter is understanding this point: while
external conditions and their resulting threats have changed dramati-
cally for us in the twenty-first century, our innate old brain's reactions
have not. A majority of our threats today do not come in the form of
wild animals ready to attack us in search of a meal. Today's threats
come from *humans* inflicting psychologically hurtful *dignity violations*
upon one another.

The effect of this legacy on our "family" relationships

What does this mean for us, all members of the same human family?
It means that when push comes to shove, when we perceive that we
are being offended or hurt by others—when someone violates our
dignity—our instinctive, self-protective hardwiring tells us that what
matters most is our *individual* well-being and survival, not the relationship's survival. Our instinct for self-preservation is stronger than our
instinct to preserve the relationship. In other words, when we feel some-
body is hurting us by violating our dignity today, our instincts tell us to
react just as intensely as we would have 100,000 years ago—either fight
or flee. When our old brain instructs us to flee, we pull out of the relationship in order to protect ourselves. Most of us will recognise this feeling.
Have you ever felt like just ending a relationship, or at the very least
walking out the door, when you were in the middle of a heated argument
with your partner? That is the "flee" survival pattern taking hold.

When our protective old brain instructs us to fight, we are pulled to
denigrate the other person and seek revenge. Our instincts want us to
eliminate the threat by either fighting back or withdrawing from the
relationship and we have the inborn capacity to do that. We seem to
intuitively know how to belittle and criticise others. Of course, intel-
lectually we all know that in the end this only sets up a cycle of hurtful

dignity violations. But try convincing the old brain of that. It does not want us to pause and reflect on what has happened. It is not designed for problem-solving. When our old brain leads the charge, all it wants is to protect us from more harm. It does not care about the consequences of its actions. It only cares about eliminating the source of the injury—either by fighting or withdrawing from the relationship.

To protect ourselves, we are hardwired to either fight or flee when we perceive a threat is looming. At the same time, evolutionary biologists tell us, another part of our ancestral inheritance is the desire to be in relationship with others because being in relationship gave our ancestors survival advantages (Jacobs, 2003). As social beings, our ancestors were dependent on one another for almost all aspects of daily existence. They hunted together, gathered together, and shared in all of the overwhelming tasks of survival. They were so dependent on one another that if a member of the community was cast out for any reason, his or her life was in peril. The individual's connection to the group was necessary for survival (de Wall, 2009). And here is the link to our present-day desire to be treated with dignity: in order to stay connected to others, in order to not be kicked out of the group and into the cold, harsh environment, our early ancestors had to be seen in a favourable light by the community. The desire to be held in esteem and to be respected by others meant you'd be able to stay with the clan, and this, in turn, meant survival to our early ancestors. In our old brains, formed 100,000 years ago but still residing in us today, it continues to feel as if being treated with dignity and being able to survive is intricately linked.

This is why being treated well is so important to us. In modern terms, this is why negative judgment feels so bad. This is why it is so difficult to receive critical feedback about our behaviour without it triggering our old brain's fight or flight response. Threats to our dignity put the old brain in charge of our reactions. We have an "instinct" to react to comments that feel damaging to who we are. So, as discussed above, this instinct often makes us want to fight or flee, both reactions that damage relationships—but at what cost?

The dramatic tension

Historically these old brain reactions helped to ensure our *individual* survival and the survival of our genetic material into the next generation. Today these same reactions have the potential to wreak havoc on our relationships. In fact, their very existence creates a profound human dilemma for us. What we need for survival (a connection to others), can also feel like the greatest source of threat to our survival (when the connection becomes hurtful). These two survival needs can live comfortably side by side when all is well in the world—when we're getting along just fine. The problem obviously comes when we begin to threaten each other's dignity—when the relationship threatens our sense of worthiness. Then the trouble begins. This dramatic tension between the need to be connected to others and the need to protect ourselves from the other's possible hurtful attacks explains why relationships are so hard. Our sensitivity and vulnerability to being injured by others, and our ability to injure them—both part of our evolutionary legacy—sets us up for struggles in our relationships. Relationships break down when the need for individual self-protection overrides our need for connection. We'll walk away from a relationship—be it political or personal—if it begins to feel threatening or does not serve our individual desire to be held in esteem and respect. From the individual perspective, individuals break down when their need for connection overrides their need for self-protection. How many times have we compromised our own dignity—not reacting to being violated—for the sake of maintaining a relationship?

Better to be safe than sorry

You can see how our evolutionary legacy has wreaked havoc on our relationships. The very mechanism that evolved to protect us from individual harm—our fight and flight instincts—has created so much human suffering by enabling us to justify our undignified behaviours towards others. Our self-preservation instincts predispose us to hurt one another and favours disconnection over connection. Better to be safe than sorry. Is it any wonder why intimacy feels so threatening and vulnerable? It's a setup for being injured or re-injured.

And it is safe to say that we have all been injured in some way, given the reality that I have described above. We are at a point in our human history where the awareness of what is acceptable treatment of one another is at a fairly primitive level because our instincts justify our hurtful behaviours. Many of our parents, teachers, siblings, and even religious leaders were blind to the negative impact they had on us when we were at our most vulnerable—when we needed their love and attention the most. Without awareness of how easily small children can be hurt and how fragile their sense of worthiness is, many of us grew up with a shattered sense of dignity (Herman, 1992). The early emotional imprint of unworthiness resides deep in the recesses of our old brain, which is why the *feeling* of unworthiness is so hard to shake. It is like being branded. Children don't evolve the part of the brain that enables them to analyse and reflect on what has happened to them until much later in their development. All their emotional memories get stored in the primitive brain centres.

And families are not the only source of early dignity violations. Our cultures are excellent breading grounds for toxic beliefs that some people are superior to others. Whether it is racism, classism, sexism, or any number of other harmful "isms", their effects are the source of so much self-doubt and human suffering. It appears that we are better equipped to harm others than to love them.

So even if you grew up in the perfect family (and I am still looking for such a person), you have most likely been traumatised by dignity violations in one way or another and have questioned your worthiness. Our common human family has suffered great injuries because we have yet to become aware of the capacity for harm that grows out of our woundedness. A dignity violation creates a wound that produces a self-protective reaction that is in turn wounding of others. That's how the instinct works and in the strict sense, by no fault of our own. It's part of our evolutionary legacy. The important point is, it may not be our fault, but what are we going to do about it?

We might have entered the world with strong self-protective and potentially harmful instincts, but we did not enter the world with an awareness of how much we hurt one another in the process of our own defence. In fact, we often feel justified to "get even" or lash back. Awareness is not an instinct. It requires reflection and self-knowledge. In the end, it may not be our fault that we are hardwired to hurt one another in the service of self-protection, but it is our responsibility to control it. Is not our capacity to become aware of the consequences of our actions part of what make us uniquely human? Knowing this gives us dignity.

One thing I do not want to do in this chapter is to contribute to the shame that we all know so well by pointing out how instinctively hurtful we can be to one another. On the contrary, I believe we have to take the shame out of that acceptance. We have all been hurt in our lives, we all know the crippling feeling of unworthiness. By virtue of being human, we have most likely inflicted pain and suffering on others.

In fact, there's liberation in the acceptance that part of being human means we have instincts that, when activated, can be harmful to others. We have to keep in mind that those instincts evolved to annihilate the source of threat. When these ancient urges are triggered in us, it does not mean that we are bad. It means we are experiencing one aspect of our humanity that wants us to survive over anything else. These instincts do not invite us to examine the consequences of our actions. All they want is to eliminate the source of the threat.

There is nothing inherently shameful about protecting oneself. The problem is that the instincts are not serving us as well today as they did for our ancestors. They create overkill reactions that are not appropriate to our present threats and they trigger us to violate the dignity of others. The good news is that we can employ another part of ourselves and *know* that we have other resources for handling threats to our well-being. Taking responsibility for our instincts is part of the process of breaking free from the destructive aspects of our evolutionary legacy, enabling us to make conscious choices about how we want to be in the world.

The struggle for dignity: the I and the Me[1]

Before we can really understand dignity, we need to understand something more about ourselves as human beings. Most of us spend a good part of our time looking for dignity outside of ourselves, putting it into the hands of others. If we're in public and someone embarrasses us in front of other people, we feel ashamed and bad about ourselves. If we're at work and our boss excludes us from an important meeting, we feel bad. If we're at home and someone in our family criticises us, then we suffer. If someone treats us unfairly, we have an immediate reaction: our heart starts pounding and our temperature rises. This is true for all of us, because there is a part of us that I call the "Me" that gets hurt when other people treat us badly. We feel it. We are vulnerable to the way people treat us.

I find it useful to think of the "Me" as the part of us driven by the forces of our evolutionary legacy, which are often unconscious. It is the part that is enslaved by its need for *external* validation of our worthiness. The "Me" cannot feel good about itself or worthy of esteem unless it hears it is worthy from sources outside of itself. It is vulnerable to judgments and criticisms and reacts to these threats to its worthiness and self-esteem by defending and protecting itself. There is a general feeling that one is not "complete", that there is always something more one has to do to feel good about who one is.

The "Me" is generally distrustful of others, and never lets go of the fact that they have the potential to hurt. When situated in the "Me", our inner world is dominated by concerns about the self: Am I good enough? How do I compare to others? Am I acceptable to others? Do others see me as a good person? The development of the "Me" is dependent on our relationships and the kind of validation we get (or do not get) from them.

At the same time, when someone gives us a compliment, or acknowledges that we have done a good job, then we feel good. Either way, if we're praised or if we're criticised, we feel both. And that's the "Me", the part of us that looks for validation and approval from people outside of us. The "Me" is also the part of us that gets into trouble with others. It's the part that wants to "get even" when someone hurts us—the part that wants revenge. This need for revenge gets us into trouble because by getting back at the other, we end up violating the person's dignity, not to mention that we also violate our own. This is how the unconscious cycle of indignity works—you violate my dignity, my defences get activated, and I end up violating yours.

But there is another part of us that is as true as the "Me". This other part, what I call the "I", is worthy of dignity, no matter what. It is our personal anchor that no one can take away from us.

I call this other part the "I". It is the *enduring* aspect of ourselves that knows itself to be unconditionally worthy of esteem and respect. When situated in the "I", there is no such thing as a good self and a bad self; the "I", by virtue of being part of the human family, is unconditionally worthy. It does not depend on external validation of who it is and does not need acknowledgement of its right to hold itself in esteem. The "I" just *is*. Some say this is the spiritual aspect of the self, which is connected to everything else in the universe—it is part of the miracle of nature and human existence.

When we are firmly situated in the "I", the world is a wonder to us. We are *curious* about everything—from ourselves and others to the multitude of mysteries of the world around us. We are joyful, creative, we feel complete. We thrive on loving connections and, in so doing, are full of excitement about our mutual human potential.

Being connected to others is our natural state. We are seekers of love, truth, wisdom, and our ultimate purpose. All this makes for a rich and penetrating life that is not content skimming along the surface of existence. It is a life fueled by purpose, grace, and loving connections, not only to others but to the natural world and beyond. The development of the "I" is more a question of becoming *aware* that it exists and accepting the truth about who we are, and that we are unconditionally worthy. Knowing this about ourselves makes it possible to see the same unconditional worthiness of others. Being fully situated in the "I" means we understand that we are all worthy of dignity as part of our birthright. The "I" keeps us steady when someone threatens or hurts our "Me". It's the part of us that we can always come back to when our dignity has been violated. It's the part of us that stops our "Me" from wanting to get even with the person who hurt us. It is stronger than the "Me". It has the power to resist the temptation to seek revenge. It has the power to maintain our dignity no matter how badly someone treats us. It knows that we do not want to let the bad behaviour of others determine how we act. It knows that we have the inner strength to not become violent. A big part of dignity is restraint.

The "I" knows what the "Me" cannot because it has the ability to watch the "Me" in action. When the "Me" takes over our behaviour, it has little capacity to reflect on itself. It is the "I" who can obey the injunction to "know thyself". And most of all, it knows that by extending dignity to others, it strengthens its own.

The goal is to achieve a working relationship between the "I" and the "Me". Because we are human, we cannot expect to eliminate our need for praise and approval from others. It feels good and we all enjoy it. Nor can we expect to not feel it when someone hurts us. We need to develop a pathway between the "I" and "Me" so that when the "Me" gets injured, the "I", with its loving and nurturing nature, is instantly put on alert to help soothe the wounded "Me".

What part do you identify most with? The sad reality is that every time I present this material to participants in my dignity workshops, the majority of people say that they are situated in the "Me" most of the time. They realise how much of their internal world is focused on gaining acceptance of their worthiness and esteem from others. We are trapped in a set of circumstances where we are looking for validation from each other and feeling incomplete without it. We all want the kind of dignity that the "I" can give us, but instead we are looking for it from others. Why do we do this? Why does it feel so automatic to look for the validation of our worthiness outside of ourselves?

It appears to be another default reaction—something we do without thinking. And in fact, it is. Remember how I explained earlier that the need to be seen in a favourable light had survival value for our early ancestors, and how that got passed down to us like a dominant gene? It comes so naturally for us to look to the outside for approval because it is part of our evolutionary legacy. But like all the rest of our default reactions, this one's usefulness in the present needs to be examined.

Today, in the twenty-first century, do we really need the approval of others in order to survive? Obviously, the answer is "No". At the same time, there is nothing wrong with enjoying the approval of others. The problem comes when we depend on it *exclusively* to fulfill our dignity. But because the need for it is hardwired in our genes, it *feels* like a question of survival when someone treats us badly. This is when we need to be in touch with the "I" part of ourselves. We need to remind ourselves that no one can take away our worthiness and inherent value. And we can also look to others to help us with this. Rather than look to others to make us feel worthy, their role is to remind us of our worthiness, to help us remember what we already know.

This knowledge about ourselves—that we possess within us both the "I" and the "Me"—helps us understand why it is so easy to get into conflict with one another. Our "Me"s collide and we are ready to protect ourselves no matter what, even at the cost of our own dignity. It is a very high price to pay. If we can learn to recognise and accept the more combative, aggressive, and competitive aspects of ourselves, and know that we have the power within us to control them, then we are more than half-way to living a life of dignity. Such important learning cannot be left to chance. Sadly, up to this point, we have had little to no education in how to achieve dignity and to extend it to others.

No one taught us how

One of the reasons why we do not know how to be in relationship with one another in a dignified way, apart from the obstacles set up by our evolutionary legacy, is that we have never been exposed to any formal education in how to be in a healthy relationship. There is no course we can take to help us with one of the most important aspects of our lives—how to get along with and treat ourselves and others with dignity.

We have never learned how to handle our knee-jerk default reactions to feeling threatened by others—let alone why we have them to begin with. Given that many of us have endured significant early childhood violations to our dignity, I wonder how, without assistance, mentoring, a teacher, instruction, and good reading material—in short, *education*—we could possibly experience relationships as potential sources of love, understanding, and mutual growth.

The main point is: we need education in building dignified relationships just as we need to learn to read and write. Our own lives and the lives around us show us that. Knowing the skills that make dignified relationships work does not come naturally. What comes naturally is self-preservation. This awareness gives us permission to be a little gentler with ourselves and others, recognising the daunting challenges we *all* face in our struggles to feel worthy and to live with one another in a dignified way.

What we are up against

Relationships have the potential to make us feel our best and to make us feel our worst. They make us feel our best when our dignity (our sense of being worthy and seen in a favourable light) is assured. And they make us feel our worst when our dignity has been violated. Attacks on our dignity are often the reason relationships break down. There's a simple reality at work here: when people feel their dignity has been honoured, when they have been treated well, they feel good about themselves in that relationship. When people feel good about themselves in a relationship, the relationship is more likely to endure. However, the shift from feeling good to feeling bad, from civility to hostility is only a dignity violation away.

The next section describes the essential elements of dignity—concrete ways to honour the dignity of others.

The essential elements of dignity[2]

This section describes the essential elements of dignity—concrete ways to honour the dignity of others. If we honour these essential elements when we interact with others, they are triggers to connection. If we violate these essential elements when we interact with others, they are triggers to disconnection.

Understanding the essential elements enables us to:

1. Name and identify concrete ways to either honour or violate some-one's dignity.
2. Name and identify the dignity violations we experience. This helps us to make sense of why we might feel bad after an interaction with someone. It helps us understand that the source of the bad feeling could be a dignity violation—and it helps us label the *type* of dignity violation we experienced.
3. Name and identify dignity violations for which we are responsible. This helps us understand why others may feel bad after an interac-tion with us. It helps us see our mistreatment of others as dignity violations—and it helps us label the *type* of dignity violation we com-mitted. It helps us become more aware of the consequences of our actions on others.
4. Recognise when we are honouring the dignity of others.

The essential elements of dignity are:

- Acceptance of identity—Approach people as neither inferior nor superior to you; give others the freedom to express their authen-tic selves without fear of being negatively judged; interact without prejudice or bias, accepting how race, religion, ethnicity, gender, class, sexual orientation, age, disability, etc., are at the core of their identities. Assume they have integrity.
- Inclusion—Make others feel that they belong at all levels of relation-ship (family, community, organisation, nation).
- Safety—Put people at ease on two levels: physically, where they feel free of bodily harm; and psychologically, where they feel free of con-cern about being shamed or humiliated, and feel free to speak with-out fear of retribution.
- Acknowledgment—Give people your full attention by listening, hearing, validating, and responding to their concerns and what they have been through.
- Recognition—Validate others for their talents, hard work, thought-fulness, and help; be generous with praise; show thanks and grati-tude toward others for their contributions, ideas, and experience.
- Fairness—Treat people justly, with equality, and in an evenhanded way, according to agreed-upon laws and rules.

- Benefit of the doubt—Treat people as trustworthy; start with the premise that others have good motives and are acting with integrity.
- Understanding—Believe that what others think matters; give them the chance to explain their perspectives, express their points of view; actively listen in order to understand them.
- Independence—Encourage people to act on their own behalf so that they feel in control of their lives and experience a sense of hope and possibility. Use your power to empower rather than to disempower others.
- Accountability—Take responsibility for your actions; if you have violated the dignity of another, apologise; make a commitment to change hurtful behaviours.

Developing a conscious awareness of when we are either violating or honouring dignity in interactions with others takes time and practice. It also takes time and practice to become aware when we experience a violation of our dignity. As a way of illustrating the transformative possibilities of the essential elements of dignity, I would like to relate an interaction that took place over twenty years ago.

The story of Rahima and Don

My colleagues and I had organised a dialogue workshop for students from the Middle East living in the Boston area. A young Palestinian student (I will call her Rahima) hardly spoke. A Palestinian friend of hers argued with an Israeli student (whom I will call Don) about the way Palestinians were treated when they attempted to make the border crossing between the West Bank and Israel. Rahima sat nearly motionless as she listened; only her eyes shifted back and forth between the interlocutors. Her Palestinian friend was getting frustrated. He said, "If you think we are not treated like dirt, dress up as an Arab and try making the crossing yourself."

As my colleague was about to intervene in the continuing, unproductive argument Rahima interrupted the men and asked to speak. She looked at Don, the Israeli, and without any hint of judgement in her voice said to him, "I can see that you are having trouble believing my colleague. Let me tell you a story that might help you understand what he is trying to convey."

"When I was about six years old, my grandfather told me that we were going to the old city of Jerusalem to visit a friend he had not seen for many years. I remember thinking at the time that my grandfather was old, and I wondered if he wanted to go to see his friend in order to say goodbye. The thought made me sad, because I loved my grandfather, yet I was also excited to accompany him on the journey.

"He was a prominent member of our community in Ramallah; everyone respected him. People young and old would come to him for advice—he was the unofficial mediator. I was proud to be his granddaughter.

"When we approached the border crossing, a young Israeli soldier asked my grandfather to get out of the car. I was terrified. The soldier was carrying a big gun, and I didn't know what was happening. At one point, I saw my grandfather trying to explain something to the soldier, and started yelling at him. I couldn't believe it. I jumped out of the car, went up to the soldier and said to him, 'What are you doing? Don't you know who he is? He's my grandfather! You can't talk to him that way.'"

The room went silent. Rahima put her face in her hands and sobbed. We waited.

Don was the first to speak he turned to Rahima and told her how sorry he was that she and her grandfather had to endure that humiliation. His voice was trembling as he explained to her how difficult it was for him to take in her story. "As an Israeli, I believe in my heart that we are good people, fighting a painful war that we have to fight in order to maintain our Jewish identity in the future for the Jewish people. I feel the righteousness of our cause. If I accept what you say, that we are going about this fight in a way that is not righteous, in a way that is profoundly harming you and your people, then it forces me to look at my own identity and say, 'Who am I? What am I doing?' I cannot take in your experience and keep my sense of who I am intact at the same time. Because I now have no doubt that what you say is true, I have to swallow a bitter truth: that the way I have constructed my identity up to this point is causing great suffering for the Palestinian people."

In all the dialogues I had facilitated before and all I have facilitated since, I have never witnessed such bravery. Don made himself vulnerable in front of his fellow Israelis, in front of the Palestinians at the table, and in front of the rest of the participants. We were all speechless. There was nothing left to say. Words do not belong in such moments of reverence.

Conclusion: leading with dignity

Our desire for dignity resides deep within us, defining our common humanity. If our capacity for indignity is our lowest common denominator, then our yearning for dignity is our highest. And if indignity tears relationships apart, then dignity can put them back together again.

Our ignorance of all things related to dignity—how to claim our own and how to honour it in others, has contributed to many of the conflicts we see in the world today. This is as true in the boardroom and in the bedroom as it is in politics and international relations. It is true for all human interaction. If we are to evolve as a species, there is no greater need than to learn how to treat each other, and ourselves, with dignity. It is the glue that could hold us all together. And it doesn't stop there. Not only does dignity make for good human relationships, it does something perhaps far more important—it creates the conditions for our mutual growth and development. It is a distraction to have to defend oneself from indignity. It takes up our time and uses up our precious energy. The power of dignity, on the other hand, only expands with use. The more we give, the more we get.

There is no greater leadership challenge than to perform that role with dignity, helping us all to understand what it feels like to be honoured and valued and to feel the incalculable benefits that come from that experience. The leadership challenge is at all levels—for those in the world of politics, business, education, religion, to everyday leadership in our personal lives. Peace will not flourish anywhere without dignity. There is no such thing as democracy without dignity, nor can there be authentic peace if people are suffering indignities. Last but not least, feeling dignity's power—both by honouring it and locating our own inner source of it—sets us up for one of humanity's greatest gifts— the experience of being in relationship with others in a way that brings out the best in each of us, allowing us to become more of what we are capable of being.

Notes

1. First articulated by philosopher William James in *The Principles of Psychology* in 1890.
2. Originally proposed in *Dignity: The Essential Role It Plays in Resolving Conflict* (Hicks, 2011).

References

Barkow, J. (2006). *Missing the Revolution: Darwin for Social Scientists*. Oxford: Oxford University Press.

de Wall, F. (2009). *The Age of Empathy: Nature's Lessons for a Kinder Society*. New York: Harmony.

Goleman, D. (1995). *Emotional Intelligence*. New York: Bantam.

Hicks, D. (2011). *Dignity: The Essential Role It Plays in Resolving Conflict*. New Haven, CT: Yale University Press.

Herman, J. (1992). *Trauma and Recovery*. New York: Basic.

Jacobs, G. D. (2003). *The Ancestral Mind*: Middlesex, England: Viking.

James, W. (1890). *The Principles of Psychology*. New York: Henry Holt.

Pinker, S. (2001). *The Blank Slate: The Modern Denial of Human Nature*. Middlesex, England: Viking Penguin.

Restak, R. (2003). *The New Brain*. Emmaus, PA: Rodale.

CHAPTER TWO

Some psychoanalytic reflections on the concept of dignity*

Salman Akhtar

ignity is an elusive concept. Upon encountering the term, we feel an intuitive familiarity with its nosological contours. But when asked to put our "understanding" into words, we fumble, wander in and out of various conceptual alleys, and return with lexical baskets that are empty. Solace comes from finding out that the concept has been mired in controversy, ambiguity, and imprecision since its appearance centuries ago. Taken up largely by philosophers, the notion of dignity has led to considerable debate and division. Some, like Frederick Nietzsche and Arthur Schopenhauer, reject it outright, considering it a redundant and pompous façade for man's sagging self-esteem. Others, like Immanuel Kant, Francis Bacon, and Thomas Aquinas, champion the concept and offer painstakingly detailed discourse on it.

---

*This chapter was originally presented as part of a panel on dignity at the American Psychoanalytic Association meetings in New York on 18 January 2014.

More recent opponents of the validity and usefulness of the notion of dignity include Ruth Macklin (2003) and James Griffin (2002). And, more recent proponents of the concept include George Kateb (2011) and Michael Rosen (2012). The interesting fact though is that even the proponents do not seem to agree on what it is that they are talking about and to what realm the concept they are advancing applies. Four areas of discord exist. Formulated as questions, these include:

- Is dignity a specifically human trait or is it inherent in all that exists in this world, including animals, plants, and even inanimate objects?
- Is dignity confined to the morally upright, the socially powerful, and the aesthetically refined, or is it an asset of all human beings, since they carry an inviolable transcendental kernel within themselves?
- Does the concept of dignity have religious overtones or is it a secular concept, even though existing on an "anagogic" (Silberer, 1914) level?[1]
- Can an attitude of religious humility be consonant with dignity or is surrender to God contrary to human dignity?

Clearly the field is rife with descriptive and conceptual conundrums. It might serve us well, therefore, to briefly go over the various definitions of dignity that exist in philosophical and, to a lesser extent, in psychoanalytic literature. Familiarity with them seems necessary for addressing the sociocultural and technical implications of this concept.

Various definitions

The dictionary definition of "dignity" comprises of such phrases as "the quality or state of being worthy, honored, or esteemed ... high-rank, office, or position ... a legal title of nobility or honor ... [and] formal reserve of manner or language" (Mish, 1987, p. 354). This amalgam of respect, status, and restraint is uplifting but leaves the concept somewhat ambiguous. Matters become murkier when we approach the philosophical definitions of dignity. In citing them, I borrow heavily from Rosen's (2012) meticulous and thorough survey of this literature. In his summary, the following definitions make their appearance:

- Cicero (106 BC-43 BC) considered that it is the capacity for self-reflection and thoughtfulness that separates human beings from other species and gives them dignity.

- St Thomas Aquinas (1225–1274) gave an explicit definition of the concept, stating that "dignity signifies something's goodness on account of itself" (cited in Rosen, 2012, pp. 16–17). In his view, dignity is not restricted to human beings and all things created by God possess their own dignity.[2]
- Francis Bacon (1561–1626) emphasised that dignity is not associated with social status and that it is by painful and laborious effort that man achieves the elevated and respectable quality of dignity.
- Immanuel Kant (1724–1804) wrote extensively on dignity. He seemed to present many, occasionally divergent, views on the subject. One view is implicit in this passage: "In the Kingdom of ends everything has either a *price* or a *dignity*. What has a price can be replaced by something else as its *equivalent*; what, on the other hand, is raised above all price and therefore admits of no equivalent has a dignity" (cited in Rosen, 2012, pp. 20–21, italics in the original). This view permits, I assert, the extension of the concept of dignity to a breathtaking piece of art, a soulful poem, or even a single line from a poem (for instance, "what is sadder than a train stopped in rain?" by Pablo Neruda or "there is a door that I have closed till the end of this world" by Jorge Luis Borges), or a lilting movement in music. Kant's other, more restrictive view, curiously, is enunciated later in the same paragraph: "Morality, and humanity insofar as it is capable of morality, is that which alone has dignity" (cited in Rosen, 2012, p. 21). A third view could be derived from Kant's declaration that "autonomy is the ground of the dignity of human nature" (cited in Rosen, 2012, p. 21). This view would make dignity akin to a sense of agency, be it physical, intellectual, or moral. However, Rosen (2012) reminds us that Kant's use of the word "autonomy" was different from its contemporary meaning of self-determination; it referred to a willing commitment to the path of morality. What thus appears to be Kant's third view gets rapidly subsumed in his second view, though not without a remnant trace of ambiguity. What remains certain is that Kant's view of dignity does not depend upon God; in fact, he regarded religious submission to be antithetical to human dignity.
- Friedrich Schiller (1788–1805) regarded dignity as an aesthetic quality. For him, dignity was evident through "tranquility in suffering". Moreover, unlike Kant who thought genuinely moral behaviour emanated from strenuous thinking and making difficult choices, Schiller underscored the "grace" with which a person acts morally without any kind of internal struggle. Schiller declared that "Just as grace is

the expression of a beautiful soul, so dignity is the expression of a sublime disposition" (cited in Rosen, 2012, p. 35).

• Reinhold Niebuhr (1892–1971) emphasised the elements of thought and free will in his view of dignity. He held that the dignity of man consists of his capacity to rise above the laws of nature and, at times, even those of logic and reason in order to help others and for the betterment of society at large.

Moving on from the philosophical terrain to the realm of psychoanalysis immediately makes one aware of the paucity of literature on this subject. The word "dignity" does not appear in the indices to the complete works of Sigmund Freud and Melanie Klein. Nor is it mentioned in the painstakingly detailed glossaries of Bion's (Lopez-Corvo, 2003) and Winnicott's (Abram, 2007) writings. None of the major psychoanalytic dictionaries (Akhtar, 2009; Auchincloss & Samberg, 2012; Eidelberg, 1968; Laplanche & Pontalis, 1973; Moore & Fine, 1968, 1990) contains a definition of dignity. And, the PEP Web[3] yields only seven papers (Abelson, 1978; Abelson & Margolis, 1978; De Rosis, 1973; Margolis, 1978; Shabad, 2000, 2011; Zachary, 2002) which contain "dignity" in their title. And, frankly, not all of these have something significant to offer. Nonetheless, these meager morsels demand to be savoured.

De Rosis (1973) equates dignity with a kind of psychic wholeness by which the individual can maintain his or her nascent being and yet remain able to be influenced by others. The freedom to be oneself exists alongside ongoing engagement with others. To constantly retain these two modes of being is the essence of dignity. This results in living deeply and fully "within the scope of interplay" (p. 18) between the private self and the object world. And, it is only then one can have a sense of value as a unique individual as well as a responsible partner in the wider circle of humanity.

Abelson (1978) views dignity as emerging from accepting responsibility for one's actions and from insisting upon one's rights as a person, including the right to one's psychic privacy. In a provocative assertion, Abelson finds seeking psychotherapy (or, for that matter, psychoanalysis) incompatible with personal dignity. Indeed, in his view, expecting someone else to help with one's psychological trepidation entails a denial of responsibility for one's affect and action, hence a loss of personal dignity. Abelson's stance touches upon, but does not fully embody, the poignancy of Francis Bacon, who stated that "by indignities, men come to dignities" (cited in Rosen, 2012, p. 15). Abelson is criticised by Margolis (1978; Abelson & Margolis, 1978) who points out that no forfeiture of dignity is warranted if psychic pain needing remediation is clearly generated by others' actions. Moreover, while it is acceptable that a person be morally responsible for his actions, this does not mean "that one ceases to be a person when events and actions involving one as a putative person are, *at times,* causally accounted for in terms of forces over which he lacked sufficient control or knowledge or which involved inconsistencies with his sincerely avowed reasons and intentions" (Margolis, 1978, p. 222, italics in the original).

Two other psychoanalysts have commented upon the concept of dignity. Shabad (2000) equates dignity with self-respect and finds some instances of spite and opposition as the ways to regain dignity.[4] Though Shabad does not cite him, the view he is advancing echoes Winnicott's (1956) concept of "antisocial tendency" whereby outrageousness becomes a vehicle for the unconscious hope for psychic repair by the environment. Zachary (2002), in discussing the psychic shifts that occur in the wake of menopause, uses the term "dignity" to convey resilience and growth in the face of developmental crises.

In addition to the foregoing papers derived from the PEP Web, there are the pioneering contributions of Marcovitz (1970a, 1970b) and the quite recent work of Marcus (2013). Since Marcovitz's contribution is truly pioneering in this realm, I will devote considerable space to it. Delivered as a plenary address to the Southeastern Pennsylvania Mental Health Association on 4 November 1966, and published four years later (1970a), this paper is a *tour de force*. Noting that dignity is both an intrapsychic and social phenomenon, Marcovitz made the following powerful declaration.

> I believe that the development and maintenance of the dignity of the individual human being, both his own sense of worth and its reflection in the attitudes of others toward him, is a necessity to give meaning to existence, to make life worth living. It is simultaneously a prerequisite, a constituent and a sign of mental health. Its failure to develop, or its diminution, as well as the efforts to gain or to regain it, are most important aspects of various forms of mental illness as well as of other problems of personality or behavior that are unhealthy or destructive. (p. 120)

Marcovitz, rather courageously, emphasised that the feeling of having some superiority over others is often necessary in order to have a sense of dignity. Even the oppressed and the conquered can thus retain dignity by harbouring contempt for their tormentors. However, there also exist healthier avenues to sustain one's dignity under adverse circumstances: these include humour, art, music, and religion.

Among the fundamental components of dignity, Marcovitz listed (i) self-respect, (ii) self-assertion, (iii) a sense of power and agency, (iv) a sense of justice, and, significantly, (v) "an amalgam of pride and humility" (p. 124). He added that:

> There is another important ingredient to dignity—the feeling of being part of something important, something worth living for, fighting for, sacrificing for. The struggle to produce the kind of changes one aspires to will itself contribute to the dignity of all those involved in it. (p. 120)

Marcovitz also spoke of how large sections of society that live in states of poverty and deprivation are encumbered on a daily basis with indignities of life. He outlined (1970b) pathological (e.g., narcissistic hedonism, drug-induced oblivion, violence) and healthy (e.g., creativity, education, sports) measures to combat such threats to self-esteem. Finally, Marcovitz addressed the impact of gender upon the experience of dignity. He stated that:

> Although it is true that men envy women and in rare cases men want to become women, men are rarely ashamed of being men— they are usually ashamed of not being man enough, and use all sorts of means to enhance the dignity which depends on their picture of masculinity. With women the problem is different—it is not only that they envy men, but that they are ashamed of being women. Both of these shames, that of men and that of women, originate in the anatomy and in the weakness of childhood. Then social and cultural differences tend to increase or to diminish these primary feelings of shame. In the culture of poverty the woman's position is enhanced so that it is easier for her to get over her shame and to have dignity, because she is the prime wage earner and the head of the family; whereas the man's feeling of inadequacy tends

> to be fostered and he is forced into various symbolic or substitute or exaggerated forms of masculinity. In the middle classes the women have a more difficult time getting over their primary shame and in accepting their femininity with dignity. They tend to have more complicated forms of the problems of attaining a feeling of worthiness. (p. 126)

To be sure, these comments are dated and both social and psychoanalytic perspectives have moved ahead. But, Marcovitz deserves credit for at least confronting the gender-based dimension of dignity head on. He is an exception, since all the philosophical and psychoanalytic writings on dignity skirt the fact that many cultures and many religious traditions have accorded women less dignity than men. And, in certain parts of the world, this remains true to this day.

Jumping from the earliest to the most contemporary contribution to the concept of dignity, we find the views of Marcus (2013). He equates dignity with a proper sense of self-worth and self-respect, and declares that

> A person with a dignified being is one who exhibits behaviour that is "worthy of himself" and does what needs to be done to shield himself from emotional wounding and other forms of harm. Dignity is also the state of being worthy of respect, esteem, or honour. To treat others with dignity involves, among other things, not psychologically or physically harming them. (p. 136)

A psychoanalytic exponent of the twentieth-century French philosopher Gabriel Marcel (1889–1973), Marcus notes the centrality of the traits of integrity, fraternity, and freedom in the former's concept of "inalienable dignity" (Marcel, cited in Marcus, 2013, p. 137) of human beings. Marcel was passionate about the human striving towards a life of beauty, truth, and love, as well as towards the protection (and restoration) of the sacred from the intrusions of technology and totalitarianism. He emphasised that dignity is not associated with social class, but with compassion, empathy with the suffering of others, and courage to resist tyranny. Such courage, in turn, does not reflect a mere affirmation of the self but emanates from a deeply awakened sense of morality. All in all, Marcel's concept of dignity subsumes integrity, autonomy, compassion, self-respect, courage, and a firm conviction in the sacred nature of life. With the thoughts of a Catholic philosopher presented to us by a Jewish psychoanalyst, we find ourselves at a propitious confluence of the two strands (philosophical and psychoanalytic) with which we began our consideration of how to define the notion of dignity. Time now to put the pieces of this puzzle together.

An attempt at synthesis

By bringing together the foregoing philosophical and psychoanalytic observations together in a harmonious gestalt, we end up with three types of dignity. While subtle overlaps between them exist, these categories actually refer to different phenomena, exist on different levels of abstraction, possess different evocative potentials, produce different praxis, and have different degrees of proximity with psychoanalytic metapsychology. A close look at the three categories I am proposing here would confirm my assertions of their distinct nature.

Metaphysical dignity

This refers to the view that all that exists in this universe is sacred and inherently worthy of respect. All human beings have dignity but dignity is not limited to human beings. Animals, plants, and inanimate objects also have dignity; their intrinsic coherence, purpose, and role in the mysterious operations of nature confer such honour upon them. The imperious lion, the majestic elephant, the somber pyramids, the mesmerising Taj Mahal, and yes, even an old oak tree, a beautifully carved grandfather clock, and an intricately woven Persian rug possess dignity. Searles' (1960) lamentably unread treatise on the non-human environment and Bion's (1965) concept of "O" undergird what I have termed "metaphysical dignity" here. The former offers a detailed analysis of how our ecological surround and the physical objects as well as the big and little animals that populate it silently contribute to our psychic development and functioning. The latter posits the omnipresence of absolute truth which is inherent in the universe and can be readily found by an unthinking mind (yes, you read it right; Bion declares that truth and even thought itself pre-exists the human mind which can only elaborate upon it, not create it). The advantage of the concept of "metaphysical dignity" is that it yields a sense of tenderness and consideration for all things; a Buddhist calm flows from the heart to the entire universe.[5] The disadvantages of the concept is that it is too broad, can be taken to absurd extremes (e.g., conferring dignity on a mosquito, a broken shoe-lace, a sewage pump),[6] and poses the risk of putting unrelated phenomena (e.g., respect for plants and for human freedom) on an equal footing.

Existential dignity

This refers to the view that only the human species possesses dignity. The argument states that since only human beings are capable of forging discontinuities with nature and also evolving and subscribing to an inner sense of morality, they exist on a higher plane than other species. This sentiment is evident in the Holy Quran's declaration that "We have bestowed dignity on the children of Adam and conferred upon them special favours above the greater part of our Creation" (17: 70). Each single human being is bestowed with dignity simply by belonging to a distinguished species and also partly because being human implies the capacity for transcendence within the hearts and souls of each individual. The psychoanalytic concept akin to existential dignity is that of "belief-in-species" (Erikson, 1975). This concept proposes that an individual must possess and safeguard the understanding that all human beings belong to the same species, Homo sapiens, and therefore share the same characteristics; the tendency to divide a human being into more or less human, to the extent of considering some people infra-human or non-human, is "pseudo-speciation", which assaults the basic commonality and dignity of human beings. The advantage of the concept of "existential dignity" is that it propels equal respect for all human beings; the notion of fundamental human rights, equality of all human beings, and justice for all arise from this very substrate. The disadvantage of the concept is two-fold. First, by restricting dignity to only human beings, it can unleash wanton and remorseless exploitation of animals, things, and nature at large (Kateb, 2011). Second, by imparting dignity to every single human being, it risks obliterating the important moral difference between the oppressed and the oppressor, and the cruel perpetrator and the innocent victim. Think about it. Does the ruthless Nazi officer with a bayonet share the same sort of dignity as his hapless captive?

Characterological dignity

This refers to a constellation of personality traits that are largely derived from the epigenetic unfolding of human psychic development and therefore might not exist in all individuals to comparable extent. These traits include integrity, restraint, authenticity, empathy, self-esteem, and courage. Seen this way, dignity is not a given but a developmentally "earned" attribute. An implication of such thinking is that while an infant might have "metaphysical" and "existential" forms of dignity, he or she lacks "characterological" dignity. Even when a separate and coherent sense of self first emerges (Mahler, Pine, & Bergman, 1975), the child can be seen to have a sort of "proto-dignity" at best. Much ego growth and mastery of many developmental tasks is required before full "characterological" dignity appears on the horizon.

The individual with such dignity can stick to moral pathways, tolerate states of fear, immerse himself in the subjective experiences of others, maintain appropriate caution and reserve, express himself with elegance, and remain true to his own core beliefs. Marcovitz (1970a, 1970b) stands heads and shoulders above the psychoanalytic contributors to such delineation of dignity. However, since characterological dignity denotes a composite of self-respect, confidence, integrity, inner morality, authenticity, and courage, all those who have addressed these topics implicitly contribute to the understanding of this type of dignity. It is not possible to list all such contributions but mention must be made of Freud's (1923b, 1924d) and Jacobson's (1964) writings on superego, Benedek's (1938) concept of "confident expectation", Rangell's (1954) delineation of poise, Erikson's concepts of "integrity" (1950) and "care" (1982), Winnicott's (1960) proposal of true self, and the recent psychoanalytic papers on courage by Levine (2006), O'Neil (2009), and Akhtar (2013a). The advantage of the concept of "characterological dignity" is that being a personality trait, it can be psychoanalytically studied and, with improved child-rearing, can be cultivated more and more often. The disadvantage of this concept is that it facilitates a certain kind of psychic élitism; some people are seen as having dignity (or, at least, more dignity) while others as lacking it. Such division creates the potential (however unintentionally) of prejudice and discrimination against the latter group and, worse, deliberate jettisoning of disliked individuals and minorities into the less-dignified category.

Further synthesis of these three perspectives becomes feasible if we lump the first two categories (metaphysical and existential) together and designate the resulting concept as "dignity in the broad sense" of the word and call the remaining category (characterological) as "dignity in the narrow sense" of the word. Precedent for such classification does exist in psychoanalysis in the forms of "reality principle in broad sense" and "reality principle in narrow sense" (Hartmann, 1956, 1964) and "self-psychology in broad sense" and "self-psychology in narrow sense" (Kohut, 1977). Yet another way of thinking about these three groupings (metaphysical, existential, and characterological) is to consider them "perspectives" rather than categories per se. At the same time, it cannot be overlooked that no matter how neat the nosological packaging of the concept of dignity, some slippage inevitably occurs.

Technical implications

The foregoing elucidation of human dignity has enormous sociopolitical implications. The concept forms the backbone of the theory of human rights. In civilised societies, such rights include those pertaining to freedom of speech, freedom of religion, freedom of association, freedom of movement, entitlement to one's privacy, and access to due process of law. Inherent in human rights is a commitment to the equality of all human beings. Each human being has the same and equal rights. The state cannot abridge or deny the rights of any individual and cannot treat any person as a second-class citizen or practice discrimination against any group by law. Such understanding of the dignity of each human being and of the human species in general plays a vital role in the United Nation's Universal Declaration of Human Rights of 1948, the Geneva Convention of 1949, and the Constitution of the United States. With various hues and nuances, each of these documents insists upon the dignity of human beings, even in dire circumstances such as imprisonment, judicial retribution, and war.

Such profound matters and debates surrounding them (Kateb, 2011; Rosen, 2012), however, are not daily concerns of the practicing psychoanalyst. Nonetheless, dealing with the most private and sensitive core of human psychic life and the "boundary crossings" (Gabbard & Lester, 1995) inherent in such enterprise necessitates that the analyst be mindful of dignity-related issues in the clinical situation. In my way of thinking, there are four ways in which concerns about dignity crop up in the course of our work.

Safeguarding the dignity of the analytic space

The expression "analytic space" has both literal and metaphorical dimensions. On the literal level, it refers to the waiting room and the consulting room. The former mostly constitutes a space for private, introspective reverie (Wolman, 2007) but can be used for all sorts of different psychic purposes by patients (Abassi, 2014; Kieffer, 2011). The latter, that is, the consulting room, is where the "real" work of analysis takes place. Elsewhere, I have written in detail about the diverse manners in which the analyst's office (and the physical objects contained in it) impact upon the clinical process (Akhtar, 2009, pp. 113–133). I have elaborated upon the dimensions of location, comfort, authenticity, and constancy of the analyst's office and the analyst's need to safeguard its holding functions. Here, however, I want to emphasise that a certain "metaphysical dignity" characterises the consulting room and imparts to it a sacred quality. The wall next to the couch becomes a containing limit, the *objets d'art* acquire the status of "mnemic objects" (Bollas, 1992), the furniture and the lamps offer themselves as objects of "non-human transferences" (Akhtar, 2009). The inanimate is a silent ally of the analytic process. Hence, it must be treated with dignity and its sacredness protected from intrusions of the profane.[7] To put it bluntly, accoutrements of instinctual gratification (e.g., condoms, pornographic material, bottles of alcohol) must not be stored in the nooks and crannies of the analyst's office nor should activities of direct instinctual gratification (e.g., sexual intercourse, physical violence) take place inside the analytic office, even outside of the clinical hours and even if involving individuals other than patients. The principle of abstinence applies not only to the analyst's attitude during clinical work but also to his or her respect for the analytic office. If an analyst smokes pot, masturbates, or has sex with someone in the office, memory traces of such acts continue to haunt the space and pervert its sacrosanct nature. Two lines from the renowned Urdu poet, Jan Nisar Akhtar (1914–1976) come to mind in this context:

> "Aayeene ke aage na badalna kapde
> Aayeene mein aks reh be jaate hain sakhi"[8] (1972)

Needing to protect the dignity of the analytic space, however, goes beyond its literal level. On a metaphorical level, analytic space refers to the dialectically created, psychic realm of discourse between the unconscious of the patient and the unconscious of the analyst (Akhtar, 2013b; Bolognini, 2011; Freud, 1912e). This space is not static. It shrinks and expands. It deepens and becomes shallow. It might seem ephemeral but it is always there and must be treated with dignity. Quick, clever, and deep interpretations might impress the patient but often foreclose the analytic space and preclude the emergence of the "waiting beast" (Coltart, 2000) from within the depths of the patient's psyche. Treating the analytic space with dignity warrants patience, respect for the essential Otherness of the patient, and keeping tight reins upon the analyst's "compulsion to interpret" (Epstein, 1979).

Protecting the dignity of the analytic process

Two points must be made clear at the outset here: one, that the analyst must possess, display, and behave with "characterological dignity"; two, that the analyst is, by the very nature of his role, open to be moulded, constructed, destructed, formed, deformed, and even defiled (to a certain extent) by his patient's transferences. Both these points are well-accepted. The rub comes when the patient's projective intrusions (and, at times, real life actions) begin to collapse the analytic space and violate the core dignity of the analytic process. Undoubtedly the patient, in a state of frustration and rage, can call his Jewish analyst a "kike", his African-American analyst a "nigger", his Hindu analyst a "monkey-worshipping asshole", and his Muslim analyst a "fucking Arab terrorist". But when such attacks are cold, calculating, and chronic, and when the patient's speech becomes a predominant vehicle of instinctual discharge, matters take a different turn. Pertinent in this context is the following observation of Ella Freeman Sharpe (1940):

> The discharge of feeling tension, when this is no longer relieved by physical discharge, can take place through speech. The activity of speaking is substituted for the physical activity now restricted at other openings of the body, while words themselves become the very substitutes for the bodily substances. (p. 157)

This applies to the sharp and narrow-minded interrogation by the malignantly paranoid, blood-curdling screams of the severely borderline, and the lascivious "dirty talk" of the defiant pervert. The latter, though on the surface referring to matters erotic, is also at its base hostile. And, in so far as such verbalisations (perhaps better called vocalisations) turn speaking into acting, they constitute attacks on the dignity of the analytic process. The existence of hostility in such talking is approached by Aulagnier (2001) from a novel perspective.

> If one considers the auditory function, what one notes is the absence in this register of any system of closure comparable to the closing of eyelids or lips, or to the tactile retreat that muscular movement allows. The auditory cavity cannot remove itself from the irruption of sound waves; it is an open orifice in which, in a state of waking, the outside continuously penetrates ... [consequently] the voice-object may so easily become the embodiment of the persecutory object. (p. 60)

The point to remember here is that such behaviours on the part of the patient are attacks against the analyst's dignity as an analyst (not so much as his or her dignity as a human being, though that too might be involved to a certain extent). It is therefore that such behaviours must be curtailed. Elsewhere (Akhtar, 2013b), I have dealt in detail with technical measures (including refusal to listen to certain kinds of material) indicated under such circumstances. Here, it would suffice to say that it is the analyst's responsibility to protect his dignity as an analyst, his dignity as a person, and, above all, the dignity of his clinical work.

Maintaining contact with the patient's dignity

Besides transference, countertransference, and therapeutic alliance, the analytic pair is also involved in a real relationship. Constituents of it are manifest in their loyalty to the frame (e.g., punctuality, regularity, payment of fees) and the spirit (e.g., respect for complexity, quest for knowledge, and a fundamental attitude of decency and affection towards each other) of their work. Noted by a number of authors (Freud, 1954; Greenson, 1967; Stone, 1954, 1961), such "real relationship" demands that the analyst must not ignore the patient's "existential dignity" at any point. The occasions where the analyst's diligence in this regard is tested vary. An admittedly incomplete list consists of the following:

- The patient is in an advanced state of pregnancy and, at the end of one session, needs assistance to get up from the couch.
- The patient has severe postnasal drip and cannot lie down on the couch, and wants to sit up.
- The patient is a doctoral student and has been regular in attendance and payment. She learns that, for the purposes of her dissertation, she has to spend six weeks in another country. Since this is not to occur for another four to five months, she expects that a long notice like this would mean that she does not have to pay for the sessions missed.
- The patient belongs to a religion other than that of his analyst and cannot keep two appointments due to certain observances. He thinks he should not be charged for those sessions.
- The patient reports that he eats his snot on a regular basis.
- The patient notices that the analyst is quite sick. The analyst has been quiet about this but the patient has learned from the grapevine that the analyst has a terminal illness. Then, one day as the session ends, the patient notices that the analyst's face is quite ashen, he is very weak, and having difficulty getting up from his chair. He asks the analyst what is the matter.

All these situations might have individualised responses to them that would be appropriate. No one attitude can be legislated for as being correct. But these situations do have something in common. They test the resilience of the analytic technique and provide opportunities for treating our patients with the dignity they deserve. In accepting their basic rights as human beings, and their entitlement to empathy, respect, and honesty, we preserve their dignity. Simply put, we assist the pregnant woman in getting up from the couch, let the patient with postnasal drip sit up, not charge the doctoral student and the religious Other for the missed sessions, listen with equanimity to the one who eats snot, and let the patient know the truth about our not being well. If, however, we exert psychoanalytic autocracy, hide behind "proper" technique, and remain stonily silent or turn interpretive in these circumstances, we end up offending them to their very core. We must not forget that respect for the patient as an autonomous and worthy individual is central to our clinical work. The views of the French philosopher, Emanuel Levinas (1906–1995) turn out to be the most reliable guides for appropriate conduct in the sort of situations mentioned above. Levinas (1961, 1981) states that ethical relatedness to the Other requires recognition of and respect for difference. Erasing self-other distinction leads to totalisation and sets the stage for domination and control. Commitment to dialogue, in contrast, endorses a relation between self and Other while accepting the "strangeness" and autonomy of both parties. No partner in a dialogue has all the answers and each can enrich the process between them. Needless to add that judicious accommodations to frame and offering well-titrated "gratifications" that might emanate from such an attitude do not oppose the interpretive work of psychoanalysis.[9] In fact, they strengthen the possibility of such work to continue.

Empathising with the indignities faced by the patient

Many of our patients suffer from indignities, either those that were afflicted upon them during childhood or those that are their lot as adults. In an impressive confluence of ideas, the psychoanalyst Leonard Shengold and the political theorist George Kateb address the devastating impact of being robbed of one's dignity upon the human mind. Shengold (1989) designates the result of assaults upon human dignity as "soul murder". Deliberately inflicted by an individual upon the (usually dependent and weaker) other, such trauma consists of (i) attack upon the capacity for rational thought, (ii) erasure of the victim's identity, and (iii) brain-washing that leads to confusion in the victim's mind about what actually took place and a belief that what did take place was highly pathological. Kateb (2011) makes similar observations within the sociopolitical context and I take the liberty of quoting him at some length.

> Beyond oppression, there are systems of suffering that are so extreme as to efface the personhood of individuals and leave only biological entities that do anything to survive, at whatever cost to those around them and to their own dignity. Degraded human beings therefore lose their identity as human beings and as particular persons, at least for a significant stretch of time. They have been forced to lose almost all uniquely human and personal characteristics. Thus through no fault of their own, they no longer manifest

the reason for which incomparable dignity is assigned to human beings. The assault on dignity has achieved its aim when the every possibility of the idea of human dignity is forced out of the mind of the victim by extreme suffering. (p. 20)

Kateb emphasises that since such existential loss often fails to register on the victim, it is the responsibility of the observer to highlight the evil treatment. Now, this is as true in the setting of one nation, one tribe, one ethnic group (usually the majority) abusing the other nation, tribe, or ethnic group as it is in the less magisterial but no less sinister setting of one individual being abused by another. Here the validating role of the psychoanalyst gains paramount importance. Take a look at the following situations.

- The patient reports that during his childhood, his enraged father would ask him to lie still on the floor while he took a few steps back, came rapidly towards him, and kicked him with full force in his head.
- The patient reports that after his mother's death when he was five years old, his maternal grandfather sodomised him, saying that this should make him feel close to his deceased mother; the grandfather declared himself to be the substitute for the boy's mother.
- The patient says that his wife routinely calls him "scumbag", worse than an animal, psychotic, antisocial, and so ugly that she feels like vomiting each time she looks at his face.
- The patient, an international medical graduate from the Far East, reports sitting in a departmental meeting where senior faculty members were unrelentingly mocking the name of one Dr. Ha who had applied for a job there.
- The patient is eighty-three years old and often loses control of his bowels, soiling his underwear. He cannot see or hear as sharply as before and feels ashamed about his shuffling gait and stooped posture.[10]

To a greater or lesser degree, all the situations cited above call for validation from the analyst that the patient's dignity is or was being endangered. Of course, deciphering the meanings of each event to each particular individual will be necessary and would form the cornerstone of the psychoanalytic approach. However, such work must be preceded by "affirmative interventions" (Killingmo, 1989) that are intended not at unmasking what lies under the surface but at establishing plausibility that the patient's anguish is valid and meaningful. The confirmation that the patient's dignity is threatened paradoxically restores the valued asset.

Concluding remarks

In this contribution, I have surveyed the wide-ranging literature on the topic of dignity. I have reviewed its definitions in philosophical and psychoanalytic writings and attempted to synthesise them by outlining three categories of dignity which can be seen as phenomenological clusters, points of views, as well as levels of abstraction. These are (i) metaphysical dignity, which extends the concept of dignity beyond the human species to all that exists in this world, (ii) existential dignity, which applies to human beings alone, and (iii) characterological dignity, which applies to some human beings more than to others. I have detailed some pros and cons of each category and acknowledged the limitations of my classification. Finally, I have elucidated the sociopolitical and therapeutic implications of the dignity concept, though my emphasis has remained upon the latter.

I now wish to conclude by briefly taking up three matters that exist on the remote but challenging periphery of the topic at hand. The first pertains to whether someone's dignity can be trampled upon without their conscious or unconscious surrender to such assault. The second pertains to dignity's link with goodness. The third pertains to the role of dignity in certain kinds of suicide. As far as the first issue is concerned, it seems that during infancy and childhood when one is weak and dependent, and in concentration camps and terrorising totalitarian regimes, human dignity can be crushed even without the individual's participation in such abuse. However, in adult-life situations and in relatively calm social circumstances, one has to almost willingly surrender one's dignity in order for the tormentor to be really successful. The fact is that an adult retains choice, and this is especially true when people can undertake collective revolt against oppression and occupation. While true of many populations of today's world, the following poem by Chogyam Trungpa (1998, p. 5) captures this sentiment in the context of the Tibetan occupation by Chinese forces.

> The red flag flies above Potala,
> The people of Tibet are drowned in an ocean of blood;
> A vampire army fills the mountains and plains,
> But self-existing dignity never wanes.

The second matter pertains to the connection between dignity and goodness. The components of dignity (integrity, morality, authenticity, poise, self-respect, and courage) have a remarkable overlap with what I have elsewhere (Akhtar, 2011) delineated as the components of human goodness (restraint, epistemic enthusiasm, gratitude, concern, empathy, authenticity, generativity, and faith). Dignity and goodness thus appear closely related. And we witness their confluence in the lives of Gandhi, Martin Luther King, and Nelson Mandela, to name but a few shining stars of humanity. But do all "good people" have dignity? Or, is there some additional element that imparts the aura of personal dignity to an individual? More fortitude? More charm? A certain kind of noble reserve? Physical grace? Frankly, we do not know. Further complexity is added when we consider whether "bad people" can exude dignity. Forgive my audacity but might we consider Don Corleone, the Mafia boss from Mario Puzo's (1969) novel, *The Godfather* (and his celluloid incarnation in the person of Marlon Brando), as possessing dignity? He was restrained. He was authentic and courageous. He had a certain sort of integrity and, in his own way, was even "moral". So would we be correct in assuming that he, and other high-level gangsters and criminals like him, have dignity? We cringe at that thought but a moralising countertransference is hardly a sufficient response to this question. It is not easy to spot the boundary between the charisma and power resulting from pathological narcissism and the transcendental calm emanating from morally anchored concern for others, deep empathy, and genuine fortitude. Keeping these two phenomenological postures blurred is the hallmark of messianic cult-leaders in whom pseudo-humility cloaks omnipotence and charm masquerades as kindness. Clearly more thought is needed about the presence or absence of dignity under such circumstances.

Finally, there is the link between dignity and certain kinds of suicide. Sociopolitical and ethical debates regarding the practice of euthanasia and the self-righteous crusades of Jack Kevorkian (1928–2011) notwithstanding, the question whether killing oneself can, at times, be the only way left to preserve one's dignity, is important. Within psychoanalysis, two passages help us think about this matter. One is by Klein (1935) and the other by Winnicott (1960). Talking of the suicidal individual, Klein states:

> In committing suicide, his purpose may be to make a clean breach in his relation to the outside world because he desires to rid some real object—or the "good" object which the whole world represents and which the ego is identified with—of himself, or of that part of his ego which is identified with his bad objects and his id. (p. 276)

This is "morally-clean" or altruistic suicide. Self-destruction is undertaken because it appears undignified to go on burdening others with one's needs and demands. Many suicides in the context of incurable terminal illness fall in this category.

Another pathway that links personal dignity and suicide is to be found in the following passage from Winnicott (1960).

> The False Self has as its main concern a search for conditions which will make it possible for the True self to come into its own. If conditions cannot be found then there must be organized a new defence against exploitation of the True Self, and if there be doubt, then the clinical result is suicide. Suicide in this context is the destruction of the total self in avoidance of the annihilation of the True Self. When suicide is the only defence left against betrayal of the True Self, then it becomes the lot of the False Self to organize the suicide. This, of course, involves its own destruction, but at the same time eliminates the need for its continued existence, since its function is the protection of the True Self from insult. (p. 143)

In simpler words, this amounts to saying that if one has no hope whatsoever left to lead a life of authentic self-expression (an important component of dignity), then it makes sense to end one's life. One might agree or disagree about the applicability of such dynamics to acts of political martyrdom but its operation in certain personal situations appears convincing. In fact, an admixture of the altruistic motive outlined by Klein (1935) and the self-preservatory motive outlined by Winnicott (1960) often underlies the suicides of great people who, due to old age, illness, and infirmity, find themselves unable to lead a life of dignity.

While examples can be given from many realms of human enterprise, it might be humbler to cite only those from within our own field. Prominent psychoanalysts who thus chose to leave this world at their own command include Paul Federn, Bruno Bettleheim, Nina Coltart, Thomas Szasz, and, long before all of them, Sigmund Freud himself. Suffering from cancer, living in chronic pain, tolerating repeated surgeries, sustaining himself on injectable opiates, becoming unable to talk, turning foul-smelling due to infection towards his final days, and feeling rejected by his beloved dog, Jofi, Freud asked his physician, Max Schur, to give him a lethal injection of morphine (Gay, 1988). He had led a rich and highly accomplished life and his time to exit this world had come. He could have lived a few more days, perhaps even a few more weeks or months. But rather than cling to mere biological survival, he elected to exercise power over his destiny, including how and when his life would end. Being the *mensch*[11] that he was, Freud rejected lingering with indignity and chose a death of dignity.

Notes

1. Silberer originated the term "anagogic interpretation" for a mode of decoding symbolism that brings out its universal, "transcendent", and ethical dimension. Unlike the customary psychoanalytic tendency to decipher symbols along personal and sexual lines, *anagogic* (Greek for "to bear upwards") interpretations elevate the concrete into the spiritual.

2. Generally speaking, the three Middle Eastern religions (Judaism, Christianity, Islam) have a hierarchy whereby God, angels, prophets, and man—all, and in that order—exist above animals. Eastern religions (e.g., Hinduism, Buddhism, Jainism) do not subscribe to such a view. Their God resides everywhere and can exist within human beings as well as within animals. As a result, they ascribe greater dignity to animals.

3. The PEP Archive (1871–2008) contains the complete text of forty-six premier journals in psychoanalysis, seventy classic psychoanalytic books, and the full text and editorial notes of the twenty-four volumes of the *Standard Edition* as well as the eighteen-volume German *Gesammelte Werke*. PEP Archive spans over 137 publication years and contains the full text of articles whose source ranges from 1871 through 2008. There are approximately 75,000 articles and 8,728 figures that originally resided in 1449 volumes with a total of over 650,000 printed pages.

4. Although Shabad uses the expression "spite" throughout his paper, righteous opposition to assaults upon one's dignity need not be termed as such. Rosa Parks' (1913–2005) refusal to yield her seat to someone only because of their being White did not have a spiteful quality. It was a gesture of robust self-assertion to maintain her dignity.

5. For details on how contact with one's own dignity opens one's heart and eyes to the dignity of all creation, see the October 2008 special issue of *Soku Gakkai International Quarterly: A Buddhist Forum for Peace, Culture, and Education.*

6. A Buddhist friend of mine responded to this statement by asking why these things should not have dignity. The mosquito and the sewage pump are doing what they are required to do. And, the broken shoelace is like a poet who has had a stroke. Simply because he is no longer able to write poetry, do we withdraw our respect for him?

7. The word "profane" is derived from the Latin *profamus*, itself comprised of "pro" (before) and "famus" (temple). In other words, "profane" means something that has to be left outside of the temple.

8. An admittedly inelegant translation is "Don't change clothes in front of the mirror; images of your nudity would linger in it long afterwards."

9. The word "gratification" has been unduly maligned in psychoanalytic discourse. One reason for this is the lack of distinction in many analyst's minds between the satisfying prohibited and id wishes versus meeting developmentally unrealistic appropriate ego needs (Akhtar, 1999, for needs wishes).

10. See Lax (2008) for what she calls the "indignities" of getting really old.

11. A Yiddish expression, *mensch*, denotes an honest, courageous, reliable and strong person.

References

Abassi, A. (2014). *The Rupture of Serenity: External Intrusions into the Psychoanalytic Space*. London: Karnac.

Abelson, R. (1978). Psychotherapy and personal dignity. *Psychoanalysis and Contemporary Thought*, 1: 203–216.

Abelson, R., & Margolis, J. (1978). A further exchange on psychotherapy, personal dignity, and persons. *Psychoanalysis and Contemporary Thought*, 1: 227–235.

Abram, J. (2007). *The Language of Winnicott: A Dictionary of Winnicott's Use of Words* (2nd ed). London: Karnac.

Akhtar, J. N. (1972). *Ghar Aangan.* New Delhi, India: Maktaba Jamia.

Akhtar, S. (1999). The distinction between needs and wishes: implications for psychoanalytic theory and technique. *Journal of the American Psychoanalytic Association, 47*: 113–151.

Akhtar, S. (2009). *Comprehensive Dictionary of Psychoanalysis.* London: Karnac.

Akhtar, S. (2011). Goodness. In: *Matters of Life and Death: Psychoanalytic Reflections* (pp. 1–28). London: Karnac.

Akhtar, S. (2013a). *Good Stuff: Courage, Resilience, Gratitude, Generosity, Forgiveness, and Sacrifice.* Lanham, MD: Jason Aronson.

Akhtar, S. (2013b). *Psychoanalytic Listening: Methods, Limits, and Innovations.* London: Karnac.

Auchincloss, E. L., & Samberg, E. (Eds.) (2012). *Psychoanalytic Terms and Concepts.* New Haven, CT: Yale University Press.

Aulagnier, P. (2001). *The Violence of Interpretation; From Pictogram to Statement.* London: Brunner-Routledge.

Benedek, T. (1938). Adaptation to reality in early infancy. *Psychoanalytic Quarterly, 7*: 200–214.

Bion, W. (1965) *Transformations.* London: Karnac, 1984.

Bollas, C. (1992). *Being a Character: Psychoanalysis and Self Experience.* Hove: Routledge.

Bolognini, S. (2011). *Secret Passages: The Theory and Technique of Interpsychic Relation.* (Trans. G. Atkinson). London: Karnac.

Coltart, N. (2000). *Slouching Towards Bethlehem.* New York, NY: Other Press.

De Rosis, L. E. (1973). Self-esteem, dignity, or the sense of being. *American Journal of Psychoanalysis, 33*: 16–27.

Eidelberg, L. (Ed.) (1968). *The Encyclopedia of Psychoanalysis.* New York, NY: Free Press.

Epstein, L. (1979). Countertransference with borderline patients. In: L. Epstein & A. H. Feiner (Eds.) *Countertransference* (pp. 375–406). New York, NY: Jason Aronson.

Erikson, E. H. (1950). *Childhood and Society.* New York, NY: W. W. Norton, 1963.

Erikson, E. H. (1975). *Life History and the Historical Moment.* New York, NY: W. W. Norton.

Erikson, E. H. (1982). *The Life Cycle Completed: A Review.* New York, NY: W. W. Norton.

Freud, A. (1954). Psychoanalysis and education. *Psychoanalytic Study of the Child, 9*: 9–15.

Freud, S. (1912e). Recommendations to physicians practising psychoanalysis. *S. E., 12*: 109–120. London: Hogarth.

Freud, S. (1923b). *The Ego and the Id. S. E., 19*: 1–66. London: Hogarth.

Freud, S. (1924d). The dissolution of the Oedipus complex. *S. E., 19*: 171–188. London: Hogarth.

Gabbard, G. O., & Lester, E. P. (1995). *Boundaries and Boundary Violations in Psychoanalysis*. New York, NY: Basic Books.

Gay, P. (1988). *Freud: A Life for Our Time*. New York, NY: W. W. Norton.

Griffin, J. (2002). A note on measuring well-being. In: C. J. L. Murray, J. Salomon, & C. Mathers (Eds.), *Summary Measures of Population Health: Concepts, Ethics, Measurement and Applications* (p. 31). Geneva, Switzerland: World Health Organization.

Greenson, R. (1967). *The Technique and Practice of Psycho-Analysis*. New York, NY: International Universities Press.

Hartmann, H. (1956). Notes on the reality principle. *Psychoanalytic Study of the Child, 11*: 31–53.

Hartmann, H. (1964). *Essays on Ego Psychology*. New York, NY: International Universities Press.

Jacobson, E. (1964). *The Self and the Object World*. New York, NY: International Universities Press.

Kateb, G. (2011). *Human Dignity*. Cambridge, MA: Harvard University Press.

Kieffer, C. (2011). The waiting room as a boundary and a bridge between self-states and unformulated experiences. *Journal of the American Psychoanalytic Association, 59*: 355–349.

Killingmo, B. (1989). Conflict and deficit: implications for technique. *International Journal of Psychoanalysis, 70*: 65–79.

Klein, M. (1935). A contribution to the psychogenesis of manic depressive states. In: *Love, Guilt and Reparation and Other Works—1921–1945* (pp. 262–289). New York, NY: Free Press, 1975.

Kohut, H. (1977). *The Restoration of the Self*. New York, NY: International Universities Press.

Laplanche, J., & Pontalis, J. -B. (1967). *The Language of Psychoanalysis*. New York, NY: W. W. Norton.

Lax, R. F. (2008). Becoming really old: the indignities. *Psychoanalytic Quarterly, 77*: 835–857.

Levinas, E. (1961). *Totality and Infinity* (Trans. A. Lingis). Pittsburgh, PA: Dusquesne University Press.

Levinas, E. (1981). *Otherwise than Being* (Trans. A. Lingis). Pittsburgh, PA: Dusquesne University Press.

Levine, S. (2006). Catching the wrong leopard: courage and masochism in the psychoanalytic situation. *Psychoanalytic Quarterly, 75*: 533–565.

Lopez-Corvo, R. (2003). *The Work of W. R. Bion*. London: Karnac.

Macklin, R. (2003). Dignity is a useless concept. *British Medical Journal, 327*: 1419–1420.

Mahler, M. S., Pine, F., & Bergman, A. (1975). *The Psychological Birth of the Human Infant: Symbiosis and Individuation*. New York, NY: Basic.

Marcovitz, E. (1970a). Dignity. In: M. S. Temeles (Ed.), *Bemoaning the Lost Dream: Collected Papers of Eli Marcovitz, MD* (pp. 120–130). Philadelphia, PA: Philadelphia Association for Psychoanalysis.

Marcovitz, E. (1970b). Aggression, dignity, and violence. In: M. S. Temeles (Ed.), *Bemoaning the Lost Dream: Collected Papers of Eli Marcovitz, MD* (pp. 131–149). Philadelphia, PA: Philadelphia Association for Psychoanalysis.

Marcus, P. (2013). *In Search of the Spiritual: Gabriel Marcel, Psychoanalysis, and the Sacred*. London: Karnac.

Margolis, J. (1978). Psychotherapy and persons: reply to R. Abelson. *Psychoanalysis and Contemporary Thought, 1*: 217–226.

Mish, F. (Ed.) (1987). *Webster's Ninth Collegiate Dictionary*. Springfield, MA: Merriam Webster Publications.

Moore. B., & Fine, B. (Eds.) (1968). *A Glossary of Psychoanalytic Terms and Concepts*. New York, NY: American Psychoanalytic Association.

Moore. B., & Fine, B. (Eds.) (1990). *Psychoanalytic Terms and Concepts*. New Haven, CT: Yale University Press.

O'Neil, M. K. (2009). Commentary on "courage". In: S. Akhtar (Ed.), *Good Feelings: Psychoanalytic Reflections on Positive Emotions and Attitudes* (pp. 55–63). London: Karnac.

Puzo, M. (1969). *The Godfather*. New York, NY: G. P. Putnam's Sons.

Rangell, L. (1954). The psychology of poise—with a special elaboration on the psychic significance of the snout or perioral region. *International Journal of Psychoanalysis, 35*: 313–332.

Rosen, M. (2012). *Dignity: Its History and Meaning*. Cambridge, MA: Harvard University Press.

Searles, H. (1960). *The Nonhuman Environment in Normal Development and in Schizophrenia*. Madison, CT: International Universities Press.

Shabad, P. (2000). Giving the devil his due: spite and the struggle for individual dignity. *Psychoanalytic Psychology, 17*: 690–705.

Shabad, P. (2011). The dignity of creating: the patient's contribution to the "reachable enough" analyst. *Psychoanalytic Dialogues, 21*: 619–629.

Sharpe, E. F. (1940). Psychophysical problems revealed in language: an examination of metaphor. *International Journal of Psychoanalysis, 41*: 201–220.

Shengold, L. (1989). *Soul Murder: The Effects of Childhood Abuse and Deprivation*. New Haven, CT: Yale University Press.

Silberer, H. (1914). *Problem der Mystik und ihrer Symbolik*. Leipzig, Germany: Hugo Heller.

Stone, L. (1954). The widening scope of indications for psychoanalysis. *Journal of the American Psychoanalytic Association, 2*: 567–594.

Stone, L. (1961). *The Psychoanalytic Situation: an Examination of its Development and Essential Nature. Freud Anniversary Lecture.* New York, NY: International Universities Press, 1977.

The Holy Quran (Ed. & Trans. A. Y. Ali). Lahore, Pakistan: Ashraf Publications, 1968.

Trungpa, C. (1998). *Timely Rain: Selected Poetry of Chogyam Trungpa* (Ed. D. I. Rome, Trans. A. Ginsberg). Boston, MA: Shambhala Publications.

Winnicott, D. W. (1956). The antisocial tendency. In: *Collected Papers: Through Paediatrics to Psychoanalysis* (pp. 306–316). New York, NY: Basic, 1958.

Winnicott, D. W. (1960). Ego distortion in terms of true and false self. In: *The Maturational Processes and the Facilitating Environment* (pp. 140–152). New York, NY: International Universities Press, 1965.

Wolman, T. (2007). Human space, psychic space, analytic space, geopolitical space. In: M. T. S. Hooke & S. Akhtar (Eds.), *The Geography of Meanings: Psychoanalytic Perspectives on Place, Space, Land, and Dislocation* (pp. 23–45). London: International Psychoanalytic Association.

Zachary, A. (2002). The menopause: dignity and development at the end of the reproductive cycle. *Psychoanalytic Psychotherapy, 16*: 20–36.

CHAPTER THREE

Philosophical perspectives: dignity as *arche* and dignity as *telos*

Kenneth A. Richman

E ven the most casual examination of the literature on dignity reveals multiple meanings and concepts. Akhtar identifies three (Akhtar, Chapter Two, this volume), others four (Killmister, 2010) or five (Häyry, 2004). Rather than count concepts of dignity, I identify two families of dignity concepts: dignity as *arche* and dignity as *telos*. *Arche* draws on the idea of an origin or source, as in "archetype" or "archeology." Dignity as *arche* refers to the dignity inherent in a being that is the source (the *arche*) of our duties to that being. *Telos* is a concept meaning goal or target. A teleological explanation of something cites its purpose or intended outcome. Dignity as *telos* is the endpoint (*telos*) that we try to promote in our patients and in ourselves. These concept families may have many members, some bearing closer resemblance than others, but, at their core, concepts of dignity do or should belong to one or the other.

Notes on method

My project is one of conceptual analysis (broadly construed). "Dignity" is a familiar word that captures a familiar concept. As with many concepts, objects, beliefs, and actions that we commonly accept without reflection, a closer look can make the concept of dignity seem foreign, complex, even incoherent. The goal of conceptual analysis is to instigate this sort of disruption in our thinking and suggest ways of putting the pieces together again.

Conceptual analysis is just one way of subduing a difficult concept. Some concepts have become so corrupted that it is reasonable to eliminate them from certain discussions entirely. For instance, among the present cohort of college students the concept of an opinion seems to be completely muddled. Due to influences beyond my control (McBrayer, 2015), many of my students believe that there can be no such thing as a true opinion. This is, of course, contrary to the way "opinion" has been used historically and the way it continues to be used in philosophy. The conviction that opinions could not be true (or even that all opinions are false) appears so firm that I ask students in my bioethics classes to refrain from using the word "opinion" altogether.

Another approach would be to stipulate a definition of "dignity" as a technical term. Declaring "dignity" a technical term would free us from the limits of common usage. This can be useful when we have no better word for the idea we want to capture. However, stipulating a technical definition would not help us understand what people mean by "dignity" in other contexts.

Our work here is meant to be descriptivist rather than revisionist. That is, we will seek to characterise an actual concept of dignity—the way "dignity" is used in the real world—rather than to change this usage by suggesting a revised version of the concept. At the same time, on consideration, we may find that some real-world uses of "dignity" look like misuses under the theory. There is no need for our theory to accommodate every actual use of the word. After all, the meaning of a concept is what allows us to distinguish situations where it applies from situations where it does not apply. Potential for misapplication is thus a consequence of having any meaning at all. The meaning of a term tells us both when it applies and when it does not apply. Our cat concept tells us both that Garfield is a cat and that Lassie is not one.

Even descriptivist theories will thus be revisionist when it comes to some particular instances. Judgments about examples should be adjusted when they fail to fit what the theory indicates. On the other hand, if core examples are rejected by the analysis under consideration, the analysis most likely needs to be revised. Adjusting theory to fit specific examples and adjusting our judgments about specific examples to fit the theory is a balancing act that philosophers call reflective equilibrium. In addition, where there are multiple meanings to a term, as I argue there are with "dignity", a key component of the analysis will be disambiguation between or among these.

Dignity as arche

By "dignity as *arche*" I will mean the feature of humans (and possibly some other entities) that makes them valuable in themselves. It is the basic origin, the source, the *arche*, of human value. Dignity as *arche* is akin to moral standing or moral worth. Dignity in this sense can be seen as inalienable. We might also think that, like an old-fashioned pension, it "vests". That is, once we have dignity in this sense we do not lose it even if we lose capacities or other features.

While dignity "is often seen as hopelessly amorphous or incurably theological" (Foster, 2014, p. 417), Kant derives dignity as *arche* without invoking explicitly theological commitments. Kant does this in at least three ways.[1]

In one move, Kant writes that some things have price and other things have dignity (Kant, 1959, p. 53). On this view, dignity does not consist in being on the extreme end of the price scale; humans do not a have "a price above rubies". Instead, dignity is an entirely different kind of attribute, one that does not admit of degrees. One cannot have more or less of it, and it serves as the rock bottom *arche* of value in the world.

In a related move, Kant claims that we are all sovereigns in the kingdom of ends (Kant, 1959, p. 52). Sovereigns are lawgivers, the sources of rightness and wrongness. As autonomous rational beings, we have the ability—indeed, the responsibility—to use reason to determine and embrace moral law. The universality of rationality means, on this picture, that each of us should come to the same determinations about right and wrong. In this way, we are all sovereign kings and queens in the moral realm, each providing, individually and in unison with the others, moral law.

The second formulation of the categorical imperative presents another related move: treat humanity, whether in yourself or in others, always as an end in itself and never as a means only (Kant, 1959, p. 46). Indeed, many philosophers refer to this formulation as the principle of dignity. It means that we should never use people, at least not without at the same time respecting their inherent value. It is not permissible to treat a person as if she were only good because she helps us to get something else. People are good in themselves, independent of their being useful.

In Frances Hodgson Burnett's (2000) *A Little Princess*, Sara Crewe illustrates appreciation for the dignity of human beings through her interactions with the servant girl Becky. Sara begins her time at Miss Minchin's seminary rich as a princess. She makes respectful overtures to Becky, who insists on complying with social expectations that servants be subservient. Not long into the story, Sara's wealth evaporates and she is left penniless and at the mercy of the mean-hearted Miss Minchin. There is no doubt that Miss Minchin had been using Sara as a means only. Sara immediately loses all the trappings of her previous status, and becomes a fellow servant living in a bare room next to Becky's in the attic they imagine as a revolutionary Bastille. Sara explains to an astonished and still very deferential Becky: "I told you we were just the same—only two little girls—just two little girls. You see how true it is. There's no difference now. I'm not a princess anymore" (Burnett, 2000, p. 88).

The Kantian would agree with the claim that the two girls were the same all along, but not in the way Sarah describes. Rather than being the same in a lowly way, their dignity as *arche* makes them both princesses. Ronald Dworkin explains this Kantian idea as follows: given that "… objective importance cannot be thought to belong to any human life without belonging equally to all, … it is impossible to separate self-respect from respect for the importance of the lives of others" (Dworkin, 2006, pp. 16–17).

Later in *A Little Princess*, we see how Sarah recognises the dignity of a "beggar child" whom Sarah thinks of as "one of the populace" (Burnett, 2000, p. 156). On one of her forced errands, tired, hungry, wet, abused, Sara finds a fourpenny-piece in the dirt outside a bakery and decides to spend it on some hot cross buns. These are one-a-penny hot cross buns, but the woman in the bakery generously puts six buns in the bag in exchange for the fourpence. Sarah gives five of the buns to the miserable girl begging outside the bakery. The baker reacts:

"Well, I never!" she exclaimed. "If that young un hasn't given her buns to a beggar child! It wasn't because she didn't want them, either. Well, well, she looked hungry enough. I'd give something to know what she did it for." (Burnett, 2000, p. 159)

But of course Sara did not do it *for* anything. That is, she did not give away her precious buns as a means to some end. She gave away her buns because she recognised the dignity of the beggar child, the other girl's status as an end in herself. (Sara's action may also have reflected her own need to act out her self-image as a dignified princess, but this does not take away from her treatment of the other girl as an end in herself.)

We can also see recognition of dignity as *arche* in the willingness of the nurses at Boston's Beth Israel-Deaconess hospital to provide treatment to Dzhokhar Tsarnaev, who was entrusted to their care under the presumption that he had committed the crimes surrounding the 2013 Boston Marathon (Gastaldo, 2013). Even those horrific acts, which also disrupted daily life in the whole region, could not strip this patient of the dignity that is the source of moral worth for human beings.

Theologically based concepts of dignity fall into the concept family of dignity as *arche*. Consider, for example, these words from Pope Leo XIII's Encyclical Letter on the Condition of the Working Classes (quoted in Häyry, 2004):

No one may with impunity outrage the dignity of man, which God Himself treats with great reverence … Nay, more, in this connection a man cannot even by his own free choice allow himself to be treated in a way inconsistent with his nature, and suffer his soul to be enslaved … (Pope Leo XIII, 2000, pp. 35–36)

For Pope Leo XIII, the source of human dignity would be that humans are made in the image of God. The ethical implications of this "'Image of God' doctrine" (Craig, 1997, p. 10) are precisely what is captured in the non-theological second formulation of the categorical imperative: treat no one, not even yourself, as a means only.

In Akhtar's tristinction among concepts of dignity (see Chapter Two, this volume), metaphysical dignity and existential dignity are concepts of dignity as *arche*. However, my perspective suggests a re-thinking of Akhtar's claim that "by imparting dignity to every single human being, [existential dignity] risks obliterating the important moral difference between the oppressed and the oppressor and the cruel perpetrator and the innocent victim" (Akhtar, p. 31). Dignity as *arche* attributes just as much dignity to the "the ruthless Nazi officer with a bayonet" as to "his hapless captive" (Akhtar, p. 32) With respect to dignity as *arche*, the problem is not that the officer has no dignity or less dignity, but that he is committing outrage against the dignity of man, both in himself and in his captive. Levine (Chapter Ten, this volume) would see this as "dignity abdication", but dignity as *arche* does not allow one to abdicate. The officer cannot truly alienate himself from his own dignity, and cannot damage the dignity of any human in the sense of dignity as *arche*. There is no doubt, however, that he has damaged his own dignity as *telos*.

Dignity as telos

Dignity as *telos* refers to the state of the person, self, or patient that we aim to achieve. This concept resonates with Aristotelian rather than Kantian traditions.[2] The *telos* of a thing is its goal, its aim, its final cause, "that for the sake of which" (Aristotle, 1947, p. 194b). The *telos* of an activity is also said to be "the good" for that activity:

> Every art and every inquiry, and similarly every action and pursuit, is thought to aim at some good; and for this reason the good has rightly been declared to be that at which all things aim. (Aristotle, 1947, p. 1094a)

The *telos* of an acorn is to grow into a mighty oak tree. It is rare for an acorn to achieve this, but being a mighty oak is, nonetheless, the good at which acorns aim.

Although "*telos*" can be translated as "end", it is not necessarily the last phase in the development of a thing, but the fullest realisation of its nature. The acorn that fulfills its *telos* by becoming a mighty oak continues on even as its magnificence fades.

Akhtar captures dignity as *telos* beautifully in his gloss on what he calls characterological dignity: "This refers to a constellation of personality traits that are largely derived from the epigenetic unfolding of human psychic development and therefore might not exist in all individuals to a comparable extent" (Akhtar, this volume, p. 32). This way of conceiving dignity invokes concepts of nobility and poise. It also very clearly portrays dignity as a type of health, well-being, or flourishing.

Maslow's concept of self-actualisation also belongs under this umbrella. Maslow identifies as good "Anything that conduces to th[e] desirable development in the direction of actualization of inner human nature" (Maslow, 1954, p. 115). Maslow argues that realisation of potentialities, which "may be either idiosyncratic or species-wide" (Maslow, 1954, p. 126), is required for full psychological health. Therapy, for Maslow, is whatever facilitates progress toward the *telos* determined by our individual versions of human nature (Maslow, 1954, p. 115).

Authenticity and resilience, which would include maintaining a core sense of self even in the face of adversity, appear to be significant features of dignity as *telos*. (Compare Akhtar, Chapter Two, this volume; Maslow, 1954, p. 129; Underwood, 1975, p. 148.) We see this also in Sara Crewe's ability to maintain a strong, positive self-image even in the context of mistreatment:

> "Whatever comes," she said, "cannot alter one thing. If I am a princess in rags and tatters, I can be a princess inside. It would be easy to be a princess if I were dressed in cloth of gold, but it is a great deal more of a triumph to be one all the time when no one knows it." (Burnett, 2000, p. 136)

Under a concept of dignity as *arche*, Sara's status as a princess is not hard to maintain. This status cannot be lost. However, maintaining dignity as *telos* while being deprived of food, sent out into the cold without adequate clothing, and being told again and again that she is worthless, is the epitome of "the triumphant nature" (Maslow, 1971, p. 52, quoted in Underwood, 1975, p. 149) of the self-actualising person.

We can use the distinction between dignity as *arche* and dignity as *telos* to unpack some of the rich ambiguity found in particular claims about dignity. For instance, Foster writes: "A prison warden who forces a prisoner to eat his own feces isn't primarily affecting the dignity of the prisoner. But he's massively eroding his own" (Foster, 2014, p. 423). On our scheme, the dignity that is eroded by his behaviour is his own dignity as *telos*. Although treating oneself badly is generally not recognised as a culpable offence, it is, of course, unhealthy and unfortunate. The assault on the prisoner's dignity as *telos* is one aspect of what makes the warden's behaviour blameworthy, especially as it would take remarkable strength of character for the prisoner to maintain his dignity as *telos* in the face of this treatment. The warden's behaviour is also blameworthy because he is failing to respect (committing an outrage against) dignity as *arche* in both his prisoner and himself. Again, failure to respect dignity of the other is generally blamed more than failure to respect the dignity of the self.

When Sara tells Becky that they are both just two little girls, Becky's response also resonates with both aspects of dignity. Becky replies "Whats'ever 'appens to you—whats'ever—you'd be a princess all the same—an' nothin' couldn't make you nothin' different" (Burnett, 2000, p. 88). Becky's statement seems to reflect a great respect for Sara's dignified character (dignity as *telos*), which appears so well seated as to be resilient in the face of any assault. There is also a class-based essentialism lurking here. Becky does not consider herself worthy of respect, but sees dignity as *arche* as something that cannot be taken away from Sara. This suggests that, contra Kant, Becky sees herself and Sara as different sorts of beings.

Clinical implications

Dignity as *arche* tells us that patients have moral worth no matter what. Patients can lose their connection to that status in themselves, but clinicians never should. The simple implication of this concept is that the clinician should help restore the patient's recognition of and respect for her own dignity.

We are the *arche*—the source—of moral value because of the core human capacity to choose and to act on the basis of reasons and values. We are therefore most fully connected with our dignity when we are able to take responsibility for our choices and values. This means acting authentically, where our actions flow from and are attributed to the self rather than being or being seen as controlled by someone or something else. As Lear puts it, "Psychoanalysis encourages a person to work through the particular meanings by which he lives his life: nothing is to be taken for granted or accepted merely on authority" (Lear, 1998, p. 206). For those who are capable or can become capable of taking responsibility, accepting meanings for one's life merely on authority is a failure to connect with the dignity of the self.

Kant tied human choice and values to rationality. In the psychoanalyst's more complicated milieu, the patient must also come to own her impulses and drives. According to Lear, "… failing to accept responsibility for my drives makes me vulnerable to pathology" (Lear, 1998, p. 174). The clinical goal of harnessing these drives to the individual's value-based choices serves as a way to give the patient's dignity as *arche* its rightful place. Achieving this goal requires "crafting a narration, which captures a reinterpreted life" (Tauber, 2010, p. 197). This narration is a reinterpretation in so far as it involves revision and clarification of the values, choices, and drives that shape the story, and attributes them unequivocally to the patient.

Giving dignity as *arche* its rightful place in this way is essential for promoting dignity as *telos*. No one can achieve self-actualisation without recognising herself as the source of value and choice in her own life. Indeed, the ways in which a person establishes the details of her individual version of dignity as *arche* determines her *telos* and points toward its realisation. Promoting dignity as *telos* involves empowering patients to act on (to make real) the values and choices that flow from the self as *arche*—the self as the source of value in the world and as the force driving her life narrative.

Attending to dignity as *arche* and dignity as *telos* in the patient will not be a linear process. It will, instead, be more like the reflective equilibrium mentioned in the notes on method above. An individual's values become evident through her actions even as those values give rise to those very actions. In this way, the result provides evidence of what gave rise to it:

> It is in the healthy, functioning adult that the inquiring scientist can discover the principles or organization of that species. Only then can he understand what the youthful striving to acquire form was a striving toward. (Lear, 1998, p. 214)

Uncovering the individual's version of dignity as *arche* and identifying the goals that define dignity as *telos* for that individual requires an iterative process of successive examination and revision of each in turn.

I started out by aiming for a descriptivist account of dignity. I believe the distinction between the two families of dignity concept describe actual uses of the concept. The application may, however, seem to stray. My description of dignity as *telos* clearly resonates with authenticity and integrity, concepts that involve internal consistency and maintaining the self as the locus of control. It also reflects the Aristotelian notion of flourishing as realisation of one's nature, although the Aristotelian sees nature on a species level rather than as varying from individual to individual.

It might be less clear how dignity as self-actualisation (another aspect of dignity as *telos*) reflects the common understanding of dignity as a feature of people who are dignified. When we attribute dignity to a senator, king, or pope, we certainly suggest that the person has achieved an honourable manner, a way of being in the world that reflects wholeness and flourishing. This sort of dignity can be lost (unlike dignity as *arche*), but one could not be very dignified if that dignity were easy to dislodge.

The dignity of the truly dignified person is stable and robust. Whether the self-actualisation I describe above is stable and robust in the same way is an empirical matter. However, it is reasonable to expect that the coherence, integrity, and authenticity that comes with living a life consistent with one's goals would be stable and robust. Do those who have achieved or are striving to achieve their *telos* elicit admiration the way individuals whom we call "dignified" do? Again, we can only speculate, but intuition suggests that they do.

Further challenges lurk in the waters of dignity. One concern is how to ground dignity as *arche* for all and only those to whom it properly applies. If we stipulate criteria for having dignity (such as rationality), we leave out some who should be included. Allowing that dignity vests keeps in those who once satisfied the criteria. Vesting does not, however, take care of those who have never satisfied the criteria, and it seems wrong to ground the dignity of vulnerable people on analogy to the "better specimens" of humanity. On the other hand, if we attribute dignity as *arche* to any human being we must address the status of human embryos, which raises other challenges.

Identifying two themes in our dignity concepts helps to identify the dignity-related tasks for the psychoanalyst. These are to help patients recognise, connect with, and respect their own dignity as *arche*, and to help them realise their own dignity as *telos*.

Notes

1. This is not intended as a scholarly treatment of Kant's texts. It is, however, meant to reflect Kantian themes—ideas that at least have Kant as their *arche* and that will be recognised as Kantian by philosophers. See Pfordten (2009) for a scholarly discussion of the role human dignity plays in the range of Kant's work.
2. As with the Kantian discussion above, this is intended to reflect Aristotelian themes in the service of exploring the concept family dignity as *telos*. It is not intended as an exposition of Aristotle.

References

Aristotle (1947). Nicomachean Ethics. In: R. McKeon (Ed.), *Introduction to Aristotle* (pp. 935–1126). New York, NY: Random House.

Burnett, F. H. (2000). *A Little Princess*. New York, NY: Scholastic.

Craig, E. (1997). *The Mind of God and the Works of Man*. Oxford: Oxford University Press.

Dworkin, R. (2006). *Is Democracy Possible Here?* Princeton, NJ: Princeton University Press.

Foster, C. (2014). Dignity and the ownership and use of body parts. *Cambridge Quarterly of Healthcare Ethics, 23*: 417–430.

Gastaldo, E. (2013). Nurses talk about caring for Dzhokhar Tsarnaev. *USA Today*, 20 May. Available at: http://www.usatoday.com/story/news/nation/2013/05/20/newser-dzhokhar-tsarnaev-nurses/2326539/.

Häyry, M. (2004). Another look at dignity. *Cambridge Quarterly of Healthcare Ethics, 13*: 7–14.

Kant, I. (1959). *Foundations of the Metaphysics of Morals*. (L. W. Beck, Trans.). New York: Bobbs-Merrill.

Killmister, S. (2010). Dignity: not such a useless concept. *Journal of Medical Ethics, 36*: 160–164.

Lear, J. (1998). *Love and its Place in Nature*. New Haven, CT: Yale University Press.

Maslow, A. H. (1954). In: R. Frager, J. Fodiman, C. McReynolds & R. Cox (Eds.), *Motivation and Personality* (Third Edition). New York, NY: Harper & Row.

Maslow, A. H. (1971). *The Farther Reaches of Human Nature*. Oxford: Pergamon.

McBrayer, J. P. (2015). Why our children don't believe there are moral facts. http://opinionator.blogs.nytimes.com/2015/03/02/why-our-children-dont-think-there-are-moral-facts/?_r=0. Date accessed: 15 June 2015.

Pfordten, D. V. D. (2009). On the dignity of man in Kant. *Philosophy: The Journal of the British Institute of Philosophical Studies, 84*: 371–391.

Pope Leo XIII (2000). *Encyclical Letter of His Holiness Pope Leo XIII on the Condition of the Working Classes: Rerum Novarum*. Boston, MA: Pauline Books.

Tauber, A. I. (2010). *Freud, the Reluctant Philosopher*. Princeton, NJ: Princeton University Press.

Underwood, R. L. (1975). Freedom and dignity in A. H. Maslow's philosophy of the person. *Zygon, 10*: 144–161.

CHAPTER FOUR

Dignity (1966)*

Eli Marcovitz

W hy was the topic "Dignity" given to me by a Mental Health Association? Obviously, there is an implicit assumption that the quality of dignity is one of the characteristics of a healthy individual. But there are many who believe that interest in the individual is now passé, a manifestation of nineteenth-century bourgeois-capitalist socially-mobile middle-class attitudes, out-of-time in our modern civilisation of automation, over-population, big-money multidiscipline team research and mass destructive potential. To think of the individual is reactionary at worst, old-fashioned and ineffective at best. Move masses and individuals will be affected secondarily, hopefully in ways that will spell progress, improvement, and a better life.

---

*This paper was given as an address at the 15th Annual Meeting of the Mental Health Association of Southeastern Pennsylvania, Philadelphia, 14 November 1966.

The fact is, there may be elements of truth in this attitude. But, like so many either-ors, it offers only a part-truth. It seems to me we are in the fortunate position of being able to have both: interest in the mass and in the individual.

Personally, I believe that the development and maintenance of the dignity of the individual human being, both his own sense of worth and its reflection in the attitudes of others toward him, is a necessity to give meaning to existence, to make life worth living. It is simultaneously a pre-requisite, a constituent, and a sign of mental health. Its failure to develop, or its diminution, as well as the efforts to gain or to regain it, are most important aspects of various forms of mental illness as well as of other problems of personality or behaviour that are unhealthy or destructive.

Webster defines dignity in terms of the individual's state of being worthy, honourable, noble, and of his manifestation of concomitant characteristics; and also in terms of his rank and station in the social hierarchy and the degree of estimation in which he is held by others.

It is as if one can say either "I have dignity or worth because of my innate or personal attributes" or "I am dignified or made worthy by my rank or by the esteem or acknowledgment of others." Sometimes one can both have dignity and be dignified; but these do not necessarily go together.

Since dignity is both an intra-psychic and a social phenomenon, we will constantly find ourselves shifting our attention back and forth between both sets of forces, especially since each influences the other. Usually self-esteem is enhanced by the esteem of others, and self-esteem usually plays some part in evoking esteem from others.

From the definition, with words such as "nobleness, excellence, honorable", it is obvious that the concept of dignity was originally a quality associated only with a member of the elite, someone with power, possessions, and prestige. Such an abstraction could appear only in a well-structured hierarchical society, in which it was inconceivable to attribute worth to the lower classes. After all, remember the meanings of "worth". We unconsciously equate "what are you worth" and "are you worthy". Personal attainments, endowed status, and value judgments usually get confused. In accordance with that attitude, someone without possessions, without status, could not be deserving or worthy of either and, therefore, could have no dignity.

Effectiveness and ethics are hard to separate. The "right" way to do something can be either "effective" or "morally good", or both, and "it is wrong" can mean either "ineffective" or "morally bad", or both. But it takes some degree of maturity and sophistication to differentiate these meanings and to recognise that success is not always a just reward and that failure is not always a deserved punishment.

Similarly "dignity" is an ambiguous concept because it embodies this lack of distinction between attainments and deserts. But this ambiguity is a characteristic human mode of thinking.

Worth is relative. In the hierarchy of all groups, practically everyone can find someone to disdain. The "dain" in "disdain" comes from the same root as "dignity". So, the feeling of having some form of superiority over some others is usually necessary in order to have a sense of one's own dignity. The ubiquitous phrase "all men are equal, but some are more equal than others" recognises this universal fact of human society. Only those who are aware that there is no one and will never be anyone lower to look down on lack all self-esteem and fall ill with apathy. But this occurs only in very special situations of extreme helplessness, for example, abandoned or abused infants, debilitating illness, hopeless degrading incarceration, and the helplessness of old age. Ordinarily human society is so complex that no one need be in all regards and in all relationships "low man on the totem pole". There are ways of turning the tables on the superiors from subtle ways the superiors may not even recognise, through achievement in various fields, to varying degrees of overt insubordination, even to violent revolution. Even conquered peoples may keep their sense of dignity through a feeling of contempt for their conquerors. But in order to maintain dignity, one has to have had some. Montaigne wrote, "My reason is not obliged to bow and scrape, that is for my knees." It takes great wisdom to feel a sense of dignity without the feeling or the insignia of superiority.

Somewhere deep in the human mind there is a conviction that children of the nobility inherit the qualities of nobility. Myths and fairy tales from all over the world tell of the legitimate prince who could be recognised though he was reared by peasants, and of the princess who could be identified because her sleep was disturbed by the presence of a pea under a dozen mattresses. Only the legitimate son of Uther Pendragon could draw Excalibur from the anvil.

Today it would be difficult to maintain that only royalty is born with innate dignity. With the spread of the ideals of individual liberty and equality, the concept of dignity has changed also. It is no longer a prerogative of the nobleman and a sign of his superiority. It is now potentially an attribute of all mankind.

For the beginnings of dignity we must return to the infant. He may or may not be born with the dignity of rank, but to have eventually an inner sense of dignity he must experience the feeling of being nurtured, protected, and valued as if he were a king. By the time he is two, a child can give an impression of dignity—when he has mastered walking and running, when he has developed some control of his body functions, when he has some independence and has reserve with strangers but not anxiety.

The next step in the attainment of dignity is learning about the world and people and acquiring the skills necessary for successful adaptation. By adaptation I am not referring only to the process of conforming to the demands of the world. Adaptation also includes the ability to change the external situation to make it more nearly meet one's own demands. Adaptation takes different forms in different environments. In our culture, for most people it requires productive or useful work and the making of a living. Without this there is no dignity, and there is nothing so shattering to dignity as being out of work. But for a significant part of the population this doesn't hold. How does one maintain dignity based on work in the world of chronic unemployment or marginal employment and the welfare cheque? There is alcohol or drugs, there is the cult of masculinity, including delinquency and varying forms of violence. There is the open flouting of the standards of higher social groups, even to dethroning the ideal of work itself. In short there are all sorts of complicated methods that people use to combat the feeling of lack of worth in comparison with those fortunate enough to have been born into or to have achieved higher social and economic status in our society.

Human dignity also requires the development of standards, ideals, ethics, and responsibilities, as well as the ability to stand off and evaluate oneself with justice and humour. Humour can be a great weapon in the struggle to maintain dignity in the face of overwhelming forces. Freud opened his essay on humour with the remark of a criminal on his way to the gallows on a beautiful Monday morning. "Well, the week's beginning nicely." Throughout history oppressed or degraded groups have used humour as a defence against indignity. There is an ancient story of a royal personage travelling through a village who saw a peasant who bore a remarkable resemblance to himself. He called him over and asked, "Did your mother ever work at the palace?" to which the peasant replied, "No, your highness, but my father did."

Besides humour, poor and oppressed peoples have used various forms of art, music, and religion to express their identity and creativity. These creative activities provided pleasure as well as means of expressing aggression in ways that would escape punishment. Only by such means could they create a climate for dignity that saved them from mental and moral disorganisation.

Another necessary component of dignity is aggression. Konrad Lorenz in his recent book *On Aggression* observes that friendship, loyalty, love between two individuals occur only in species with high degrees of intra-specific aggression. I believe the same can be said for dignity. Without the potential for and the command of aggression, there can be no dignity.

In ordinary usage people think of aggression as unprovoked attack, as behaviour that is destructive, anti-social, and unacceptable. This is only one possible form. I conceive of aggression in terms of a spectrum of different forms of relationship. Unless one is aware of these differences and designates specifically the type one is referring to, there can be unending misunderstanding and disagreement and breakdown of communication.

The word *aggression* derives from the Latin *ad gradior*, to walk to or towards. So my first category is simply *activity*, movement. Spontaneous passivity is non-aggressive. But passivity which is reactive, in opposition to someone else's wish or demand, is a form of aggression which relates to the second category—*self-assertion*, the demarcation of boundaries, of what is me and mine. My third category in aggression is *mastery*, which consists of the use or exploitation of others for one's own purposes. This implies the continued existence of the object, and may even necessitate its careful protection. Fourth is *hostility*. This involves the injury or destruction of the object as a step towards the attainment of some other goal. It includes hunting for sport or food or removing a rival or destroying any frustrating object. Then comes *hatred*, which in my experience is always directed against the representative of the evil which one repudiates in oneself, or against the betrayer who has been loved, or against one who has caused shame and dishonour.

Dignity requires the aggression that is in self-assertion. Other forms may also contribute; for example, in some cultures honour requires vengeance. Self-assertion must vary in the course of a person's development.

First there must occur the awareness of one's own boundaries, the differentiation between the "me" and the "not me", with the power to determine what becomes part of the "me" and what is rejected as "not me". This means also the power to resist intrusion, including the power to spit out what mother forces into one's mouth. The first boundaries are of the body itself, then of possessions and territory. Boundaries widen to include one's knowledge and skills, the people with whom one identifies, one's goals and ideals. There is a general law about boundaries: there is a constant tendency for them to spread. But our space on this earth is limited. We do not yet have that Utopian society of abundance in which everybody can have whatever he wants without encroaching on the boundaries of others. Conflict of interests, testing of limits, is universal and inevitable. This does not mean there cannot be co-operation, especially against the next order of stranger; but without the ability both to seek wider boundaries and to resist intrusion there can be no dignity. Only after one has the certainty of this potential can one choose not to use it and still maintain dignity. If one has not stood up and fought in childhood, it takes great fortitude to learn how to stand up and fight in more adult ways later. It takes experience to learn to choose effective means of self-assertion, to know when violence is just and effective and when other means may be better, in both senses—morally and adaptively. Sometimes, however, it seems as if advocates of violence are attempting to realise the never-never lands of delirium and fanaticism. It seems as if these are inevitable detours which must be explored in all human movements at some price of suffering and destruction. But hopefully there is enough reality-sense in most people to force the dreamer to wake eventually, if the price is too great and the rewards too little.

Dignity is sometimes confused with Pride. They are not identical. Dignity is rather an amalgam of Pride and Humility, a just knowledge of one's powers and limitations. Humility is a necessary ingredient because its absence indicates the feeling "I have no limitations"—this is megalomania—the delusion that one is God.

Humiliation is the destroyer of Dignity, but it is difficult to humiliate the man who has humility. Humility is a protection against the destruction of dignity. To humiliate is to dishonour, to degrade, to expose weakness. We talk of someone being "stripped" of honours, of rank, of dignity. This connotes that all these are like clothes which cover the weak and lowly state which is part of the essence of every human being, the state in which he was born.

Dignity and Power are interdependent. When Hitler wanted to eliminate the Jews he first had to take away their power to resist. The first steps were devoted to gradually increasing humiliations, as well as of gradual removal of rights, possessions, and of freedom of movement, all designed to strip them simultaneously both of power and of dignity. This made resistance impossible, so that finally they could be led like lambs to the slaughter.

Power is always an essential to dignity, even where on the surface it seems lacking. An infant acclaimed king immediately has dignity, resting on the power of those who declare allegiance to him. I remember the dignity of the man in his eighties who remarked, when a young relative noted his difficulty in walking and asked how he was, "I am fine, but my legs no longer serve me." This is the power to surmount one's own weakness. Power involves both the ability to exert force and the ability to endure force, to control and to resist being controlled.

With the help of the power of one's ideals and responsibilities and with the help of the rewards and punishments of the world, we learn to control our drives, our passions, and our appetites. With the aid of our inner drives and worldly considerations, we learn to master our otherwise overwhelming conscience, and we learn to resist the inordinate demands of the external world by calling on the inner strengths of our drives and of our ideals.

Dignity depends on a balanced use of all these powers. Balance does not mean remaining constantly in a state of rigid moderation, but rather the ability to return to a state of equilibrium after a movement in any direction—a controlled giving up of control. This is like the difference between a dive and a fall off a high board. One has dignity and the other is collapse. One should also be able to divest one's self of dignity in order to play, as long as one retains the choice of time, place, and person.

Dignity has many faces, and it changes with time. The dignity of the young exploring child is different from that of the questioning adolescent, or from that of assured maturity, or from the wisdom of old age. And the dignity of the woman is different from that of the man.

This brings us to Shame, the brother to Humiliation. Humiliation comes from outside, and we can learn to avoid it, but shame is carried around inside—the constant drain on dignity. Fundamentally shame depends on a conviction, conscious or unconscious, of an inborn weakness or inferiority. One is in constant danger that this will be exposed, if it isn't already obviously visible. Then will come ridicule, humiliation, shame. These are among the most painful experiences possible. Every child feels it to some degree, but some individuals and some groups are subject to much greater trauma tic experiences of being shamed. To diminish the effects of shame, each child has to have experiences which will develop the feeling of acceptance with some degree of pride in himself and his origins, including family, ethnic group, nationality, or religious background. Before one can come to a realistic judgement of one's self, one has to swing between over- and under-estimation. Children feel both extremes—they know their weakness and they try desperately to believe in their greatness—if not of themselves then of their parents or their group or nation—something about them has to be the best. The current preaching among the Negroes of pride in black-ness is long overdue. It is to be expected that for some time it must carry the conviction, "We are the best." How long has it taken the Whites to begin to get over that notion? We can't expect other groups to be able to do without it.

Acceptance and a sense of worth in one's self also involves gender. Although it is true that men envy women and in rare cases men want to become women, men are rarely ashamed of being men—they are usually ashamed of not being man enough, and use all sorts of means to enhance the dignity which depends on their picture of masculinity. With women the problem is different—it is not only that they envy men, but that they are ashamed of being women. Both of these shames, that of men and that of women, originate in the anatomy and in the weak-ness of childhood. Then social and cultural differences tend to increase or to diminish these primary feelings of shame. In the culture of poverty the woman's position is enhanced so that it is easier for her to get over her shame and to have dignity, because she is the prime wage earner and the head of the family; whereas the man's feeling of inadequacy tends to be fostered and he is forced into various symbolic or substitute or exaggerated forms of masculinity. In the middle classes the women have a more difficult time getting over their primary shame and in accepting their femininity with dignity. They tend to have more compli-cated forms of the problem of attaining a feeling of worthiness.

I have already said that even under indignity one may retain an inner feeling of dignity. But each man has his limit. The Gospel states that, after indignity and humiliation, at the third hour, when He was fas-tened to the cross, Jesus said, "Forgive them, Father, for they know not what they do." In spite of indignity He rose above His tormentors and retained dignity. But at the ninth hour, just before He died, He cried, "Lord, Oh Lord, why hast Thou forsaken me?" Six hours of torture on the cross had reduced Him to a forsaken child, His dignity gone. If the stress is great enough or specific enough no man can resist regression and with regression the collapse of dignity.

Dignity then does not depend only on the qualities of the person himself. Anyone can be robbed of dignity. The corollary is that dignity can be conferred. Honour and rank can be bestowed and then command respect regardless of personal qualities. In the Army everyone is taught, "You are not saluting the person, you salute the rank." But still it is the person with the rank who gets the salute.

In our culture, with our egalitarian credo, we have mixed feelings about the dignity of rank or position. We both support it and jeer at it. We can't really make up our minds whether everyone should be expected to strive for his own status and dignity, or whether everyone should have the right to equal dignity a priori.

Dignity can rest on any of these: Being, Knowing, Doing, Creating, and Im pressing. Except for the first, Being, they all imply Power. "Being" carries the meaning "I am worthy just because I am." Many years ago, in describing marijuana addicts in the Army I wrote, "A great many form a compensatory image of themselves as superior people, above the rest of the world in their appreciation of 'Life' and all its sensual experiences. The rest of the world, the 'squares', allow themselves to be limited to the earth, whereas they can transcend it. In this they take on the traditional attitude of the creative artist, but without the need of even making a pretense of creating. They themselves are the superior creation, and they do not feel any need to justify their existence by soiling their hands with work. A frequent remark was 'I wasn't cut out for work.'"

I did not appreciate then that I was describing a form of dignity also attributed to the sons of aristocracy. The intoxicant addictions always are an attempt to deny the lack of dignity, by seeking the *dream* of power and fulfillment. LSD has an even more subtle appeal to the sense of Dignity in Being. According to Timothy Leary, to experience a transformation of oneself and of the world, a distortion of all perceptions, of time and space, with the feeling of recalling not only one's own life back into the womb but also back through one's ancestors to the primeval ooze, to come through such ordeals provides a sense of mystic powers which in the past required long periods of pain, of abnegation, and of inner self-searching, to attain. Now in our modern advanced civilisation anyone can buy a five-dollar instant mystical experience—instant dignity. However, to judge from the statements of Leary and other proselytizers for LSD, it seems to act like a super-vitamin on the universal human fantasies of omnipotence. The illusion of being superhuman is such a seductive temptation—much more attractive than the difficult task of learning one's real potentials and limitations, as well as those of the world. One can be modern and rebellious, expand one's boundaries to the infinite and create a wonderful new world, all with a drop of LSD No wonder it is almost irresistible. LSD is a powerful cerebral poison, and it is foolish to use it and criminal to encourage others, particularly young college people, to use it, outside of the strictly controlled conditions of medical research, until its usefulness and dangers are much more fully understood and controllable than they are so far.

Throughout the discussion today there is shocking evidence that large sectors of our community, those who live in poverty, and within what Oscar Lewis calls "the culture of poverty", are deprived of many things, including dignity. In our urban society such a degree of indignity and degradation must affect the whole community. Not only are "they" deprived but "we" are deprived. If our own sense of dignity has anything to do with our sense of being human, then we must cherish the dignity of all other humans. Abraham Lincoln said, "A man is not a horse because he was born in a stable."

Certainly we know that the "culture of poverty" carries with it an unusually high incidence both of physical and mental illness and of violent and destructive behaviour against others as well as against the self, together with limitations on intellectual development even relating to the use of language. All of these manifestations relate to the ever-present necessity of living in the moment. It is a luxury beyond the means of many in the "culture of poverty" to postpone an immediate pleasure or an immediate relief of any tension in favour of considering possible future consequences.

In my opinion the most significant psychological consequences of the culture of poverty are due to the fact that the reality situation offers no premium for postponement. Existence is carried on at the level of the pleasure-pain principle. There is no room for the development of what we would call the reality-principle. The reality-principle involves controls of drives, postponement of gratifications, endurance of tensions, consideration of and preparation for the future, and requires the development of language, thinking, and foresight. The conditions of urban slum living give little opportunity for such development, and this has little relationship apparently to the origins of the ethnic groups living in the slums of the world's large cities. The pleasure-pain principle is the reality-principle of the slum. By the time a slum child starts school he is already handicapped in his relationship to language in comparison to children in other sectors of the population. As a consequence his intellectual potential has already been diminished. Projects such as Head Start and Get Set are designed to try to reduce this initial educational handicap. But the effect of growing up within the culture of poverty seems to produce many of the characteristics we ordinarily consider child-like—and which really depend on living in the immediacy of the pleasure-pain principle. Secondarily, of course, the slum-dwellers with these handicaps of ego development interact with the real situation of poverty which demands immediacy of response and there is the inevitable vicious circle from which few ever emerge. Their needs for dignity are expressed, therefore, in ways we associate with the immaturity of youth. But under the circumstances of their lives, this can hardly be different.

Social, economic, and cultural conditions affect the structure, function, and relationships in the family. These in turn affect the development of each person in the family. There is no question that to create conditions in which all people have the opportunity to develop mature dignity, profound social, economic, and cultural changes are necessary. The question is whether these changes will be permitted to occur through an evolutionary process.

Changes are difficult and always either too fast or too slow. They should not be sought or fought for to produce a Utopia. That always means fanaticism, violence, and disillusion. There cannot be for anyone a promise of fulfillment of all needs and desires, nor of freedom from Conflict, distress, or fear. Changes should be designed to produce conditions under which all people have the opportunity to develop their potential, to live somewhat more in accordance with the reality principle and to attain the dignity which that entails.

There is another important ingredient in dignity—the feeling of being part of something important, something worth living for, fighting for, sacrificing for. The struggle to produce the kind of changes we have indicated will itself contribute to the dignity of those involved in it.

In summary, the development of dignity based on reality rather than on fantasy requires models and experiences—models of values and strength with which to identify, and experiences of successes and of usefulness. These come primarily from the family, from peers, and from the school, as well as from other groups and situations, such as the religious community, outstanding figures in real life or in fiction, or from mass-communication media. But poor family situations, crowded and inadequate schools, experiences of ridicule, humiliation, and failure, all tend to cripple the development of dignity.

Yet human beings are so complex that there are always exceptions.

In closing, let me recall to you Hamlet's order to Polonius about the players, "Let them be well used", Polonius' "My lord, I will use them according to their desert", and Hamlet's reply, "God's bodikins, man, much better: use every man after his desert and who should 'scape whipping? Use them after your own honour and dignity; the less they deserve the more merit is in your bounty."

Dignity, like justice, must be accorded to others, as well as valued for oneself, if the political and philosophical ideal of the importance of the individual human being is ever to become a universal reality, or even continue to exert some force in human society. We owe dignity to others but we must each win it for ourselves.

CHAPTER FIVE

Of whom shall we speak? Psychoanalytic reflections on dignity*

M. Gerard Fromm

> When there are so many we shall have to mourn,
> when grief has been made so public, and exposed
> to the critique of a whole epoch
> the frailty of our conscience and anguish,
> of whom shall we speak?

These are the opening lines of W. H. Auden's magnificent elegy "In Memory of Sigmund Freud" (1940), begun just after Freud's death on 23 September 1939, three weeks after the Nazi invasion of Poland. They were also the opening lines of the first issue of the *International Review of Psychoanalysis* forty years ago this year. I begin with these lines because, within them, there is the great juxtaposition of what

---

*This chapter was originally presented as part of a panel on dignity at the American Psychoanalytic Association meetings in New York on 18 January 2014.

Davoine and Gaudillière (2004) call the Big History and the Little History, the catastrophic social upheaval of the day and the loss of one person, someone who was "doing us some good", says Auden. Just as in Mark St. Germain's play *Freud's Last Session* (2011), we are at the historical end of the "Long Weekend" between the World Wars, and the horrors set in motion 100 years ago this year are about to resume with unimaginable fury. In that context of immeasurable loss, "Of whom shall we speak?"

But Auden's poem does more than remember, honour, and elaborate Freud; it asserts, and it argues for, an answer to this question: that we shall speak of someone who stands for the dignity—and, to be sure, the complexity—of the individual. This is the first point—actually a two-part one—I want to make: that psychoanalysis as a field of study—as an institution, if you will—*stands for* the dignity of the individual. A corollary of "Of whom shall we speak?" is "To whom shall we listen?" Psychoanalysis answers that resoundingly in favour of the individual. Further, psychoanalytic treatment embeds dignity as a *clinical provision* into that individual listening.

I will return to the Big History of Auden's opening stanza—and to the task of the *International Review*. For the moment, though, let me move to some lines just before his closing stanza.

> [B]ut he would have us remember most of all
> to be enthusiastic over the night,
> not only for the sense of wonder
> it alone has to offer, but also

> because it needs our love. With large sad eyes
> its delectable creatures look up and beg
> us dumbly to ask them to follow:
> they are exiles who long for the future

> that lies in our power, they too would rejoice
> if allowed to serve enlightenment like him,
> even to bear our cry of "Judas",
> as he did and all must bear who serve it.

In these three stanzas, Auden brings us to another question: "Who shall speak?" The answer is the "delectable creatures" of the night, who see—indeed see with sadness—but by themselves are dumb.

Exiles—like Freud—whom we can bring into what Auden calls "the bright circle ... of recognition". I've often begun dream seminars with these lines. To me, they speak to a core psychoanalytic stance later articulated by Charles Rycroft in *The Innocence of Dreams*:

> [T]he dreaming self utters meanings from a timeless, total posi-
> tion ... while the part of the self that receives dream-messages
> occupies a preempted, prescribed position localized in a par-
> ticular time and place, and possesses a preconceived notion of
> itself which is at risk if it listens seriously to dream-meanings.
> (1979, p. 148)

It was Freud's genius to discover that *these* were the voices that might "serve enlightenment"—the repressed voices, the dream voices. For Auden, Freud's method was simple, to some degree shared between author and subject, and gets to the question of "How we shall listen?":

> ... he merely told
> the unhappy Present to recite the Past
> like a poetry lesson till sooner
> or later it faltered at the line where
>
> long ago the accusations had begun,
> and suddenly knew by whom it had been judged,
> how rich life had been and how silly,
> And was life-forgiven and more humble

In the method of free association (Bollas, 2002), psychoanalysis dignifies both the recital and the faltering. It rests on the "good faith" assumption that the patient is doing his or her best and that, at the place of faltering, curiosity rather than judgement is the provision. Auden calls this provision "love"; so does Winnicott: love meaning the "positive interest taken" (1954, p. 285), he says in his paper on the analytic setting. It seems to me that dignity also has a place in this conversation. Free association as a methodological foundation asserts that part of ourselves is naturally working toward health, and it gives worth to—which may be the definition of dignifying—the seemingly less important and defensively discarded thoughts hidden in condensation or set aside in displacement.

Even further, I would argue that dignity is implicit in a technical stance of neutrality, abstinence, and relative anonymity—sometimes controversial concepts these days. This gets to what André Green (1999) called "the work of the negative". Beyond the basic ethic of not using the patient, these technical principles—to be sure, lived out in the context of a therapeutic alliance—dignify the rejected, the negated, the hated and self-hated parts of a person, parts that are also dumb, if more angry than sad, parts that will lead the patient's conscious self to accuse us of betrayal if we try to listen seriously to the whole person. Our bearing its "cry of 'Judas'", in Winnicott's terms (1969) surviving it and making sense of it, transforms our attitude of dignity into something less thin, something more muscular because experiential, something even bi-directional, more real because really suffered.

In that Winnicott paper, the full statement—in his list of twelve aspects of the analytic setting—goes on to include hate too, hate "honestly expressed … in the strict start and finish and in the matter of fees" (1954, p. 285). In Auden's poem, at Freud's death,

> Only Hate was happy, hoping to augment
> his practice now, and his dingy clientele
> who think they can be cured by killing
> And covering the garden with ashes.

Winnicott's "hate" is of a different order. It is in the service of discovery rather than covering over. It reifies a boundary across which he hopes to meet the parts of a person *they* have covered over. This boundary of separateness invites the patient's hate, and it allows for the critical experience of the analyst's not being killed off in the service of the patient's preserving—as though preservation would cure—the tenuous relationships of his or her inner world. For Winnicott, his survival brings joy, to which we would add dignity, to the patient as a whole person and to the therapeutic relationship, which now can be trusted—almost in the engineering sense—to hold the full weight of the patient's affectivity (Fromm, 2012a1). If dignity is about worth, the "worthy opponent" dimension of treatment is worth noticing.

* * *

But as Auden says, "To be free is often to be lonely." When we broaden our field of vision, we so often discover that the patient has indeed unconsciously participated in being killed off in the service of curing a troubled family, and progress becomes intertwined with loyalty, fear, and grief. I have spent my career at the Austen Riggs Center, a small psychiatric residential treatment centre in Stockbridge, Massachusetts. Its treatment programme is unusual in today's world: four-times-weekly psychoanalytic psychotherapy in a completely open and voluntary therapeutic community setting. It's actually a beautiful setting, given its location in the Berkshire Hills. But to enter a psychiatric hospital, even one on Main Street, Stockbridge, and to enter a treatment relationship with its patients, is to follow Freud, who, in Auden's words

> ... went his way
> down among the lost people like Dante, down
> to the stinking fosse where the injured
> lead the ugly life of the rejected

"Where the injured lead the ugly life of the rejected". The insult of rejection is added to the basic injury, and then lived out as ugliness. We see this in our society and we see it in psychiatric hospitals. And we learn that what families cannot bear within themselves, what must be refused as "not us", is often located in, indeed assigned as an unconscious role to, one of its more vulnerable members—who then live out life as a form of refuse, across the "borderline" of what's acceptable in the ordinary social world (Fromm, 2012b1). These are the patients who find their way to Austen Riggs: patients with enormous self-structure and self-esteem problems, with flagrant, scattered symptomatology, desperate for both identity and help, or with profound withdrawal to a dark place on the other side of the fosse.

At the beginning of Riggs' psychoanalytic history, one of its fellows wrote a paper describing burgeoning crises with younger more acting-out patients. The times were "out of joint", so to speak. The nursing staff longed for the good old days of Dr. Riggs' ten mental health commandments, the quaint New England town remained sleepy and still a bit puritanical, and the newly arrived senior analysts were beginning to realise that neutrality was no way to administer a hospital. The writer went on to a remarkable—and to my mind, hilarious—statement: "Then the historic decision was taken to talk the situation over with the patients" (Christie, 1964, p. 458). This daily "talking it over with the patients", beginning with four volunteers from both groups, became the core of the therapeutic community programme, and remains codified in Riggs' statement of its mission and vision (Austen Riggs Center website). Apropos of this paper, the second sentence in the mission statement is: "The focus throughout … is on the importance of human relationships and the responsibility and *dignity* of the individual", and the first sentence of the vision statement speaks to "the *dignity* of the individual, the importance of human relationships and the centrality of a sense of community in an increasingly complex and fragmented world."

Dignity is an embedded provision in this programme, a "corrective emotional" structure and point of view about people, available as a counter-weight to the patient's original system. But, as I have suggested earlier, engaging the negative is also a dignifying action. In the daily life of the community, projective dynamics inevitably occur, among patients and between patients and staff. Patients' troubles are played out and staff anxiety is as well. Dignity here, within the community's work, as distinct from the psychotherapist's work, has to do with the staff's commitment to considering symptomatic eruption in group and systems terms. As I wrote elsewhere, "Acting out by any member of the community not only affects the total community (which is important in its own right); it also represents something for everyone, something dissociated from conscious dialogue and yet central to understanding the group's having gotten off-task in some way" (Fromm, 2012a2, p. 192).

Interpreting this in terms of the system restores the holding environment it simultaneously tests. The commitment here is to a "How are they right?" stance (Shapiro & Carr, 1991), not an abdicating "You're right, because you are a patient (or a staff member)", but in what way is the other right? This sense-making perspective—that of an "interpretive democracy" since any member can offer the sense they see in what's happening—lives out a "psychological equality" (Kennard, 1998, p. 127), and may lead to powerful learning in the here-and-now for both the community and the patient (or sometimes the staff member) who is carrying an issue for the group, with whatever degree of personal distress and compromised functioning.

A colleague in the social conflict field (Waslekar, 2012) commented recently that troubled societies suffer from three deficits: "a development deficit, a democracy deficit, and a dignity deficit." One could make the case that a treatment programme that facilitates the living out of democratic principles—that each person's voice matters, that finding one's authentic voice is a good thing, and that participation in decisions by which one is affected is both just and healthy—is not only dignifying but inherently therapeutic. Winnicott once quipped that an adult is a person with a point of view. As I wrote earlier,

> A democratic frame of reference invites a person toward discovering his or her point of view, toward declaring it publicly, toward listening to the points of view of others and, in doing so, toward learning more, surrendering or standing one's ground. It faces its members with problems of difference, conflict, and compromise, with moments of decision that both join and separate one from others, and with the requirement to re-join, after the battle so to speak, in order to carry on something larger than the self, namely, the total community's life. This terrain—between one-ness and two-ness (on the way to third-ness)—is the political equivalent of that developmental territory leading up to the depressive position.... Patients in this kind of programme are challenged in the place they most need to develop, that is, toward taking authority in a world of others rather than simply being subject to the authority of others or attempting to dominate them. The open setting for the therapeutic community structurally recognises the separate authority of the patient group, the authority of a citizen-consumer rather than a quasi-employee, and rather than a patient role in which authority is simply surrendered to the staff. It requires a partnership between an authorised patient group and a receptive staff group in order to maintain its functioning and maximise the treatment benefit. It also requires staff leadership to hold this authority differentiation, to work with it, and to lead reflection about democracy-eroding inter-group dynamics. (Fromm, 2012a2, pp. 199–200)

A number of years ago at the daily community meeting a member said emotionally, "I feel so guilty. I'm here and others whom I care about can't be." Another said, "Yes, but when we bring our feelings to each other and share them, as you're doing in this meeting, it makes it more bearable." The former speaker was actually an experienced nurse, devastated by the loss of two colleagues during a financial crisis. The second speaker was the patient chairperson, elected to lead the meeting for an eight-week term. To quote again from my paper on therapeutic community, "New patients, new staff, and professional visitors at the Community Meetings regularly have the experience of asking themselves, 'Was that a staff member or a patient who said that?' This is a powerfully de-centering moment"—a moment of dignity if you will— "in which patients become in their daily participation what others think of as staff. They then can come to see, with whatever mixture of exhilaration and chagrin, that patienthood is a role, not an intrinsic aspect of person—a realisation basic to the process of taking authority" (Fromm, 2012a2, p. 203), which itself is critical to sustaining and cultivating one's own sense of dignity.

* * *

And then there is the irony of severe psychopathology: that what began as refuse sometimes holds in trust, if you will, essential information about a family's fragmented history. The "ashes" sprinkled over the garden are sometimes the ashes of death, the detritus of unbearable and unthinkable family trauma, unconsciously transmitted to the next generation, who then live it out in symptomatology (Davoine & Gaudillière, 2004; Fromm, 2012b1). From a different context, the psychoanalyst Lawrence Gould (2002), reporting his experience as consultant to the United States Holocaust Museum, relates a frequent occurrence, which I discuss in the afterword to *Lost in Transmission* (2012b2, p. 212).

> An aged man, in a rumpled jacket, goes to the information desk, hands the receptionist a box, and says, "Will you hold this for me?" The box turns out to contain, in the example Dr. Gould cited, the tattooed skin that this man had cut from his arm when he was freed from the concentration camp and which he had kept hidden for fifty years. "I'm going to die soon; I haven't told my family about this and I don't want them to find it," he says; "Will you hold it for me?" This is a most unusual definition of a "holding environment", but a critical one. Because, to the degree that the traumatized person cannot contain his experience, it is lived out in one way or another in his or her family, and to the degree that it cannot be contained or metabolized there, it relies on—it absolutely needs—institutions to hold its objects, its affects and the evolving societal narrative, into which traumatized people may bring their experience. The Holocaust Museum serves that purpose for an aging generation of survivors and their families ...

A psychiatric hospital sometimes serves that purpose for patients and families struggling with their own private holocaust, one that itself may well relate to the horrors of the Big History. A patient's becoming found—so to speak—in this transmission of trauma opens a space for grief both in oneself and in the family, for pity in its more honourable sense, and for genuine understanding of the people on whom one's own sense of self has depended and from whom the transmission of trauma has taken place. The most profound and dignifying endpoint of this process is the inscription of emotional truth into the narrative of the generations, honouring one and liberating the other. When things go well, the patient is, in Auden's words, like one of those

> ... long-forgotten objects
> revealed by his undiscouraged shining
> returned to us and made precious again

* * *

Let me offer now one of those "delectable creatures" of the night. "In my dream, there was a hospital that looked like a lighthouse. Ariel Sharon was being wheeled in on a stretcher. He was very ill. But the treatment in this hospital was bizarre: the patients were hung upside down, and that helped them get better." This was not the dream of a patient; rather it was the dream of a member of a group relations conference in the Netherlands. With their focus on the here-and-now operation of the unconscious among people engaged in collective work, these conferences represent a most powerful form of applied psychoanalysis, which both deepens and turns upside-down its members' understanding of everyday, pseudo-rational group behaviour. Indeed, the above dream, reported in a closing plenary, came to represent the total shift in perspective people had come to in their conference learning; their understanding of organisations had been profoundly turned upside-down. It also represented the really daunting challenge of re-entering, and talking to ordinary people in, the so-called right-side-up world.

The Riggs therapeutic community programme, as an example of "the inmates running the asylum", is part of the upside-down world, as is the perspective above about the patient's holding traumatic family experience in trust. For a number of reasons, including Erik Erikson's inspiration over many years, we at Riggs found that we wanted to offer something from this rich and unusual set of experiences with quite disturbed patients, something that would bring these experiences out of the intensive focus on a few individuals and into interaction with others. So, we created the Erikson Institute for education, research, and application. This is the link to the task of the *International Review*, which was also about application, a task now incorporated into the *International Journal*.

It's not an easy task though, especially if we think back to Auden's lines: "When there are so many … of whom shall we speak?" On the one hand, psychoanalysis stands for the dignity and complexity of the individual; on the other hand, in doing so, how do we take into account the problem of scale, the "so many" who are outside our purview? Years ago, a young psychologist, attending an Erikson Institute training conference, said at its closing: "This conference has been like oxygen to me. I'm taking a very deep breath and going to try to make it last as long as I can in my work back home." What a powerful statement, and what a daunting task! More usually, we encounter professionals who cannot listen to a psychodynamic perspective at all, but not because it isn't persuasive to them; on the contrary, to the extent that they are captivated and moved by it, they must reactively dismiss it. A version of cognitive dissonance comes into play. They cannot let themselves value what they do not have the resources, within their treatment systems, to carry out; the guilt would be too great. They feel what the singer Sinead O'Connor expressed in a song many years ago: "I do not want what I haven't got" (1990).

This is one of our many problems, one that does indeed relate to the dignity of the "so many" who are suffering. In my own work, I have found myself inclined toward psychoanalytic application in the direction of understanding the dynamics of organisations—in essence the task of helping troubled holding environments and its trapped members see more clearly how they have become stuck in what Wesley Carr (personal communication) called the dynamic but tangled "undergrowth" of the organisation. I've also had the good fortune of working with the psychoanalyst Vamık Volkan, in his effort to bring psychological understanding to societal conflict. Dr. Volkan (1997, 2004) has over many years articulated extremely valuable concepts for this kind of understanding: "chosen trauma", "deposited representation", and "societal regression", among many others. Perhaps a vignette from a recent intervention will illustrate the importance of dignity to the process.

This event took place not long ago in Northern Ireland. A small facilitating team was invited to meet with twenty or so people who represented all the major political parties as well as a range of civic leadership. The context was a recent eruption of destructiveness surrounding the limits on flying the Union Flag over Belfast City Hall. Engaging the negative was inescapable in this meeting. Simply a facilitator's hearing and speaking to the frank expression of shame seemed to make it real and to trigger rage: "I hate it that you said something about shame; there is so much shame here that if we let ourselves feel it, we would all kill ourselves."

But as the gathering was coming to an end, the facilitating team also noted progression in the conversation: increased emotional engagement; increased person-to-person talk; increased strength in the voices of the civic leadership; the emergence of the political leadership's speaking as persons; and the appearance of bridging issues. In the final session, a young unionist said to a nationalist: "You want us to join you but, when we don't, you interpret that as our problem, rather than asking us *why* we don't join you." He was pointing out how curiosity was lost to presumptions and a too quick certainty. The unionist added: "Why do you want us to respect your dead? I respect my own dead; I don't need you to respect them." Then, another nationalist, speaking with real feeling, answered his question: "I'll tell you why. When I was growing up, people didn't even acknowledge that my mother and father and grandmother even existed, and when they did, they treated them like dirt. So, if they weren't respected in life, I want them respected in death." A senior NGO leader joined with the facilitators: "That's what they mean by the *ghosts of the past*", and then said to the nationalist: "I won't remember much of the political talk here, but I will never forget what you just said."

Indignities, humiliations, and trauma go way back in this group, but being deeply heard goes a long way too. To me, a psychoanalytic framework on trauma and a process that engages the live—and often negative—feelings dignifies all involved by virtue of our experiencing, surviving collectively, and attempting to give words to the deep pain behind these feelings. Perhaps only psychoanalysis valences this play of opposites—the engagement of destructiveness in the service of healing. Listen to Auden in his final stanza:

> One rational voice is dumb....
> [In this line, Freud has joined the delectable creatures who "beg/ us dumbly to ask them to follow ... [and] long for the future/that lies in our power".]

... Over his grave
the household of Impulse mourns one dearly loved:
sad is Eros, builder of cities,
and weeping anarchic Aphrodite.

Auden here does not juxtapose Eros with Thanatos, as we might have
expected. Rather he juxtaposes two representatives of love: Eros the
builder and Aphrodite the anarchist, the love that brings together and
the love that does not allow itself to be killed off in a vain attempt at curing others. For Auden, both shall speak, and both deserve the dignity
of our listening.

References

Auden, W. H. (1940). In memory of Sigmund Freud. In: *Another Time*.
New York: Random House.

Austen Riggs Center website: www.austenriggs.org.

Bollas, C. (2002). *Free Association*. Cambridge: Icon.

Christie, G. (1964). Therapeutic community and psychotherapy: the Austin
Riggs Center. *The Medical Journal of Australia, 1*: 457–560.

Davoine, F., & Gaudillière, J. -M. (2004). *History Beyond Trauma*. New York:
Other Press.

Fromm, M. G. (2012a1). Impasse and transitional relatedness. In: *Taking the
Transference, Reaching toward Dreams: Clinical Studies in the Intermediate
Area* (pp. 1–19). London: Karnac.

Fromm, M. G. (2012a2). The therapeutic community as a holding environment. In: *Taking the Transference, Reaching toward Dreams: Clinical Studies
in the Intermediate Area* (pp. 187–204). London: Karnac.

Fromm, M. G. (2012b1). Treatment resistance and the transmission of
trauma. In: *Lost in Transmission: Studies of Trauma across Generations*
(pp. 99–114). London: Karnac.

Fromm, M. G. (2012b2). Afterword: lost and found. In: *Lost in Transmission:
Studies of Trauma across Generations* (pp. 215–220). London: Karnac.

Gould, L. (2002). Managing depressive anxieties: Consulting to the United
States Holocaust Memorial Museum. Presentation given at the Austen
Riggs Center, 11 January 2002.

Green, A. (1999). *The Work of the Negative*. London: Free Association.

Kennard, D. (1998). *An Introduction to Therapeutic Communities*. London:
Jessica Kingsley.

O'Connor, S. (1990). *I Do Not Want What I Haven't Got* (CD). New York:
Ensign Records Ltd.

Rycroft, C. (1979). *The Innocence of Dreams*. London: Hogarth.

Shapiro, E., & Carr, A. W. (1991). *Lost in Familiar Places: Creating New Connections Between the Individual and Society*. New Haven, CT: Yale University Press.

St. Germain, M. (2011). *Freud's Last Session*. Dramatist's Play Service.

Volkan, V. (1997). *Bloodlines: From Ethnic Pride to Ethnic Terrorism*. New York: Farrar, Straus and Giroux.

Volkan, V. (2004). *Blind Trust: Large Groups and Their Leaders in Times of Crisis and Terror*. Charlottesville, VA: Pitchstone.

Waslekar, S. (2012). Report of the 9th Biannual Meeting of the International Dialogue Initiative, London: www.internationaldialogueinitiative.com. Date accessed: 17 June 2015.

Winnicott, D. W. (1954). Metapsychological and clinical aspects of regression within the psycho-analytical set-up. In: *Through Paediatrics to Psycho-Analysis* (pp. 278–294). New York: Basic Books, 1958.

Winnicott, D. W. (1969). The use of an object. *International Journal of Psychoanalysis, 50*: 711–716.

CHAPTER SIX

Psychoanalytic approaches to dignity in children and adolescents

Robert Kravis

The consideration of dignity may be approached from several different perspectives. In this chapter I will expand on Ahktar's concept of characterological dignity (Chapter Two, this volume) with reference to the role of the body and modesty. There has been virtually nothing written in the psychoanalytic literature about children and adolescents on this topic, yet, as I shall try to illustrate, the dignity of the child or adolescent is integral in psychoanalysis, if perhaps indirectly so, both theoretically and clinically.

Developmental considerations

Webster's Dictionary defines dignity as "the quality or state of being worthy, honored, or esteemed". As Levine (2014) has pointed out, synonyms for the word "dignity" fall into two main categories: self-esteem, and inherent worth. So, taking a developmental approach, would it make sense to consider that, in thinking about children, the boundary between the two categories Levine mentions may be blurred? Specifically, self-esteem requires the prior development of a sense of self. Therefore, there can be no dignity in the sense of self-esteem which can be called inherent if inherent is understood as being present at birth. Rather, it is only when the infant is treated as worthy that the possibility of self-esteem can develop. In fact, self-esteem is co-constructed in the sense that the environment, in the person of the child's caregivers, and the child, are both active participants in this process. The child must be able to receive, process, and integrate communications of her worthiness, and the caregivers must be able to convey them to the child in a manner that is digestible.

Problems in this process can occur in a multitude of ways. From the side of the child, faulty perceptual apparatus, integrative difficulties and disturbances such as autistic spectrum disorders and pervasive developmental delay can impair the child's ability to receive and metabolise feelings of worthiness. So also can physical ailments and anomalies, and acts of fate such as the death of a parent or other close relative. In some cases, common occurrences such as the birth of a sibling, transitioning to school, or separating from a parent when engaging in activities outside the family, can become interferences to the development of healthy self-esteem. From the caregivers' side, all manner of psychological factors, including unwanted pregnancy, stressors in daily living, and idiosyncratic negative reactions to the particular child can interfere with the capacity to think of the child as worthy. Also, marital discord, tensions between and among extended family members, and a chronically ill parent or sibling are possible interferences. Again, such ordinary events as a patent's departure for work, or expressing frustration and anger, even if not directed at the child, may result in catastrophic responses on the part of the child, which lead to low self-esteem. Many more examples can be imagined on both sides of the equation.

While the psychoanalytic literature is lacking on the specific subject of dignity, there is much written about narcissism starting with Freud's 1914 paper. In this literature attention is paid to the development of both healthy and pathological narcissism, where healthy narcissism refers to the development of an internal reservoir of positive feelings that is neither impoverished nor grandiose, either of the latter being considered forms of pathological narcissism. While narcissism may be considered to be a metapsychological concept, manifestations of variations in self-esteem are its observable derivative expression. Thus, in individuals with healthy narcissism, while there may be fluctuations in self-esteem within a limited range according to external or internal circumstances, the level of narcissism remains constant.

The development of self-esteem can be viewed as one of the byproducts of internalisation whereby the child internalises the esteem in which he or she is held by his or her caregivers. There is clearly not a one-to-one correspondence between the caregivers' esteem of the child and the child's developing self-esteem as a function of the child's immature perceptual apparatus and cognitive limitations. But it is more likely that positive self-esteem will develop when the child is esteemed by her caregivers than when he or she is not. Beyond esteeming the child, it is also important for caregivers to titrate experiences of frustration and gratification. The child who is consistently left to cry for too long is likely to be too frustrated for good feelings about himself or herself to develop. And the child whose caregivers hover and soothe at the first sign of a whimper do not facilitate the development of the child's ability to internally regulate frustration.

It is also important to recognise that beyond the caregivers other environmental factors influence this process. Concepts such as "background of safety" (Sandler, 1960) stress the importance of a safe, supportive, "holding environment" (Winnicott, 1969) as a prerequisite for normal development to occur. Children growing up in a war zone or in conditions of extreme deprivation such as poverty, or who are exposed to trauma and catastrophic loss, are often too occupied with survival to develop the kinds of internalisations that would lead to positive self-esteem.

To summarise: given a safe, secure environment, intact perceptual, and cognitive apparatus, and loving, "good enough" (Winnicott, 1953) caregivers, it is likely that the child will develop the capacity to love himself or herself. Which is to say, develop healthy narcissism as evidenced by manifestations of high self-esteem such as confidence in the ability to be successful in new and challenging situations, the ability to tolerate periodic unsuccessful outcomes in work and love, satisfaction with one's body, relative ease in social situations, the capacity to love others, etc.

Self-esteem and dignity

I have considered the development of self-esteem which is largely, but not entirely, based upon the esteem in which the child is held by his or her caregivers. But self-esteem and dignity are not synonymous.

I would submit that self-esteem is a necessary, but not sufficient condition for the development of dignity. The quality or state of being worthy, honoured, or esteemed, in my view, presupposes positive self-esteem. Furthermore, to be worthy, honoured, or esteemed also supposes an other who confers this state or quality. Thus, as is the case with self-esteem, dignity is also co-constructed. It may well be that such a co-construction partially replicates the co-construction that led to the original development of self-esteem.

Returning to the discussion of narcissism, in Freud's original paper "On narcissism: an introduction" (Freud, 1914c), he introduced the concepts of primary and secondary narcissism. Primary narcissism was posited as an initial state consisting of global feelings of well-being in the infant as a function of the "cocoon" of love and protection provided by the infant's caregivers. As the infant develops, and the differentiation between self and others occurs, the infant gradually becomes aware that the feelings of well-being are not self-contained, but rather depend on the ministrations of others. Additionally, experiences of frustration and of delay of gratification, which are part and parcel of daily living, reinforce the beginning realisation that what was originally experienced as blissful is not as seamless as it first was felt to be. Hence, primary narcissism gives way to the beginnings of internal self and object representations. Freud's thesis was that once this occurs we spend the rest of our lives trying to recapture the blissful feelings associated with the primary narcissistic state. He called this secondary narcissism and felt that this was approximated through object love, as the love of the object replenishes the depleted narcissism of the person being loved. While there is still much controversy about the concept of primary narcissism, and much disagreement about Freud's thinking about narcissism, would it be too far-fetched to consider that one way of replenishing narcissistic feelings might occur through dignity? Specifically, being deemed worthy, honoured, or esteemed would surely enhance self-esteem and feelings of well-being. In fact, the attitude of the caregivers toward the child shapes the child's self-esteem. Considering the spectrum of possibilities from disregard and apathy at one end and (narcissistic) idealisation on the other, the range of possible attitudes toward the child is extensive. But an expression of love for the child that approximates the state of being in love in the adult sense of that term, seems most likely to achieve the desired result.

Dignity and the body

Anna Freud, in her classic book, *Normality and Pathology in Childhood* (Freud, 1965), introduced the concept of developmental lines. She described developmental lines as "basic interactions between id and ego and their various developmental levels". One developmental line she described was called "from irresponsibility to responsibility in body management". She articulated three main stages along this line including: 1. Turning the direction of aggression "from being lived out on the body to being turned toward the external world". 2. Development of the reality principle "together with the pain barrier and the narcissistic cathexis of the body" which serve to protect the child against external dangers. 3. "Voluntary endorsement of the rules of hygiene and medical necessities".

Essentially what is being described here is a shift from the caregivers being responsible for the management of the child's body, to the child assuming such responsibility to a reasonable extent. But I would suggest that as the child moves along this developmental line something else occurs: the child acquires a sense of pride in, and value of, his or her body. Thus, the "narcissistic cathexis" of which Anna Freud speaks serves not only a self-protective function, but also leads to the development of a sense of dignity whereby the body is treated as a valued possession that is to be protected emotionally as well as physically. Such protection includes all manners in which the body is cared for and how it is presented to the external world. Hygiene and cleanliness certainly have health components, but they also reflect the degree of care and pride which the individual takes in the body. Similarly, appropriate clothing serves the function of keeping the temperature of the body regulated, but also reveals how the individual adorns the body. Good grooming and cleanliness elicit positive reactions as does attractive, but modest clothing. Provocative clothing, excessive make-up (in both sexes), etc., may attract gratifying attention, but are not reflective of dignity, which, as stated earlier, is a co-construction of the individual's self-esteem and the impact he or she has on the observer. More specifically, a seductive presentation generally leads to a sexual response (or its derivative) in contrast to a response reflective of dignity.

I believe that it would be useful to conceptualise a developmental line of dignity. In most general terms, one might start with the naïveté of childhood in which the self-representation is not fully formed and self-esteem not yet established in a mature sense that is informed by the feelings associated with an elaborated sense of self, including both psychological and physiological components. This is followed by increasingly sophisticated layering of self-representations and by the elaborated development of self-esteem (in the context of a supportive environment). In this process the representation of the physical body and the affects linked with this representation are also further elaborated. It seems likely that as the child assumes more control and responsibility for his or her own body (and less rests with caregivers), dignity begins to develop. That this process is not a smooth one can most easily be illustrated in adolescence. It is not uncommon to see adolescents dressing provocatively, being sexually promiscuous, and putting their bodies in danger through risk-taking behaviours including dare-devil antics, drug use, and unprotected sex. This time of life may, in this context, be seen as a crisis of dignity. Hopefully these behaviours, like others at this time of life, are transitional, but some adolescents compromise their dignity in a manner from which they cannot recover. Those who sustain serious physical damage, unwanted pregnancies, or become involved in the criminal justice system are some examples.

Examining certain other violations of dignity in adulthood will help to clarify the concept. Forcing an individual to expose his or her naked body is a clear violation of dignity and as such is sometimes used to humiliate and degrade prisoners or hostages. But a more common example is found in individuals who are medical patients, particularly hospitalised medical patients. In the outpatient setting the body is put in the hands of the examining physician, and perhaps a nurse or a medical technician. Questions about basic bodily functions such as bowel and bladder functioning are asked and answered, and there may be a physical examination requiring exposure and probing of certain areas of the body in question. A hospital gown may be worn with or without underwear. At the end of the outpatient appointment the patient usually gets dressed and leaves. But in an inpatient setting, there is usually no clothing worn other than the hospital gown and any number of people, including physicians, interns, medical students, residents, nurses, and technicians may have access to the patient's body. This situation clearly deprives the patient of his or her dignity because of the exposure of the body to strangers and because of the requirement that basic bodily functions be monitored on a routine basis. Unlike outpatient treatment, inpatient treatment may require more lengthy time in the hospital and consequently more lengthy impingements on the patient's dignity.

Other, more subtle, violations of dignity occur regularly as a result of the power differential between doctors and patients. The tendency to talk down to patients, to discount their anxieties and concerns, or to treat them as an amalgamation of specific body parts or symptoms are familiar examples of this. Psychoanalysts are sometimes among such offenders as we may think and/or talk about patients in disparaging ways. The pejorative use of the diagnostic term "borderline" is an example.

Clinical considerations

The psychoanalytic attitude ideally includes respect in talking to and about patients. The case I am going to present, however, is an example of how not all patients respect the analyst's dignity. In the transference, some patients mount assaults on the analyst's dignity, often in such situations doing to the analyst what they feel has been done to them. While such cases are frequently characterised, correctly, as sadomasochistic, referring to them in this way sometimes masks the (often unconscious) intent to demean and to be demeaned by the analyst. I am making a distinction here between the sadomasochistic wish to make the analyst suffer as a source of instinctual gratification to the patient, and the patient who turns passive into active by demeaning the analyst in the manner in which the patient has felt demeaned. Such patients frequently expect to be demeaned by the analyst and, in anticipation of this, assault the analyst's dignity preemptively. Child and adolescent patients, who are still living with their primary objects and who are generally organised more primitively than adult patients as a consequence of their immaturely developed egos, tend to express such assaults in more direct, less subtle ways than do adult patients.

Case vignette

The patient, Javier, was a six-and-a-half-year-old boy brought for consultation by his parents who had concerns about school-related problems including trouble with reading and writing together with distractibility and overactivity. In addition he was reported to be highly opinionated, with little tolerance for others' viewpoints, and to need to be in control, often unresponsive to adult directives both in school and at home.

The family constellation consisted of his parents, both professionals, and his sister, three years older than he. Javier's development was unremarkable except that he was reported to have had very few words until shortly after his second birthday.

Javier's parents agreed that they had "a terrible relationship". They had not had sex in years and were not affectionate with each other. They further indicated that Javier's mother did the bulk of the parenting. She expressed resentment about this, but her husband indicated that when he tried to get involved she rebuffed him. For her part, she felt that he was too harsh and heavy-handed in his handling of the children. He, however, indicated that she was too lenient, giving the children too much freedom and failing to set limits. But, because he was working long hours and was not as available to parent as she was, he deferred to his wife's parenting style. Furthermore, while his mother was very concerned about Javier, his father was not sure that there was anything "abnormal" about him. Also, while Javier's mother reported that Javier said that he "hates Daddy" and did not want to be around him, his father stated that both children were very affectionate with him when his wife was not present, suggesting that the children were expressing a negative view of him to his wife because that was what they thought she wanted to hear. He also felt that his wife preferred their daughter, a high achiever and non-problematic child, to Javier.

Despite their differences, the parents agreed that they had been "too permissive" with Javier. His father felt that had there been clearer and firmer limits Javier would not have had any difficulties, while his mother said that she had hoped that the structure of the classroom environment would have helped him. They reported that Javier would "sell" pencils to guests who visited them and that he would also "charge" them for parking in the family driveway.

In the playroom, Javier introduced a play scenario in which he was "the evil doctor" and I was the patient. He started by "examining" me with the toy doctor's kit. In the course of this examination he wanted to actually put the thermometer in my mouth and insert the otoscope into my ears and nostrils. When I indicated that he could pretend to do so, but could not actually examine me in this way, he only reluctantly agreed after several attempts to do it the way that he wanted. After the examination I was told that I was very sick and that I needed medicine. Again, he wanted to mix up a potion from watercolor paints that I was actually to swallow, and only reluctantly agreed that I could pretend to swallow it. Once having taken the medicine I was told that it was actually poison and that I was going to die. When I expressed distress and anxiety about my fate and wondered why he would do such a thing to me, he gleefully told me that he had warned me that he was an *evil* doctor. This play was repeated with little variation throughout the three evaluation sessions. When I expressed my reservations with complying with the examination and the ingestion of medication which had previously turned out to be poisonous, I was assured that this time it would not be, only to find that I was being repeatedly deceived, much to my chagrin and to his delight.

The sadomasochistic nature of this play led me to conclude that Javier had internalised conflicts that needed to be addressed in analysis. The ease with which he entered into this play encouraged me to believe that the material would be readily accessible in analysis. I made this recommendation to his parents and they agreed with little hesitation.

During the course of the analysis I was very much aware of the sadomasochistic conflicts which were being played out in the transference. At the time, I thought of this as a combination of Javier's wish to turn perceived passive experiences into active reversals in which he was the perpetrator rather than the victim; and his need to be in control as a means of pre-emptively preventing disasters from befalling him. I had not yet consciously considered the issue of dignity, both his and mine, as it played out in the treatment. However, I believe that it is implicit in the material and in my approach to Javier and his parents. I will illustrate this with a selection of vignettes, recognising that many other themes, although important, cannot be addressed here.

In the early stage of the analysis the evil doctor play evolved to a point that consisted of Javier strapping my arms and legs to the chair on which I was sitting before performing the examination. He used masking tape to do this. I contemplated whether to allow this and decided that I would comply as I felt that I could free myself from the masking tape with little effort so that we were still in the realm of pretending I was immobilised. What I did not allow, however, was his wish to put masking tape over my mouth and eyes. The results of the examination were identical: I was very sick and needed medication. But now the medication was administered involuntarily. Because I was bound to the chair I could not resist it. My conduct in this play was based on my wish to allow Javier the opportunity to express himself as directly as possible, while ensuring that I was not actually injured or immobilised. It was my intent in doing so to keep our activities in the realm of play. Parenthetically, it was my belief that Javier's parents were not so good at doing this, and consequently allowed him more direct impulse expression than was good for him.

One day, a bit further along in the analysis, Javier came in for his appointment and asked if I had heard the latest news. When I asked what he was referring to, he told me that in the car on the way to his appointment, he and his mother had heard that Marv and Harry had been released from jail and had joined forces with Osama Bin Laden and were heading our way. When I asked about who Marv and Harry were he reminded me that they were the two men in the movie *Home Alone* who had tried to break into the home of the family who had inadvertently left behind one of their children, who then had to fend off the would-be intruders on his own. I expressed alarm at this news and he agreed that there was good reason for concern. In a later meeting with his parents I was told that Javier had become very anxious recently when he had been dropped off by the school bus after school and found that his mother was not yet home and he was locked out of the house. His mother arrived home a little later to find him in tears saying that he had worried that she had forgotten about him and was not coming home. I then understood his story about Marv, Harry, and Osama Bin Laden as an expression of the degree of his anxiety about being "home alone" when his mother was not there as expected. Although it was unusual for his mother to be late, I also understood his anxiety to reflect his feeling that he could not count on her.

Javier elaborated this scenario over the next few weeks. Although he was able to protect himself from the trio of evil doers, I was not so fortunate. They ended up capturing my mother who was then hung upside down, naked, and was tortured. I was tied up and made to watch helplessly. During the course of this scenario he commented that his own mother had a string coming out of her butt. I took this to be a reference to seeing his mother naked with a tampon string hanging down. I also noticed one day when he was bending over that his own buttocks were exposed, revealing that he was not wearing underwear. In a later session with the parents I asked about the underwear and was told by his mother that she felt that it was his father's job to buy his son underwear. The father said that his wife did all the clothes shopping for both children so he did not understand why she could not buy underwear along with the other clothes she bought for Javier. After all, he said, she bought underwear for their daughter. Javier's mother replied that a mother buying underwear for her daughter is different from buying underwear for her son. I suggested to them that for Javier not to have underwear was potentially humiliating for him and that if I noticed it, then it was likely that other children noticed it as well. I urged them to find a solution, which they eventually did.

I was also curious about why Javier was not more concerned about this. When I asked him about it he said that he found underwear "uncomfortable". I also talked with his parents about his concern, or lack of concern, about his body being exposed and in that context asked about modesty practices in their home. They indicated that Javier was not modest. He left his door open when he was dressing and did not shut the bathroom door. His sister was modest and was "grossed out" by Javier's lack of modesty. I then asked about the parents' modesty practices and was told that Javier's mother, at the advice of her own therapist, was trying to get his father to stop showering with Javier. She did not say anything about her own modesty practices. However, I had also noticed that upon opening the waiting room door to greet Javier, I would periodically find him sitting in his mother's lap facing her with his arms around her neck attempting to kiss her on the lips. When I asked him about this, Javier told me that he was very angry at his mother's therapist because his mother had informed him that her therapist had told her that it was not a good idea for her to allow this. Javier clearly had the idea that were it not for her therapist's prohibitions his mother would allow him to continue doing this.

These fragments of material illustrate Javier's assault on my dignity from the very start of the analysis. His wish to control me was expressed in the early play scenarios in which he wanted to trick me into ingesting poison and to bind my hands and feet. As the analysis progressed there was a shift from assaults on my body to the body of my mother. I was made to feel helpless, humiliated, and ashamed. In the course of experiencing those feelings I became aware of how toxic Javier felt his environment was and how he felt helpless, humiliated, and ashamed. In essence, his dignity had been compromised in the same manner in which he was compromising mine. Continued exposure to parental nudity was accompanied by the failure to adequately clothe Javier's backside and genital area, resulting in his also being exposed. His seemingly amorous assaults on his mother in the waiting room were desperate attempts to engage her. Neither parent was particularly involved with Javier. His father had left the rearing of both children to his wife who, for her part, was more interested in her daughter than in Javier.

Developmentally, there had been a kind of perfect storm. Javier had learning difficulties that, combined with the lack of admiration, or even emotional investment, from his parents, further damaged his already precarious self-esteem. Hence, the requisite components for the co-construction of dignity were not available to this boy.

Over time, Javier was able to see me as an ally and the play shifted to the use of the analytic couch as an ocean liner in which he and I would explore the sea (his mind). He was always the captain and I would periodically be sent off underwater to explore on my own. At such times the lifeline to the ship was often broken and I was at risk of drifting endlessly under the sea. But he would invariably come to my rescue. I viewed this as a reversal in the transference as it was actually I who was coming to his rescue.

In yet later play Javier was the proprietor of an "information store". If I wanted to know anything I would have to pay him to provide it. Although he at first insisted on my actually paying him, he did reluctantly accept play money. And while the computer he relied on for getting the information I wanted (about him) was frequently "down", he was able to "hack into it" and provide what I wanted to know. Thus, while ostensibly remaining in control, Javier was able to co-operate with the analysis.

I also worked with both Javier and his father on trying to cultivate a father-son relationship. Both of them were able to participate in this process and they started going fishing together at a local park. Javier had no friends and continued to be a kind of social outcast. The family did acquire a dog, to which Javier became very attached. For a period of time the analysis focused on his relationship with the dog, which he tried to get to obey him and to do tricks. His parents complained that he was unreasonable in his expectations of the dog, and that he over-stimulated the dog, which would then run wildly around the house. We worked in derivative terms considering what it might be like for the dog to bear the brunt of unfair expectations and to be overstimulated to the point where he lost control of his behaviour. He was able to join me in this work and made attempts, not always successful, to modify his treatment of the dog, showing more understanding and compassion.

In terms of dignity, the respectful analytic approach to trying to understand his inner world characterised by anxiety, fears of abandonment, low self-esteem, sibling rivalry, and rage helped Javier to think of himself as a complicated but worthwhile person. He began to develop more age-appropriate interests, including a gratifying relationship with his father and interaction with same sex peers. In addition, my enjoyment of him and of the work we did certainly contributed to the analytic co-construction of his sense of dignity.

This case vignette illustrates a situation in which there were assaults on the child's self-esteem in the form of a learning disability compounded by his comparison to his accomplished sister, and an inadequate (relative to his needs) amount of love, admiration, and involvement from his parents. Hence, both components leading to the development of a sense of dignity were compromised.

The analysis allowed Javier to express the resultant affects and conflicts in a safe environment. As the analysis progressed, the transference became the vehicle for such expression as Javier turned passive into active, challenging my sense of dignity. His delight in my misfortune and his wish to be in control were gradually interpreted: the former in terms of his internalised object relationships consisting of being either the victim or the aggressor, and, given that choice, understandably choosing to be the aggressor; the latter in terms of his need to control outcomes so that nothing bad would befall him (as it had done in the past). As we slowly began to understand his internal life, we became allies more than adversaries. As this occurred, Javier returned more nearly to a path of age-appropriate functioning and began to display a sense of dignity.

References

Freud, A. (1965). *Normality and Pathology in Childhood*. Madison, CT: International Universities Press.

Freud, S. (1914c). On narcissism: an introduction. *S. E., 14*: 67–102. London: Hogarth.

Levine, S. (2014). Panel on dignity at the American Psychoanalytic Association meetings in New York on 18 January 2014.

Sandler, J. (1960). The background of safety. *International Journal of Psychoanalysis, 41*: 352–356.

Winnicott, D. W. (1953). Transitional objects and transitional phenomena: a study of the first not-me possession. *International Journal of Psychoanalysis, 34*: 89–97.

Winnicott, D. W. (1969). The use of an object. *International Journal of Psychoanalysis, 50*: 711–716.

CHAPTER SEVEN

The dignity of one's experiences: dignity and indignity in the lives of LGBT people

Susan C. Vaughan

For some reason, death is often the first thing that comes to mind when we think dignity. The virtue of death with dignity has been extolled in stories of warriors from the earliest of times as well as more recently in movies such as *Brian's Song* and plays such as *Wit*. In its modern definition, to die with dignity is a philosophical concept that means that a terminally ill person should be allowed to die naturally and comfortably rather than experience a comatose, vegetative life prolonged by mechanical support systems (Free Dictionary, 2015). Yet for many in the LGBTQ community, the issue is less one of death with dignity than it is life with dignity—that is, a life that is natural and comfortable for that individual, a life that allows him or her to fit into the dominant culture without being defined by normative expectations about what sex and gender should mean.

Michel Foucault (1979), writing about binaries, noted that within each binary is contained a power structure or hierarchy in which one category of the binary is elevated above the other within society. For example, in the binaries White/Black, male/female, straight/gay, and cis-gender/transgender is contained a hierarchy with one pole of the binary considered superior to the other. In this example, categories of White, male, straight, cis-gender are considered superior to Black, female, gay, transgender.

In fact, in the past sixty or so years, these binaries have given rise respectively to the civil rights, women's rights, gay rights, and trans rights movements. It is the people on the "inferior" or "non-normative" side of the binary who have a need to assert their right to dignity, among other things. And in fact their leaders often have done this quite eloquently. "One's dignity may be assaulted, vandalised, cruelly mocked, but it can never be taken away unless it is surrendered," Martin Luther King, Jr. once said. While true, this fails to acknowledge that growing up in a society that is racist, sexist, homophobic, or transphobic may prevent one from ever developing an internalised positive view of the self that will make it possible to maintain one's dignity amidst psychological (and physical) assaults. Years later, King's widow Coretta Scott King noted that "Homophobia is like racism and anti-Semitism and other forms of bigotry in that it seeks to dehumanise a large group of people, to deny their humanity, their dignity and personhood." The same might equally well be said of transphobia. For too many in marginalised groups, daily life in a society in which one is on the wrong side of the binary can be an indignity in and of itself.

If we think about what dignity is not, in other words what its opposite would be, we not only define it as indignity but also, further, as humiliation, degradation, disgrace, or shame. As psychoanalysts, we appreciate especially the impact of shame—the sense that the self is inherently bad. Fostered by societal and parental attitudes as well as by interaction of the individual's mind with those attitudes, homo- or transphobia, as seen in society or the family, can easily become internalised, such that the feelings of humiliation, degradation, disgrace, and shame are directed against the self. In other words, when called a "fag" or "dyke" or "tranny" by others, the gay or lesbian or trans individual may feel humiliated and ashamed.

Assaults on dignity by society

Some brief case vignettes may serve to highlight these assaults on the self that are common for people of so-called "non-normative" (i.e., non-majority) genders and sexualities.

Alan, a twenty-seven-year-old gay man, was worried about the locker room at his gym and getting an erection there. He had once got an erection in fifth grade and, not quite understanding what it was, had felt proud that his penis appeared larger. Other older boys, understanding what was happening, had teased him about his "woody" and called him a "faggot". Alan already detested PE because he felt he was not a "jock" and he felt afraid of the rough and tumble games that were played, self-conscious about how he threw a ball and ran. So he stammered "I was just thinking about Becky [a popular cheerleader]" to throw them off and assert his heterosexuality without even knowing quite what he was doing. He then felt an internal sense of shame because he knew that this was a lie and it was part of a false self he was beginning to construct to protect himself from assaults such as "faggot".

Barbara, a thirty-year-old single lesbian in psychotherapy, told me that part of her problem as a grown woman in going to the gym was the memories it raised for her of locker rooms in childhood. She recalled in sixth grade changing in the school locker room after volleyball practice with a feeling of dread and excitement mixed together. It was a chance to see her best friend Cindy undressed, which was exciting, but it was also a time when the secret of her sexuality might spill over, which felt like an anxiety-making catastrophe waiting to happen. She was excited, yet worried, looking at Cindy's breasts with a kind of fascination that she didn't yet understand but knew was unacceptable.

These examples highlight the way in which gay and lesbian children experience a diffuse sense of aloneness and difference from peers in early life. Sometimes gender atypicality or "tomboyism" accounts for part of this difference. Unlike "sissyness" in gay men, being a tomboy is often acceptable in a society that values "male" traits, even in girls. However, many lesbian patients describe their mothers' discomforts with their athleticism and encouragement of more feminine pursuits. This sense that one is different is not neutral, for it is clear to many lesbians and gay men not only that they are different but that this difference is problematic and bad. They conclude that they should keep whatever is different hidden, sequester a part of themselves from others, sometimes even before quite knowing what that part actually is. For many gay men and lesbians, epithets such as "faggot" or "lezzie" provide the first clue as to what this badness may be. For instance, one patient I treated recalled realising that she was a lesbian when an older boy called two girls "lezzies" because they wouldn't show him their underwear.

The active, conscious suppression of aspects of the self during childhood and adolescence often gives rise to a sense of secrecy and inauthenticity as well as conflicts about what parts of the self show on the surface. In contrast to the false self of Kohut, this sense of creating a false shell to protect oneself from the assaults of peers is often quite conscious. Patients recall "studying up" on who the cute boys were that they should like, assiduously avoiding any physical contact with girls in case they are found out, dating and having sex with opposite sex partners, and generally disconnecting from their own sexual and sensual experiences in order to be "normal". But this sense of "normal" comes at a price of feeling false and disingenuous. On the one hand, being "found out" would mean being known and seen but on the other it would mean risking rejection and alienation. To make matters more complicated, lesbian children are frequently put in situations that are sexually or sensually stimulating, and many of these occur within the family itself.

If locker rooms are the nexus of confusion and challenge for the gay or lesbian child, it is clear that bathrooms are the site of trans conflict. Carin (born Cary) was a seventeen-year-old high school student when he told his mother he was trans and presented for treatment. His mother's reason for having him see me was her hope that he was not trans whereas Carin's reasons for wanting to see me were twofold: an ongoing sense of despair and suicidality, and the knowledge that she had to have a physician's letter to receive hormone therapy to transition from male to female. Carin described such an alienating sense of being in the male bathroom that she dealt with it by not drinking any fluids after eight pm the night before school and also all day during a school day so that she would not need to urinate. She also wore gym shorts under jeans so as not to have to change in the boy's locker room at all, again because she experienced such a dissonant feeling of being in the wrong locker room. Thinking about that moment of embarrassment people generally feel when they walk into the "wrong" bathroom helped me appreciate that Carin would strive to avoid this part of her daily experience.

"Assaults" and assaults on dignity by family of origin

Lesbian and gay children's identities and sense of dignity is also often affected within the family due to a prevailing societal presumption that all children are heterosexual. Mothers who would never walk around naked in front of sons routinely do so in front of their daughters, who may be lesbian, because they presume their daughters are straight and that their nudity does not represent a sexual stimulation. This is why I put "assault" in quotations at the head of this section: parents are not committing an assault of the sort that parents who are actively sexually abusing children commit. But they are unwittingly making heteronormative assumptions based on dominant cultural presumptions that children are straight (if indeed they are seen as sexual at all). Although certainly not as damaging as overt sexual abuse, this kind of daily overstimulation of gay and lesbian children does take its toll; it leaves them overstimulated physically, and having to contain the excitement they feel and to work hard at consciously constructing a protective false self to prevent others seeing that excitement. Family situations, as well as those in society, such as sleepovers that group same-gender children together, are often problematic, in terms of being overstimulating sexually, for gay and lesbian children, who often deal with this by disconnecting.

Despite the task of containing and hiding one's true self, early adolescence, when same-sex ties flourish, is often a relatively peaceful and happy time for lesbian girls and gay men. Yet this often comes to a crashing, depressing end as close friends move on to an interest in opposite gender partners. For lesbians, fathers who once treated their daughters more like sons may also withdraw as their daughters develop and their femininity becomes unmistakable. This simultaneous loss of father and close friends seems to create severe depression in a number of lesbian patients.

The results of these developmental challenges linger into adolescence and adulthood, as family "assaults" based on heteronormative assumptions can quickly change to more sinister and direct assaults. Sometimes, these assaults are just a simple function of the child being further along in self-understanding and breaking news to a parent whose sense of the child lags behind (often not surprisingly, as the child has been working hard to hide it). Still, this mismatch in where the child is and where the parent is can be a further source of pain and alienation for the child, who must witness the disappointed parent.

Many parents I have worked with report a sense of shame, and wish they could take back their reactions to their children coming out to them. "I was just surprised and showed shock and disappointment. It was like all those dreams of their wedding were suddenly up in smoke, wanting grandchildren was in jeopardy, many of my fantasies about my child in the future were challenged." Patients often recall parents saying things like "What did we do wrong?" or "I think you're making the wrong choice", or "Maybe this is just a phase", which are angering and undermining from the child's perspective. Thus I often suggest gay men and lesbians come out to their parents by letter so that the parent can absorb and digest the news before responding, to protect the patient from an unwitting assault and give the parent time to catch up. Of course, there are those families even today who reject their child completely, send them to Christian camps, alienate and disown them. And increasingly there are parents who can see and wonder about their child's sexuality and are not surprised or put off by the news that they are gay or lesbian.

Similarly, there is a wide range of parent reaction to the recognition that a child is transgender, but most are negative, including even in those parents who purport to accept the news but worry about how their child will fare in society at large (an understandable concern but one that nevertheless increases a sense of alienation in their child).

Until parents can look at their baby in a nursery and wonder if that child might be gay or lesbian or transgender and see the wealth of possible outcomes with a sense of acceptance, LGBT people will continue to face what is perhaps the biggest indignity of all: that of not being seen for who one really is. Since gay, lesbian, and trans does not necessarily show on the outside in the way that, for example, race can, without parents who can envision a range of gender and sexual outcomes for their child, the child exists in a lonely space in which important aspects of who he or she is literally cannot be mentalised by the parent. That the child might be a sexual or gender minority is simply off the table as a possibility, unrepresentable. Yet, it is just this sort of being seen for who and what one is and who and what one could become by parents in early life that creates the best chance for a child to have the kind of self-worth that allows dignity in the face of assaults on the self by society at large. Preventing the kind of internalisation of homo- or transphobia that creates assaults on the self will get easier as society becomes more accepting of gender and sexual diversity.

One interesting twist on the situation is that as more and more gay men and lesbians have children, most of whom will be heterosexual, there is a subset of people in society who have had up-close and personal relationships with gay parents. Because they are not gay themselves, these children may experience insults to their parents' dignity as unfair and untrue without the experience being highly personalised or impacting their sense of themselves.

In fact, children in general may challenge their parents' perspectives in positive ways that help further human rights and embrace the dignity of all people. Ivan, the son of gay fathers, was learning about the birds and the bees. "It takes three things to make a baby," explained his fathers. "An egg from a woman, some sperm from a man, and a womb from a woman for the baby to grow in." They were thinking of Ivan's own conception in which they used an egg donor, their own sperm mixed together, and a surrogate to carry Ivan as they explained this to him. "So that's why two men can't make a baby together," one father said. "Unless," Ivan challenged, "one of the boys used to be a girl." His fathers recounted the story with a mix of pride and shock at how much the world was evolving, for they would not have been able to generate this possibility so easily themselves.

And of course, some gay, lesbian, and trans people will be able to find within themselves a reservoir of dignity that astounds, even while growing up in a society filled with daily assaults upon their dignity. Jane and Kailey, in their twenties, were walking hand in hand in a part of their city known as especially gay when a group of college-aged men pulled alongside them in a station wagon and began slinging epithets, exclaiming "Lezzies, all you need is a good man and some dick to fix you", and "What a waste". The couple began to walk faster and to be afraid of assault or rape and their reaction only increased the name-calling and threats. Several young men piled out of the car and began to give chase on foot as the women, terrified, began to run and look for people around who could help. But the young men continued to close on them. Finally, in a stroke of genius and self-respect, Jane stopped running and began to kiss Kailey. The young men reached them, stood dumbfounded for a second, and slunk back to the car, still screaming "What a waste" as they departed. "It's not wasted", Jane, now emboldened, yelled at them as they drove off. For the couple the story became one of resilience, pride, and power in the face of societal assault on their identities.

Tempering indignities and restoring dignity to LGBT people through psychoanalytic treatment

The necessity of acknowledging problematic theory

Although it is tempting to start a section on psychoanalytic treatment with an exploration of the many potential benefits of psychoanalytic treatment for LGBTQ people, to do so would be a disservice. For it is important that, as a field and as individuals within that field, we first appreciate the harm we have wrought as analysts, whose wrong-headed theories have limited our ability to help those who come to us and have even grievously wronged them.

Along with Elizabeth Auchincloss (Auchincloss & Vaughan, 2001), I have argued elsewhere with reference to homosexuality that there are a number of problems of thinking that have led analysts down erroneous paths with regard to theory about LGBT patients. For example, the delineation of categories has been an important problem in psychoanalytic theory as it relates to homosexuality. A category that has given psychoanalysis difficulty with regard to homosexuality is the category of normality. In much of the psychoanalytic literature, homosexuality has, with disastrous ease, been linked with psychopathology, the equation between the two falsely presented as deriving from psychoanalytic methodology. A highly problematic commentary of traits runs throughout the psychoanalytic literature on homosexuality in the form of an attempt to answer the question "What are normal people like?" accompanied by the answer "Normal people are heterosexual."

Grossman and Kaplan (1988) argue that when either analyst or patient presents gender stereotypes or, by extension of their argument, any other example of trait commentary, as an adequate explanation for a behaviour or an attitude (for example, the statement "This is the way women—or men, or homosexuals, or normal people—are!"), this event should provoke a psychoanalytic investigation of a "psychopathology of conformity" (p. 353). In other words, we must wonder why the patient or the analyst, or the theorist, for that matter, accepts a conventional psychology of traits and categories as an adequate and final description of the "world as it is".

Other theoretical problems highlighted by the stormy relationship between psychoanalysis and homosexuality are that of causation and that of bedrock. By using stereotypical narratives, such as those of the oedipal configuration, in which homosexuality is seen as an abnormal and hence problematic outcome, psychoanalysts have traditionally tended to try to explain homosexual (but not heterosexual) sexuality as the result of problematic early-life relationship dynamics. In addition, since the bedrock of experience is traditionally seen as heterosexuality, homosexual desires may be chalked up as defences against problematic heterosexuality (i.e., pseudo-sexuality) as well as psychopathological. These issues of thinking play out in clinical situations all the time yet are often under appreciated by clinicians.

It is with an awareness of our profession's biases that we must hear clinical material and evaluate the experiences of our patients. We have not always allowed our patients anything like the dignity of their own experiences but have instead insisted that they not be who they are, often to their great detriment. Further, although we have come a long way in our attitudes towards LGBT colleagues, there is often still the perception of bias in applying to be a candidate, in certification, and in becoming a training analyst. We must guard against thinking that, as a field, we are finished with coming to terms with these issues within ourselves, our institutes, or our theories.

Moving beyond our history to a better way of listening

When as analysts we encounter human experiences with which we are not familiar, a common response is to feel that we need a new theory or framework for understanding these experiences. We become unsettled. Yet when we can listen with close attention to our countertransference and the ways in which psychoanalytic theory might be causing us to make problematic assumptions, we can be very helpful indeed in working with LGBT people. We should start from the radical proposition that we are dignifying the experiences of our minority patients simply by listening to their stories in an empathetic way without too much psychoanalytic formulation on our parts.

My work with Matteo shows how this kind of listening yields results. Matteo, a thirty-four-year-old single gay professional, sought psychotherapy and later psychoanalysis with me, complaining about difficulty in intimate relationships. His history was remarkable for his having been sent by his parents, between the ages of ten and seventeen, for two separate analyses in Europe, with the goal, as he put it, of "making me less sissy so I didn't turn out gay." His mother, a psychoanalyst, vociferously asserted her personal theory about the etiology of her son's homosexuality, a view buttressed by her psychoanalytic reading. She believed that his feminine identifications and preference for men were, in Matteo's words, "the best adaptation I could arrive at, with the alternative being that I would be psychotic." She banned him from loitering in the kitchen with the comforting female cook he loved, "who loved me no matter what and taught me to cook", on the presumption that his gay "problem" was being made worse by such feminine pursuits. Although Matteo had found his first analyst at age ten helpful, the analyst returned to Brazil in the middle of what sounded like a supportive treatment that did not involve an assault on his femininity. However, he was not so lucky with a second female analyst who focused on his homosexuality "as a defence against fears of the female genitals or as an immature and narcissistic developmental arrest." Although Matteo began to date girls during this analysis, he found this activity unfulfilling and began to drink, use drugs, and engage in anonymous sexual encounters with men. It intensified his sense of a false self and his shame in his true desires. Though a talented pianist, his career ended when he arrived for a performance with an orchestra too drunk to play. He quit the piano and his drug use and anonymous gay sex escalated. He sought treatment after testing HIV positive and becoming sober in AA, hoping that psychoanalysis could be a different experience than it had been in the past.

Early in treatment, it became clear that Matteo experienced interpretations from me as if he were being clubbed over the head as punishment for perceived sins or wrongdoings. However, at the same time, he persisted in an idealising transference of me as "a sage lesbian saviour" who would rescue him from the ravages of psychoanalytic theory. A split-off negative image of his mother developed simultaneously, as Matteo became preoccupied with the idea that it was her intrusiveness and "the way she came between me and my father" that had produced his homosexuality. Before a visit home, he sent his mother a copy of Richard Isay's book *Being Homosexual* (1989), believing—after seeing it on my bookshelf but not having read it himself—that it would show her a new and non-pathologising way to view his homosexuality. In short, at this point in the analysis, Matteo's personal theory of the origins of his homosexuality closely resembled that of Bieber (1988), whose paradigm of a pathogenic family constellation consisting of a close-binding mother and a distant father was turned on its ear by Isay in the very book Matteo had given his mother without having read. Clearly, he wished to blame his mother for his difficulties in intimate relationships with men, his HIV status, his substance abuse, and his general unhappiness as a gay man. As we explored the multiple meanings of his sending her the book, an image emerged of me and Matteo allied against his mother, clobbering and indicting her with psychoanalytic theories that implicated her as the cause of his homosexuality. The patient fantasised coming out to everyone in the phone book in his hometown so as to panic, humiliate, and indict his mother for her failures. When I repeatedly interpreted how his attack on his mother, supported by me as his ally, served to keep his rage and feelings of damage safely out of the analysis, his desire to punish me for the sins of analysts past, as well as for my own homosexuality, began to emerge. He began to tell me of a secret store of criticisms he had collected over time. These centered around two themes: (1) I was a damaged lesbian who was too mannish and whose defective femininity was the cause of my homosexuality. He complained, for example, that he found me "heavy-footed" and "butch" when I went to get him in the waiting room. (2) I was an analyst who secretly wished to cure him (and myself) of homosexuality. He cited my "bias" against anonymous and unsafe sex as evidence of my own hatred of homosexuality. I was unclear as to how this sense of my "bias" had emerged in the consulting room yet aware that indeed I did have a dim view of his promiscuity, not because it involved gay sex but because it put him at risk of reinfection with HIV and partners who were negative at risk of seroconverting. As issues of internalised homophobia and rage were addressed and the role of projection in shaping his views of me as a lesbian and an analyst became clearer to him, Matteo's theories about his sexuality shifted accordingly.

Approximately three years after he had given his mother Isay's book, he purchased it and read it for himself. Isay's formulations allowed Matteo to begin a new exploration of early memories of attraction to his father and of pain at his father's interest in his brother's athletic activities. He began to consider the possibility that his homosexuality might be more constitutional and innate than conflict-based. His desire to see it as primary or inborn was accompanied by increased self-reflection as to why he had previously thought of his homosexuality in terms of fault and blame. He also began to develop a more balanced positive view of me as someone who could be both a lesbian and a mature, caring person. Around this same time his mother remarked on a positive shift in their relationship and stated that his analysis must be helping. Matteo confronted her about a prior remark in which she had suggested that I, as a lesbian, would be unable to help him with sexual issues. In contrast to their previous fights about the origins of his homosexuality, this confrontation led to a productive conversation in which Matteo was able to convey his feelings of hurt. By the end of his analysis, Matteo felt that he did not know why he was gay and would probably never know. Moreover, although curious, he felt that he did not need to know. Through the work of analysis, he understood how his evolving theories of causation served to support a variety of psychological needs. He turned from this question to matters of daily intimacy, and was able to find and solidify a relationship with a male partner that he loved.

I also encountered significant bias as a candidate around the issue of taking this patient on for psychoanalytic treatment and was told I was masochistic as he would die in treatment and I would not get credit for the case. Well along in my own analysis, I was able to request a different supervisor who suggested that the patient had more problems with regard to living than with regard to dying and that even if he died while in treatment it could be a worthwhile endeavour. This case suggests how right things can go, even for patients previously damaged by problematic psychoanalytic theory, if they are seen by someone who can remain near to their experiences of the world and interested, a clinician who looks for signs of judgement within her countertransference, and questions her underlying assumptions and questions about what the patient is saying.

When I encountered Matteo in the park five years later, he was walking with his partner and their three-year-old twin son and daughter. He was beginning to teach them the piano and, given his beaming countenance in talking about them, it was clear they were his pride and joy. He remained relatively well medically for about five years, then returned for weekly treatment in the setting of some cardiac issues that were making him feel vulnerable and scared. But by this time his identity and sense of himself as a gay man and parent were solid and unshakeable. Being a patient was a new role, another aspect of identity to come to terms with, and we began to work on that new issue as he transitioned from working to being a stay-at-home dad and a cardiac patient.

Transgender and beyond: the next frontier

Although we may now be at a better place within psychoanalysis with regard to an understanding of gay and lesbian issues, analysts' beliefs about the transgender issues that have emerged publically since around the year 2000 tend to lag about twenty years behind. Yet once again they bring up the same issues about the psychopathology of conformity, our definitions of normality, our sense of what is bedrock, and our understanding of causality. Some assert that gender atypicality in children is the result of attachment disorders between mother and child.

Coates (Coates & Wolfe, 1995) notes that boys with gender atypicality often have a poignant way of expressing psychological suffering: "One three-year-old boy said during his evaluation: 'I hate myself. I don't want to be me. I want to be someone else. I want to be a girl.' Another boy volunteered: 'I hate myself. I hate being a boy. I want to die. I wish I was a girl. Why do I have to be a boy even in my dreams?'" She focuses on the role of maternal gynecological trauma and disrupted mother-child attachment in the development of the gender dysphoria and its resolution, but she also focuses on creating a safe space for "cross-gender" play and for the potential for a transsexual outcome in the child. Her barometer of progress in treatment is not resolution of gender atypicality but amelioration of emotional suffering in the child.

Yet although this perspective may be useful in work with children, as gender is in evolution, adult or adolescent trans men and women may view this line of questioning as a futile search to answer the question of why they are trans or as an attempt on the clinician's part to change them rather than as a helpful clinical endeavour. Recently, some psychoanalysts who are transgender have entered psychoanalytic training and shared their personal developmental experiences of being transgender. Writing in "Understanding gender through the lens of transgender experience" (Pula, 2015/in press), Dr. Jack Pula poignantly expresses what it was like to grow up first as a tomboy, then as a butch lesbian, and later as someone transitioning to male during analytic training:

> Many people claim that gender and sexuality are distinct entities that are too often confounded. While I appreciate the need to distinguish the two and resent the lazy confounding of both, I disagree that they are so distinctly separate. I wonder if people who say this are trying very hard to uphold the full human dignity of transgender people by making certain we are not equated with sexual perversion, as we historically have been. It is laudable and important to appreciate the full meaning of gender outside sexuality. But in my experience, through a painful and liberating analysis, and in transition, my sexuality has come fully into play as part of my gender identity.

If we want to imbue our work with transgender patients with the best chance that they will develop a sense of the dignity of their own experience, we must also be attuned to the countertransferences we face in working with them. For example, in her 2012 paper entitled "The body one has and the body one is", Lemma (2013) asserts that the transsexual confronts the analyst with a disturbing otherness and that how the analyst "looks at the patient through her distinctive theoretical lens impacts, in turn, on the patient's experience and what transpires between them." She suggests that in some cases of transsexuality the primary object(s) did not mirror and contain an early experience of incongruity between the given body and the subjective experience of gender: it remains un-mentalised and disrupts self-coherence leading to the pursuit of surgery that is anticipated to "guarantee" relief from the incongruity. Yet in suggesting the patient confronts the analyst with a disturbing otherness, perhaps Lemma discounts the strong possibility that the analyst merely reacts to the patient's self-presentation as an affront because of his or her own deep-seated need to parse people into one gender or the other.

Conclusion

In this chapter, I have tried to show that leading a dignified life as an LGBT person means weathering witting and unwitting assaults created by living as a minority in society, as well as assaults on the self within one's family of origin. I have asserted that we must carefully clear away the wreckage of the past with regard to problematic psychoanalytic theory and practice in order to make psychoanalysis useful, relevant, and, most importantly, not harmful to patients who are gender and sexual minorities. We must attend especially to countertransference, those areas of our own assumptions and discomforts that are antithetical to doing clinical work, in order to increase our patients' experiences of dignity and merit. I suggest we can start this process by trying to set aside theories about LGBT people and by just listening, and that we don't use our countertransference as an unflappable guide to what they are trying to do to us!

Society has begun to recognise the societal factor—what our laws convey about the dignity with which individuals are held. In fact, in *Windsor vs. United States*, the case that overturned the Federal Defense of Marriage Act (DOMA), Justice Anthony Kennedy (2013) cited dignity ten times. He wrote: "the State's decision to give [same-sex couples] the right to

marry conferred upon them a dignity and status of immense import."
He also stated: "When the State used its historic and essential authority
to define the marital relation [to include same-sex marriage], its role and
its power in making the decision enhanced the recognition, dignity, and
protection of the class in their own community." He explained that "by
authorizing same-sex unions and same-sex marriages, New York sought
to give further protection and dignity to that bond."

In closing, it is also important to remember that analyst/patient is
also an unequal binary, one in which the analyst is the dignitary, the
person of experience and substance, while the patient feels, or can be
made to feel, less knowing. Of course there are ways in which this is
true—the analyst must surely have expertise in ameliorating human
suffering, lessening the impact of societal and developmental influences, and creating a more coherent and less conflicted self that is experienced as having dignity in the sense of self-worth.

Perhaps Jennifer Finney Boylan, a transwoman professor at Barnard
College and the author of *She's Not There: A Life in Two Genders* (2013a),
expresses it best when she says:

> I can say that the most important thing trans people can do is tell
> their stories—in whatever venue or form we can. As my mother
> used to say, "It is impossible to hate anyone whose story you know,"
> and it is by making our stories known that other people can begin
> to understand our lives, and the challenges we face. That's how we
> change the world, I believe: one story at a time. (Boylan, 2013b)

For analysts hard at work in their offices alone with their patients, it
is always one story at a time, a story that morphs and expands in its
complexity as we understand more. Boylan directly mentions dignity
when she asserts that

> every time we have a trans person being treated with dignity and
> respect on television, or in film, or in the press, it makes things
> better—and not just for trans people but for everyone. There are as
> many ways of being trans as there are of being gay, or lesbian, or
> for that matter, straight, and we need to open up our hearts to all
> of this. There are an infinite number of ways of being human. By
> accepting the wondrous scope of gender, we affirm the vast poten-
> tial of life, in all of its messy, unfathomable beauty. (Boylan, 2013b)

As analysts we are uniquely positioned to experience our patient's suffering in our work together. To foster a sense of dignity for our LGBT patients in treatment and beyond will require the analyst's best traits of humility, an ability to contain and weather uncertainty, and an ability to hear about the range of human possibilities in an experience-near way. If we are able to withstand the pressures of our theories and countertransferences well enough, we will also surely come to appreciate the messy and unfathomable beauty in the lives of our patients. And we will ourselves be the better for it.

References

Auchincloss, E. L., & Vaughan, S. C. (2001). Psychoanalysis and homosexuality: do we need a new theory? *Journal of the American Psychoanalytic Association, 49*: 1157–1186.

Bieber, I. (1988). *Homosexuality: A Psychoanalytic Study*. Northvale, NJ: Aronson.

Boylan, J. F. (2013a). *She's Not There: A Life in Two Genders*. New York: Broadway Paperbacks.

Boylan, J. F. (2013b). Interview with Mari Haywood, 2 May. http://www.glaad.org/blog/glaad-speaks-transgender-author-jennifer-finney-boylan-her-new-memoir-stuck-middle-you. Date accessed: 28 May, 2015.

Coates, S. W., & Wolfe, S. M. (1995). Gender identity disorder in boys: the interface of constitution and early experience. *Psychoanalytic Inquiry, 15*: 6–38.

Foucault, M. (1979). *The History of Sexuality Volume 1: An Introduction*. London: Allen Lane.

Free Dictionary (2015). Farlex: www.thefreedictionary.com. Date accessed: 28 May 2015.

Grossman, W., & Kaplan, D. (1988). Three commentaries on gender in Freud's thought: prologue to the psychoanalytic theory of sexuality. In: H. Blum, Y. Kramer, A. K. Richards & A. D. Richards (Eds.), *Fantasy, Myth and Reality: Essays in Honor of Jacob A. Arlow* (pp. 339–370). New York: International Universities Press.

Isay, R. (1989). *Being Homosexual: Gay Men and Their Development*. New York: Farrar, Straus & Giroux.

Kennedy, Anthony (2013). DOMA opinion. As cited at http://www.supremecourt.gov/opinions/12pdf/12-307_6j37.pdf . Date accessed: 28 May 2015.

King, Coretta Scott. As cited at http://en.wikiquote.org/wiki/Coretta_Scott_King. Date accessed: 28 May 2015.

King, Jr. Martin Luther. As cited at http://www.goodreads.com/author/quotes/23924.Martin_Luther_King_Jr_?page=4. Date accessed: 28 May 2015.

Lemma, A. (2013). The body one has and the body one is: understanding the transsexual's need to be seen. *International Journal of Psychoanalysis,* 94: 277–291.

Pula, J. (2015). Understanding gender though the lens of transgender experience. In press. *Journal of Psychoanalytic Inquiry, Special Volume of Gender,* publication pending November 2015.

CHAPTER EIGHT

"I knew that my mind could take me anywhere": psychoanalytic reflections on the dignity of African Americans living in a racist society

Dorothy Evans Holmes

The quotation in the title for this chapter is taken from remarks by Dr. Ruth Simmons on the occasion of her appointment in 1994 as President of Smith College; she was the first African American to become President of a "Seven Sisters" school (Simmons, 1994). Dr. Simmons went on to become a beloved and immensely successful president of Brown University, the first African American to become president of an Ivy League university. She knew that her mind could take her anywhere, she said, despite the fact that she had grown up in east Texas, the daughter of sharecroppers, in the Jim Crow south, a place from which she was expected to have no other place to go. In voicing her unshakeable belief, Dr. Simmons spoke to the essence of dignity—it is irreducible human worth that persists and motivates against all odds. A human being possesses it inherently. Dignity is inseparable from what it means to be human. There is no psychoanalytic theory or definition of dignity per se. The psychoanalytic concept that comes closest is the concept of self:

> A predominantly unconscious structure at the core of the personality, which is the center of initiative, the recipient of impressions. [Its components are] the individual's ambitions, ideals, and talents ... It has its own driving force ... [If one's self is cohesive, then one experiences] an enduring sense of personal agency and initiative, continuity through time and space, stable self-esteem, values and ideals, the capacity to regulate affects and tension states, and the ability to seek out others [for mutual responsiveness]. (Auchincloss & Samberg, 2012, p. 234)

The concept of self does not fully satisfy the requirements of dignity, because the psychoanalytic concept of self allows for the self to be fragmented, to wit: "In an individual with a fragmented self, [his/her] capacities are compromised or not evident ..." (Auchincloss & Samberg, 2012, p. 234). I take the position here that dignity is a more robust construct than the self, because dignity cannot be fragmented. It is fundamental to human nature and is indivisible. Kateb (2011), in addressing that dignity can be assaulted but that its essence cannot be destroyed, said: "... a human being can never forfeit his or her dignity" (p.13). Also, the assaults from racist practices aimed at disrupting a Black person's self-worth come from societal practices as well as individual acts. Dignity is a construct that embraces that larger sphere of influence, whereas more usual psychoanalytic constructs such as self and self-esteem limit their considerations to the influence of individuals and the family. Kateb's 2011 essay on human dignity articulates how evil treatment in society, including racism, harms dignity.

Since my mid-twenties, I have been drawn to psychoanalysis—as systems of thought and as treatment methods—for its power to free the mind of its encumbrances, including assaults to dignity. Such assaults can separate a person from awareness of his or her dignity, and, thereby, such assaults can cast the dignified human being as something other than human, making his or her dignity inaccessible. It is my belief and understanding that psychoanalysis is radical enough to address and heal the rupture occasioned by inhumane treatments that are motivated to deny a person his or her dignity. In our culture, we are the descendants, perpetrators, or close witnesses of cultural atrocities that have had, and continue to have, dire effects that still course through us (e.g., slavery, the Holocaust, misogyny, homophobia, institutional racism). Only radical understandings and approaches can address these practices and their ill effects. Psychoanalysis is radical: its tools by design upset the status quo in our minds. By so doing, those tools help us find the walled-off places in our minds that contain not only our woes, but also the elements of our intactness and verve, of which our dignity is an essential element. Psychoanalytic treatment makes it possible for us to access and consolidate our qualities and capacities, and to make progress towards meeting our personal goals and ambitions. If our personal woes include distortions in our sense of who we are, as often does happen to Blacks living in racist America, psychoanalysis has the power to correct those distortions—conceptually and in clinical practice. On the conceptual side, for the reasons already stated, dignity, especially with reference to crimes against humanity and their effects, needs to be added to the concept of the self in order to have a more robust understanding of identity, self-worth, and self-esteem.

Returning to Ruth Simmons, she knew that her mind *could* take her anywhere. I am not privy to the journey by which her mind *did* take her all of the places that it did. However, undoubtedly, her powerful insight of childhood, that her mind could take her anywhere, was primary in protecting her from internalisations of the toxic and potentially soul-murdering systemic racism to which she was exposed growing up. Somehow she appears to have been protected from, or to have resolved the diminishing effects of racism on her dignity.

Given that we do not know the intricacies of Dr. Simmons' personal journey, we do not know how hard she had to fight and along what lines to claim, grow, and maintain the powers of her mind. That she became an enduring, beloved, and pre-eminently successful public figure does not mean, of course, that she was free of personal suffering, including racially. What we do know is that she had early and enduring recognition that her mind was a place containing the power necessary to propel her forward, even in the face of prevailing messages that threatened to assault her dignity. This chapter is addressed to the role clinical psychoanalysis can play when one's experience with race has deleterious effects on one's personal functioning—particularly when such experiences interfere with the rightful claim to one's dignity, self-validation, self-authorisation, and efficacy. Growing up Black in America is inherently perilous in terms of one's dignity since racism by design attempts to reduce one's worth. Historically, slavery was permissible because slaves were not considered human. Dignity is an inalienable, existential quality of being human. Due to the various civil rights advances since slavery, Blacks are, in the law, human. However, in the reality of day-to-day living, dehumanising practices have continued to this day. To wit, threats to dignity continue.

Too many people—those of colour and Whites—remain convinced that the powers of the mind are a privileged place for Whites. I proffer that the "Whites only" signs of old still "hang" too often in our societal practices, in the minds of Black and White individuals, and in cherished institutions, including institutional psychoanalysis. This chapter will, in particular, delve into how this "signage" is still evident in clinical psychoanalysis, too—as it is taught in the classroom and supervision, and as it is practiced in the consultation room. At the heart of the matter, in my view, is that psychoanalysts have identifications with, and idealizes, being privileged, in ordinary, unconflicted ways but also in ways tainted by the "isms", including racism. That is, these identifications and idealisations are connected unconsciously to racialised, gender-based and class-based dominance of one group over another, in ways unconsciously designed to strip members of the dominated group of their dignity. I will explore the psychodynamics of the phenomenon and processes by which Blacks are devalued, and become, in current parlance, "othered"—in the extreme meaning other than human, and, therefore, not possessing dignity.

First, however, as context, I will give examples of how dominance of one group over another is highly motivated and maintained with respect to gender and class. Regarding gender, forty-three years ago, Elizabeth Janeway offered a particularly astute understanding of constraints imposed on women by men. Janeway was a prescient feminist writer with a deep appreciation of depth psychology. In her 1971 book *Man's World, Woman's Place,* in relation to women's increased presence in positions of dominance, she said the reaction of men would be "… the increase of the dominance they wield already until their power grows so great they are answerable to no one. The shadow role of the dominant male is ogre."

From a specifically psychoanalytic perspective on the same subject of infringement on, and limiting of, the powers of women, Schafer has written eloquently. In 1984, he pointed out that society in general countenances "seductions into suffering" for oppressed groups. As regards women in particular he said (1984, p. 404), "De-idealization of unhappiness that is often accomplished through psychoanalysis tends to bring with it an increased readiness ... for women [to develop] lively critiques of our sexist world and adequately assertive means to resist and combat the seductions into suffering with which they are constantly surrounded." Schafer opined that the development of the capacity in women for more "lively critiques" and wellness-producing combat against sexist and misogynistic influences that constrain them, is resisted by society. I propose in this chapter that it is also resisted by psychoanalysts, ironically, given that psychoanalysis embodies the tools to foster the needed breaking away from undue constraints of any kind, internal and/or external. I will pursue some possibilities for why that is so shortly. But keep in mind that Janeway's reference to the ogre as man's unconscious role in decimating women's power and Schafer's reference to the seduction of women into suffering are ways of talking about motivation to constrain the dignity of women. In the realm of social class, we see similar phenomena. Consider the following:

> Poverty is a reaper: it harvests everything inside us that might have made us capable of social intercourse with others, and leaves us empty, purged of feeling, so that we endure all the darkness of the present day. Pleasure and suffering are proportionate to one's position in the hierarchy. I was intelligent and indigent. I was doomed if I ever sought to make good use of my mind in defiance of my class. It became clear to me that my path would be one of secrecy. I had kept silent about who I was and never mixed with the other world.

Would anyone care to guess who wrote this beautiful but melancholy passage about the ravages of internalised poverty on one's psychological well-being? Perhaps we would like to think the author is an individual in the process of developing insights gained through psychoanalysis, insights that ultimately might be freeing. Or, could the excerpt be from a psychoanalyst's process notes in a case in which she is trying to help a patient understand the real and internalised effects of poverty? Alas, neither is true. The excerpt was drawn from the work of a particularly psychologically attuned French fiction writer, Muriel Barbery. The excerpt is taken from her prize-winning 2008 novel (p. 288), the *Elegance of the Hedgehog*.

If only what Janeway offered forty-three years ago about the push-back women can expect if they try to assert the powers of their dignified selves was now quaint; if only what Barbery wrote about the ravages of poverty was just fiction. Unfortunately, the social reality and psychological impact of racism, classism, sexism, and misogyny are neither quaint nor fictional. Schafer's offerings on the necessity of working psychoanalytically with such phenomena, and the bright outcomes to be expected, are, in my view, still too absent and still too much resisted in what we teach, how we supervise, and how we work in the consultation room as psychoanalytic teachers, supervisors, and therapists. Unfortunately, psychoanalysis remains in cahoots with general society in not addressing these issues at a deep level. Therefore, it contributes to racial, gender, and class identities being either deflated unduly (assaults on dignity) or inflated unduly (a calculated misrepresentation of dignity in which falsely one makes oneself or a group more dignified than others), depending on which side of the divide you live, with unfortunate personal consequences for all.

Now, I will spell out the challenges psychoanalysts face in working with racial manifestations in psychoanalysis, beginning with some historical contributions to the lack of focused attention on race. Sigmund Freud had personal experience with racism. As we know, he grew up in virulently racist Vienna. In that culture, Jews were viewed as an inferior race, put in the same low, devalued place as Africans—both viewed essentially as subhuman and thereby not entitled to dignity. In his medical school classes and clinics, Freud repeatedly witnessed and experienced Jews being disparaged racially. In the main, Freud did not acknowledge or formulate the effects of racism on himself or on humans in general, with one exception. In his brilliant 1936 treatise on success neurosis, Freud may have been giving a bow to the contributions of class and racial factors to his success neurosis. As we know, he wrote the paper with himself as the clinical case example of success neurosis based on the dissociative symptom he suffered as he climbed the Acropolis in Athens. In that paper (1936a, p. 247), Freud said, "It seemed to me beyond the realms of possibility that I should travel so far—that I should go such a long way. This was linked up with the limitations and poverty of our conditions of life in my youth."

I find his language revealing but ambiguous and somewhat awkwardly written. In general Freud wrote elegantly. Why the ambiguous and awkward language in the success neurosis paper? Could it have been that the factors he named—"limitations and poverty"—not only contributed to his original symptom of success neurosis but were continuing to negatively impact him? Let us look closely at what he wrote. He seems to me to have said that some actual conditions of his youth—limitations and poverty—contributed to an internal view that he should not have succeeded. Poverty is a specific factor named. To what else is he alluding in his reference to "limitations"? The most intriguing thing to me about his paper is that he never answers this question. He also does not spell out the explanatory role of poverty as outlined in the body of the paper. Rather, ultimately, Freud goes on in the paper to explain success neurosis entirely in terms of how guilt from oedipal conflict taints and limits success. Others since Freud's seminal paper have updated his thinking (Marill & Siegel, 2004), and/or have expanded it to consider how conditions of poverty and/or race play a role in success neurosis (Holmes, 2006).

Most pertinent for this chapter, though, is to consider what led Freud to refrain from an explanation of how "limitations and poverty" contributed to his success neurosis? First, to what unspecified limitations was he alluding? Did he himself know? We know that on occasion, Freud did speak informally about his Jewishness and about anti-Semitism in Vienna. So, it may be reasonable to consider that among the limitations to which Freud was alluding in his paper, his Jewishness was one. However, when Freud spoke of Jewishness explicitly, he tended to minimise its importance, going as far as to say that race was only of tangential importance. At other times, he valorised his conscious mastery over adverse racial experiences, saying that adverse experiences only made him stronger. As quoted in Blanton (1971, p. 43), Freud is reported to have said, "My background as a Jew helped me to stand being criticised, being isolated, working alone". On the one hand, Freud knew of the significance of race and poverty, but on the other, he dared not to delve deeply into them; he relied only on his conscious understanding and mastery which were meaningful but not complete. My point is that such ambivalence, or any other factor that disinclined Freud to make a serious psychoanalytic inquiry into the importance and influence of factors such as race and poverty, ill-served him and the clinical science he spawned and loved.

What evidence do we have that Freud's punting on race and class ill-served him? As psychoanalysts we know that what is barred from consciousness may spring up in other ways. So it was with Freud on the subject of race and ethnicity. Freud's disavowal that his own experiences with racism impacted him negatively was proven to be incorrect inasmuch as his own internalised racism erupted when his colleague, Ernst Jones, criticised Anna Freud's analysis as incomplete in part because Freud, her father, had been her analyst. Freud responded to Jones' criticism in a letter to Eitington, as quoted in Madddox's book *Freud's Wizard: The Enigma of Ernst Jones* (Maddox, 2006). Freud said about Jones: "He is a disagreeable person who wants to display himself in ruling, angering and agitating, and for this his Welsh dishonesty serves him well" (p. 195). It is not shocking that Freud expressed unconscious racism. Any of us might. In the example given, we see evidence of spite given expression through a racist attack on Jones.

Freud's dissociative success neurosis symptom itself may bear the markings of the racism Freud internalised during his formative years but later disavowed. To discuss this possibility I need now to address the topic of being "othered" and "othering", to which I have previously alluded. The terms refer to the cultural practice of being devalued or devaluing members of cultural groups that are not the dominant one. A very simple and seemingly innocuous example is that we routinely refer to such groups as "subcultures". It is true that some groups proudly label themselves as subcultures. In all cases, though, the place of the subculture is detached from, and by choice of language, is beneath the dominant culture. Othering is a psychodynamic process that involves complex mechanisms such as motivation and defence. The process of othering aims to put the detached group, individually and collectively, in an inferior, devalued place in society. So, Freud's incredulity that he could have come so far, as symbolised in his climbing to the high place of the Acropolis, could have been a manifestation of "othering" turned on himself in which he unconsciously disrupted his climb to satisfy the requirement that he stay in a low place, that he not be the possessor of dignity that he was. Two recent psychoanalytic writers (Gentile, 2013; Tummala-Narra, 2013) have spoken pointedly to the deleterious psychological effects of othering. According to Gentile (p. 456), in giving scant attention to the place race occupies in our patients' minds and lives: "[Psychoanalysts] other the patient's cultural group. Thereby, we reduce the power of psychoanalytic witnessing of our patients' experiences with diversity."

I would only add to what Gentile said that we may do the same in considering the importance of race in our dealings with students, supervisees, and therapist-colleagues. Writing in a similar vein, Tummala-Narra (2013, p. 478) offered: "We engage in an insidious delinking process with patients around their/our 'isms' resulting in an anti-therapeutic disavowal of relevant aspects of our patient's and our own identities. We dismiss or inappropriately enfold cultural dimensions into neurotic adaptation."

I suggest that Freud may have done just that when he failed to give any further explicit and distinctive consideration to "limitations and poverty" in his success neurosis paper. Those elements seem to have become subordinated to or mingled with his consideration of ordinary neurotic adaptation in the form of oedipal conflict. The problem with such an approach is that it may constitute the elision of something that should have its own particular representation. When it comes to the various elements of our cultural and personal identities, for example, racial, class, and gender, the omission can be destructive. Tummala-Narra (2013, p. 274), clarifies this problem quite astutely: "We force into hiding what needs to be on the surface so that we can consciously and voluntarily determine the specifics of how diversity shapes the psyche … in order to analyze what is manifest … [and] what is unconscious." I would add to Tummala-Narra's argument for explicit consideration of the various manifestations of identity that only by being open to such manifestations can we know what psychical weight to attach to them in the patient's personal psychology. Also, to the extent that such factors are not worked with and brought to full conscious consideration, we leave ourselves and our patients "free" to continue to make the various aspects of our diverse identities a matter of insignificance, shame, or indignity.

There is increasing recognition in the field of psychoanalysis that it has not taken its rightful and potentially very powerful place at the table for open discussion of the effects of the "isms" on the psyche. The authors just quoted speak to the necessity to do so under the banner of the concept of "othering". Speaking on the subject with a different flavour is Emily Kuriloff, in her 2014 book *Contemporary Psychoanalysis and the Legacy of the Third Reich: History, Memory, Tradition*. In my view, the book is an eye-opener. It gives an authoritative, compelling account of how psychoanalyst emigrées from Nazi Germany and Vienna were psychically impacted and injured by Nazism, and how those injuries were never fully acknowledged by Freud and many other leading psychoanalytic figures of that time. Kuriloff's book is about how there has been no voice to speak to the personal effects of Nazism and forced migration; that voice has been silenced; the silence has been rationalised as necessary in pursuit of a positivist view of science. The author interviewed many important figures related to the subject matter (Otto Kernberg, Anna Ornstein, Tony Kris, Martin Bergmann, etc.), and otherwise researched her topic deeply, deftly, and passionately. It is a gripping and evocative book that has much to say about how analytic thinking and technique were eclipsed and distorted by the lack of discourse on how Nazism impacted the principal architects of psychoanalysis. My own opinion is that today's reticence by psychoanalysts on how the "isms" of our day (racism, homophobia, misogyny, classism, etc.) affect the psyches of all of us and the work we do derives from the gaps in shared personal reflection, theory building, and technique that Kuriloff details in her book.

Institutional psychoanalysis has been very slow to face the limited place accorded cultural factors in our theories, teaching, supervision and practice. Specifically, the American Psychoanalytic Association (APsaA; also "the American") has yet to establish guidelines for training in its approved institutes in the area of cultural diversity. Institutes are not required to report on this subject matter in the Self Studies they must prepare to be considered for accreditation or re-accreditation. Accreditation of institutes is in no way dependent on representation of cultural diversity in classes, supervision, faculty composition, or candidate recruitment and retention. However, the horizon looks more promising at present. An APsaA presidential task force has been commissioned, with funding. It will help "the American" articulate training goals and objectives with respect to cultural factors. It will also recommend institutional structures for all institutes to express their systematic and intentional plans to achieve the identified training goals and objectives with respect to cultural factors.

So far, what I am saying is that psychoanalysis has mostly refrained from using its most powerful tools to enlighten the darkened and silenced internal places in which people carry their feelings about and their uses and misuses of their and other's racial makeup. It is a broad cultural practice to do so. As to whether there are continuing problems, I say "yes", that there are three areas in which psychoanalysts have marched in step with society's exclusionary practices regarding race and other cultural factors:

1. Yes: In the past, psychoanalysts have engaged in institutional othering practices in the form of exclusionary admission policies for psychologists and the LGBT community, and in biased clinical theories
   and practices regarding LGBTs. Also, to this day, psychoanalysis has
   not systematised and institutionalised an approach to training with
   respect to race, gender, and sexuality, though it is beginning to do so,
   as just noted concerning the work of the task force. We can trace the
   history of psychoanalysis's problem with these subjects to Freud. We
   can identify ways in which not having faced these subjects squarely
   up to now has been and remains problematic. In terms of damage
   caused to psychoanalysis, Sander Gilman offered one in his celebrated
   1993 book *Freud, Race and Gender*. In that work, Gilman critiqued
   Freud's propositions about female psychology. He suggested that
   Freud's now largely discredited views on women's psyches and
   their anatomy may have represented unconscious displacements and
   projections of his own unconscious sense of inferiority as a Jew.
2. Yes: there is continuing selective mutism when it comes to exploring
   internal, psychodynamic manifestations of race in the consultation
   room. Barbery's heroine in the *Elegance of the Hedgehog* speaks to how
   the ravages of poverty have a silencing effect; Kuriloff writes similarly on the profound and collective silence by psychoanalysts about
   the most horrific racism of the twentieth century, that is, Nazism.
   Psychoanalysis has taken shelter in this place of silence. So, psychoanalysis has not used its voice to declare the damage to the psyche
   caused by the ravages of the various "isms", including their intent to
   separate humans from their dignity.
3. Yes: there is ongoing proneness to unfortunate displays of racism
   and other isms among us. I am thinking not only of examples such
   as the Freud-Jones matter noted above, but also more subtle illustrations, an example of which will be presented shortly from a treatment case.

Even for those who no longer idealise or valorise Freud, we, like Freud,
have our own needs to defend against awareness of racism and the other
"isms" in ourselves and in our patients. In my forty plus years of practice, teaching, and supervising experience, I find that the place accorded
the "isms" in what we as psychoanalysts do in our own thinking, in our
didactic teaching, supervision, and practice is still too small. Perhaps

like Freud, and reinforced by his example, we, too, are made anxious by the prospect of opening up more space, making a bigger place for the "lively critiques" and the necessary transference-countertransference engagement that would come to bear. Such engagements are likely to be full of affect. What will our countertransferences be? Will we react as Freud did when criticised by Jones, even though such responses would be anathema to our highly civilised, largely liberal psychoanalytic selves with our deeply held egalitarian values.

Collectively, as psychoanalysts, we do not shun the difficult, real, transference, and countertransference manifestations of conflicts regarding love and hate in general; nor do we shun the extremely demanding aspects of patients with more primal issues. Why, then, so much resistance when it comes to the "isms"? As Schafer opined about working with women, those freed up from oppression will once again show their worth, their dignity, and, as such, will demand a better place at the table. Psychoanalysis, past or present, is not pristine in promoting big shifts in who gets to sit at its table. The most salient example of this is the fact that until the early 1980s, the American Psychoanalytic Association excluded mental health professionals other than psychiatrists from full training (for example, psychologists and clinical social workers), except through a waiver process. Many waiver applicants viewed that process as demeaning as it appeared to be based in a view that waiver applicants were second class; paraphrasing Janeway's concept of "man's world/woman's place", the waiver experience was, "Physicians' world, psychologists' and clinical social workers' (second) place". Aggregated anecdotal data in support of waiver applicants being treated as second-class included their being able to attend classes with their physician colleagues, but being made to wait longer than them for cases, for the lengthy processing of their waiver applications; incredulity being expressed about their scholarly capabilities and aspirations; intolerance and hostile push-back being expressed when waivered candidates criticised the waiver process as discriminatory.

A combination of positive change, though slowly moving, within the American Psychoanalytic Association and a lawsuit finally levelled the playing field with respect to eligibility requirements for training. Further changes towards openness within "the American" followed the lawsuit regarding gender and sexuality. For example, led by female advocates such as Helen Meyers and Barbara Deutsch and female psychoanalytic scholars such as Marianne Goldberger, women in psychoanalysis have become emboldened through a collective awareness and expression of their dignity to demand more consideration. Their demands have been met in terms of advances in how gender issues are taught and how they are discussed in our scholarly literature. These advances have led to less bias in referral patterns based on gender. The LGBT community and Blacks are also in a continuing process of pressing for fuller inclusion and more up to date scholarship, didactics, and supervision regarding sexuality and race.

It is important to consider the push for inclusion not just as political advocacy and social justice. Rather, the inclusion of different kinds of people in our psychoanalytic communities and discourse helps psychoanalysis to stay open to and capable of synthesising more inclusive and more accurate psychoanalytic theory, didactic instruction, and supervision. Such inclusiveness, hopefully, will then foster more complete analyses—of candidates and of our patients in general. I suggest that each of the areas just named have been adversely affected by the significant blindness and closed mindedness psychoanalysts have shown to the important psychodynamics of race, racism, and the other "isms"—particularly, the dehumanising aspects of the "isms" that are motivated to deny people awareness of and expressions of their dignity.

A pointed question is now in order: How complete can theories of psychoanalysis be, how thorough and healing can our techniques be when gutted of understanding of the dignity bashing aspects of the "ism"? Please consider that, as powerful as our current psychoanalytic methods are, their power is diminished to the extent that they do not consider that dignity is an essential ingredient of that identity, and that racism is a force that aims to dehumanise and thereby negate the dignity of Blacks. As James Baldwin is widely believed to have said, "Not everything that is faced can be changed. But nothing can be changed until it is faced."

What I believe we have to face is that the efficacy of what we offer our patients will continue to be limited regarding race until we are able to open the door wide to the reality-based and latent, psychodynamic meanings of race. Current examples in our society and around the world of man's gross and severe inhumanity to man make the necessity of doing so crystal clear. I dare say, all of us carry inside of us multiple affects, thoughts, conflicts, and primal experiences of race, some conscious, some not, some owned, some disavowed. Some of us have reacted to race in ways about which we are proud; some have reacted in ways that leave us with guilt and/or shame. Most of us have probably reacted in both ways. How important these facts are in our work as therapists and teachers and supervisors thereof can only be determined per case. My argument here is that making that determination, per case, is important, no matter the racial composition of the dyad. No dyad, for example, White analyst-White patient, can be exempted from necessary curiosity about the importance of race. I have cited many times a book chapter by Michael Moskowitz (2001) in which he, a Jewish psycho-analyst, presents an excerpt from his own training analysis with a fel-low Jewish analyst. The importance of the example is that it shows that race can be an important factor in any analysis. So I will cite it again, briefly. Moskowitz stated that he had not had any direct experiences with Blacks in his youth. However, racial Blackness became manifest in a dream in his analysis. His analyst did invite associations to the Black character in the dream qua his Blackness. The analyst's openness to race led to an important discovery about the nature of the patient's transfer-ence to his White Jewish analyst whose name in Yiddish meant "black". Moskowitz thought the work could have been deeper, even, regarding his envy of Black men. Apparently, at the time of the analysis, neither he nor his analyst could deeply explore the dynamics of race-based envy of a Black man by a White man. After all, such envy is not in keeping with societally imposed understandings of the place of White men in relation to Black men. Such an understanding is of course not alien to psychoanalytic thinking, especially in the abstract, but what happens when we meet it in the consultation room, or the classroom, or supervi-sion? Often, we blink.

I will offer here a case example from one of my treatment cases. I will then conclude with what we can hope for and why it is important to keep trying to improve our efforts to rescue dignity from the bowels of racist practices.

Treatment case

This vignette is taken from the twice-weekly exploratory psychotherapy of a White man who, when he first consulted me, was a thirty-seven-year-old corporate computer scientist, married, and the father of two boys, aged six and three. He grew up in a large Southern city in the 1970s. He was cared for by a Black nanny for much of his remembered childhood. He came to treatment having suffered several years of low-grade depression and what he called procrastination. Those features intensified shortly before he consulted me following a freak accident which resulted in his toddler son having fallen from his car seat as the patient was trying to take him out of it. A similar occurrence had happened several years before, with his oldest child who was mounted on the patient's shoulders, holding on to his father with one hand and playing with a toy with the other. The patient became aware that something began to fall, perhaps the toy; the patient got discombobulated, let go, and his son fell on his head and suffered a concussion. The patient was mortified in both instances about his lack of agency and efficacy, and had no understanding of these issues at the beginning of treatment. He came across as a ponderous, obsessive, but appealingly gentle man with whom I felt empathy regarding his sadness and sense of weakness and powerlessness, even as in so many ways, he was a strong, successful professional man. I think my empathy was in part based on a sense of him as having, somehow, been disempowered from his dignity. Rather than being filled with a sense of his own prowess and confidence, he acted as if he were puny and nearly worthless in contrast to the protective father he wanted to be. The essence of racism includes the motivation to prevent Blacks from expressing their powerful, efficacious, and dignified selves. Knowing that dehumanising pressure from my own experiences living in a racist society, I empathised with my patient.

The patient's tendency to get discombobulated came to be understood in ordinary clinical terms and from the vantage point of race. In ordinary terms, it was understood as an identification with a passive, ineffective father and a mother who devalued the father and who herself could not put things together very well. She often hinted to her son that there were more important pieces to the family's puzzle than she wanted to or knew how to share. The patient discovered one of those pieces. Namely, contrary to common family belief, my patient was not his mother's first pregnancy. His mother had had an aborted pregnancy prior to marriage, which he deduced from a close examination of his birth certificate. He never asked her about that fact, saying that he knew the door would be shut to such an inquiry. For the purposes of this chapter, it is important to point out that the family dynamics just outlined resided in the patient in terms of feelings of weakness and lack of efficacy.

The reader may be curious as to how this Southern White man chose me, a Black female psychoanalyst, as his therapist. In stating why he consulted me, he eschewed any cultural factor as being important in his decision to consult me. Rather, he referred only to my "good reputation" among his referral sources. Nevertheless, important connections to race and social class emerged in the treatment in important ways. I hope the vignette to follow convinces the reader that it is important for the therapist to be open to possible racial, gender, and class factors in all cases, recognising that their importance may unfold later rather than sooner in a treatment. In this case, those factors unfolded as follows.

As the patient became more trusting in the treatment relationship, in about its sixth month, he began to be able to associate more freely, without fear of an unfortunate accident, or disturbing realisation. This greater freedom in his mind and trust in our relationship led to an exploration of his difficulties based on race. He told me for the first time that his three years younger sister was married to an African American man, and that they were about to have their first child. He said that his parents disapproved of that marriage. When asked about his own feelings, he said, with some unease, that he was not entirely comfortable himself with his sister's choice of a mate, but that he knew he was being irrational and felt ashamed about his feelings about Black people. I asked him what those feelings were. He said he thought of Blacks as powerless, poor, and undesirable. It is important to note here how the patient's racism formed along the fault line central to this chapter, that is, with the intention to strip the Black person of dignity. He quickly countered that he knew that was not accurate as a generalisation about any group, and especially that his sister's husband was as prosperous and well-educated as anyone in his own family. He noted that he also had Black colleagues in high-status positions like his own. He then looked at me very intently; and with a wry smile, he said, "And so far, I have not found you deficient." He added, "Alas, I still feel that way about Blacks in general."

I encouraged my patient to continue to be as openly curious as possible about his puzzling discrepancies regarding Blacks—discrepancies among what he felt, what he knew, and what he had personally experienced—so that we could resolve them. With this encouragement my patient became very emotional, shedding what seemed to be tears of relief, sadness, and hope. In that period of work he also mentioned for the first time his African American caregiver who had looked after him from kindergarten through most of elementary school. Mary, as I will call her, was first remembered warmly, and as greatly influential in his life, as one who, unlike his mother, answered his questions about feelings. He particularly remembered that he exclaimed to Mary how much he hated girls, and particularly, his sister. Calmly, she partially allowed him his feelings, telling him it was okay to not like girls but that he had to love family, and that she'd see him at his wedding. In re-experiencing his idealising and deeply affectionate feelings for Mary, he recalled her as a principled, strong, and dignified woman. Erotic feelings towards Mary and me in the transference began to emerge which made him anxious and guilty. He found a convenient displacement for such feelings in memories of a favourite young White teacher. He resisted understanding the displacement, given the internalised dangers of having erotic feelings for Black women. He protested that neither Mary nor I could have any deep or lasting meaning to him. After all, we were Black, and Mary was a working class servant. Mary and I became one, and given our low place in society, both in terms of race and class, we could not possibly have power and authority in his eyes, or be particularly attractive to him.

This treatment vignette is chock full of meanings. It shows how racial and class issues can emerge quickly, strongly, and obdurately, and become an integral part of a psychodynamic treatment, and that by experiencing and processing their transference and countertransference manifestations, therapist and patient can gain access to underlying feelings, issues of dignity, and conflict. However, the barriers to such work can be built quickly if what is discovered is threatening. In my patient's case, he was threatened by standard oedipal feelings and even more forbidden, oedipal feelings for a Black woman of his past and for me in the transference. As long as the oedipal aspects were not conscious, my patient could empathise with and idealise Mary as the dignified and principled person he experienced her to be, and with whom he longed to identify. Mary empathised with the patient around his angry feelings towards girls, but that empathy was eclipsed. As she said to him, you have to love family. I propose to you that Mary's restriction on whom he could hate was her countertransference, perhaps deriving from one of the pressures of being Black in a racist society.

Being hateful as a reaction to being on the receiving end of the hatred inherent in racism feels dangerous for Blacks, especially aimed towards one's own kin. Its dangers include an intensification of what comes one's way from being othered. In being racially othered as a Black person, you are disallowed meaningful expressions of power. To hate is such a power. As a Black person, punishments for such expressions are redoubled and like other intrapsychic mechanisms, often get extensively generalised. Thus, Mary cautioned her young charge, my patient, that he must not acknowledge or express his hateful feelings in his family. How did I think about and try to work with my patient in terms of race and class? My job in part was to become an even more emboldened Mary, one who did not hasten him to set aside his strongest hostilities, even when they were aimed at his sister—or at acceptable displaced objects such as me and Mary once he stripped us of feared retaliative potential by making us powerless and lacking in enduring value and authority. Considerable work was done around his need to protect himself from the hatreds reawakened in the treatment, including the racialised ones focused on me and Mary. He was able to see that in part his casting of Mary and me as powerless Black women was a projection into us of the powerlessness he felt which derived from his weak and devalued internalised parents. He was also derisive towards Mary on account of her being working class which in his mind stood for moral inferiority. We were able to trace that use of Mary to his own inner feelings of being tainted by having been spawned by a mother who had, in his estimation, shown herself to be lower class and unworthy by becoming pregnant out of wedlock. According to the patient, that fact was the family's "dirty secret".

The patient's aspersions towards the lower class were not fully developed in the treatment in part due to the fact that they arose more vividly near the end of his treatment. Another contribution to that aspect being less developed was my own countertransference limitations in that area. I resisted allowing full use of myself as the impoverished, lower class morally deficient Mary and mother in the transference. In retrospect, I realise that as regards class, with this patient, I wished to cling to a privileged status. In his treatment, this over-identification with privilege was my countertransference vulnerability. Had I been more open to this factor in the work with my patient, I may have been able to help him recognise more fully the psychodynamics of his need to focus on the poverty of Blacks. Specifically, that need was based on his own disavowed identification with his mother's dark, dirty secret of having become pregnant out of wedlock and on his own dark secret view of himself as a lower class child abuser, given the two accidents with his sons.

I hope that the offered treatment vignette shows what is possible in terms of working psychodynamically with race and class, and that it shows what is difficult in doing such work in terms of transference and countertransference manifestations. It is my view that the relative ease and/or difficulties in working with race and/or class in treatment derive from the particular dynamics of the participants in the dyad, which I have tried to outline in this case, and from societal limitations which press towards silence rather than exploration. However, to the extent that the work can be done, much may be gained for the patient personally and in relation to the world around him. Specifically, in this case, I think the patient, a White man, rediscovered his more conflict-free love of Mary, a Black woman. The work allowed for his and her dignity to be restored, and his malignant tendency towards othering (of Mary and of me in the transference) was reduced. Of course, in the consultation room, it is not our charge or our expertise to heal the world's problems directly. However, such aims may nevertheless be accomplished to some degree. In this case, it was important for my patient to achieve understanding of his various uses of Mary, and of her influences on him. It was particularly important for him to unpack how he had relied self-protectively but damagingly on her warning that he not be angry at family. In that working through process, my patient reclaimed and worked through his own anger which, through owning and taming it, became a building block in the awakening and consolidation of his own efficacy and dignity.

Conclusion

This chapter is about the necessity to lend a receptive ear and to give an expressive, informed voice to race in psychoanalytic discourse and psychoanalytic treatments. I have traced the psychoanalytic history of silence and deflection on this issue. I cast our profession's limitations in this regard as our identification with general society's limitations in regard to race, limitations based on projection and othering; limitations—to paraphrase Marianne Williamson (1992)—based on some being made to shrink so that others may shine. I have used a treatment case to show that there are constructive psychoanalytic alternatives to make it possible for our patients and ourselves to develop and maintain more secure, supple, and powerful racial identities at the centre of which our dignity is intact. As such, paraphrasing Ruth Simmons, the power of our minds will be able to take us anywhere.

I implore us to take up the call of this chapter because to do otherwise is to cheat psychoanalysis of its full radical powers to promote the development of full agency in all of our patients. According to our society's rules of racial assignment, that full agency is likely to be diminished because some are assigned too high a place and some too low—some are granted dignity and for others, assiduous attempts are made to strip it away. To make such dehumanising attempts with respect to race is a perversion and a primitive defence akin to disavowal, since dignity is inborn and cannot be destroyed. Such societal practices that persist and reside in each of us deserve respectful, informed, and persevering psychoanalytic attention and curiosity. In our society, race is the ground on which many have been denied their rightful place where they can know and embrace who they are and who they can become, freed from the constraints of destructive race dynamics. In Freud's terms, across the racial rainbow, we need opportunities to attach the right psychical weights to our racial identities. As psychoanalysts, it is important that we gain enough freedom from our various biases, including racial ones, to be able to pay attention to this difficult subject, with perseverance. Why? By so doing, we will facilitate all of our patients being able to seize the fullest possible opportunity to become masterly in authoring and living their lives. Further, we will help our patients stand with knees flexed and equipoise even though they, like us, have been buffeted by forces within and without that would seek to reduce mastery and block access to dignity. To put it psychoanalytically, I will close with two quotes, one from Aisenstein (2007), a Greek psychoanalyst who also has a strong French identity, and one from Nyong'o, an Academy Award-winning Kenyan actress who grew up in Mexico. First, Aisenstein: she uses action language for psychoanalytic therapeutic action that is particularly apropos to the subject matter of this chapter. Aisenstein says (p. 1460): "Analysis is uncompromising in relation to other therapies because … other than bringing relief from a symptom, [it] aims at aiding our patients to become, or to become again, the principal agents in their own history and thought." She ends with the following question (p. 1460): "Am I too bold in insisting that this is the sole inalienable freedom a human being possesses?" In general and with respect to how our racialised aspects affect ourselves and others, let us be as bold in our psychoanalytic thinking and work as we need to be in the interest of achieving the inalienable freedom of which this chapter speaks—to claim and reclaim one's dignity.

Also speaking to one's indelible worth, one's essential dignity, Nyong'o spoke the following when she received her Oscar for her supporting actress role in *12 Years a Slave*: "No matter where you're from, your dreams are valid".

References

Aisenstein, M. (2007). Therapeutic action. *Psychoanalytic Quarterly, 76*: 1443–1461.

Auchincloss, E. L., & Samberg, E. (Eds.) (2012). *Psychoanalytic Terms and Concepts*. New Haven, CT: Yale University Press.

Barbery, M. (2008). *The Elegance of the Hedgehog*. New York. Europa.

Blanton, S. (1971). *Diary of my Analysis with Freud*. New York: Hawthorn.

Freud, S. (1936a). A disturbance of memory on the Acropolis. *S. E., 22*: 239–248. London: Hogarth.

Gentile, K. (2013). Bearing the cultural in order to engage the process of witnessing. *Psychodynamic Psychology, 30*: 456–470.

Gilman, S. (1993). *Freud, Race, and Gender*. Princeton, NJ: Princeton University Press.

Holmes, D. (2006). The wrecking effects of race and social class on self and success. *Psychoanalytic Quarterly, 75*: 215–235.

Janeway, E. (1971). *Man's World, Woman's Place*. New York: Dell.

Kateb, G. (2011). *Human Dignity*. Cambridge, MA: Harvard University Press.

Kuriloff, E. (2014). *Contemporary Psychoanalysis and the Legacy of the Third Reich History, Memory, Tradition*. New York: Routledge.

Maddox, B. (2006). *Freud's Wizard: The Enigma of Ernst Jones*. London: John Murray.

Marill, I., & Siegel, E. (2004). Success and succession. *Journal of the American Psychoanalytic Association, 52*: 673–688.

Moskowitz, M. (2001). Our moral universe. In: D. Scharff (Ed.), *The Psychoanalytic Century: Freud's Legacy for the Future*. New York: Other Press.

Schafer, R. (1984). The pursuit of failure and the idealization of unhappiness. *American Psychologist, 39*: 398–405.

Simmons, R. (1994). First black president chosen for a "Seven Sisters" school. *Washington Post*. 16 December, A15.

Tummala-Narra, P. (2013). Psychoanalytic applications in a diverse society. *Psychodynamic Psychology, 30*: 471–487.

Williamson, M. (1992). *A Return to Love*. New York: Harper.

CHAPTER NINE

You have to be carefully taught: dignity considerations in clinical practice, scholarship, and trauma treatment

Richard P. Kluft

Introduction

Psychotherapy occurs within a societal and cultural matrix. The roles, expectations, and duties of both therapist and patient are well delineated. The psychotherapist is a sanctioned healer, a helper to the patient. The patient is expected to participate in the treatment as instructed in the service of recovery. Differentials exist in the ascribed status, knowledge, power, and prestige of helper and patient; that is, their relationship is tilted.

Further, tilted relationships, especially in the context of change-oriented psychotherapies like psychoanalysis and psychodynamic psychotherapy, contribute to changes in thinking such as distorted perceptions and transferences, those false connections driven by past experiences, both those remembered and those about which the mind is initially unaware. The patient is asked and helped to yield many characteristic forms of conscious control, and to allow defences to be challenged in order to permit the exploration of what is generally withheld from the view of others, and often from one's self as well.

Both tilt and transference, abetted by other demand characteristics of the therapeutic situation, beget regression, hopefully in the service of the ego. Therapists endeavour to prevent or at least minimise dysfunctional regressions that compromise the ego without moving the treatment forward.

Optimally, psychodynamic therapies endeavour to create an atmosphere of safety and caring, which I will summarise as a holding environment in which empathic attunement prevails more often than not. The issues and transferences of the patient and the issues and countertransferences of the therapist are monitored in accord with the therapist's training, supervision experiences, postgraduate learning, and personal treatment.

In this contribution I will argue that patients' dignity may become endangered and violations of patients' dignity may occur in surprising abundance when what we have learned to think of as good, right, and proper conflicts with other crucial considerations, and we misperceive a right versus right conflict for a clash between right and wrong.

If we understand dignity to be a birthright, stemming from a belief that all humans are imbued with value and worth, it follows that others are due considerations that acknowledge their inherent value and worth. Such consideration is deserved by others, independent of those others' attributes or accomplishments. Accordingly, individuals are always deserving of respect, even if their actions are not. (Argument summarised from Hicks, 2011, pp. 3–5.)

I will argue that "in real life" many matters emerge in the theories, teaching, and practice of psychotherapy that encourage disrespect of the actions of others, that the disrespect of the actions of others enhances the likelihood that those others will be disrespected as people, and that the treatment that follows upon that disrespect risks depriving those others of their dignity. Disrespect and indignity inflict narcissistic injuries (among others), beget the shame family of emotions, trigger the activation of shame scripts that weaken the ties between those who inflict and those who experience shame, and encourage endless iterations of unproductive acrimony and alienation (Nathanson, 1992). To anticipate what follows, disrespect undermines the according of dignity to those persons whom one disrespects. It encourages the sense that since one is right, and those one disrespects are wrong, it is permissible to bypass according them dignity and treat them poorly.

Exploring such matters within one's own profession without being unduly hurtful has proven quite a challenge. In the end, in order to avoid the risk of inadvertently causing pain to others, I have restricted myself to drawing upon less harsh, less dramatic, and perhaps less satisfactory examples from my own practice and career. I accept, none too happily, the risk of being seen as complaining rather than as elucidating the subject at hand.

While presenting a case at a psychoanalytic meeting I described an intervention I made to protect my patient from ruining her career. Four colleagues questioned my actions, and considered them inappropriate. With other hands still waving, Anton O. Kris, MD, a senior training analyst, broke in. He observed that anything unnecessarily hurtful and shaming could not be good psychoanalytic technique, and that whatever was necessary to prevent that unnecessary hurt and shame was good psychoanalytic technique (e.g., Kris, 2005). Dr. Kris captured the essence of my concerns. Sometimes one right must be allowed to trump another right in the best interests of the patient. Too often right vs. right conflicts are misunderstood as right vs. wrong conflicts with knee-jerk rapidity. Judgmental assumptions, often forms of confirmatory bias or motivated scepticism, create fertile breeding-grounds for the proliferation of dignity violations.

Patients' dignity may be jeopardised and dignity violations may be inflicted while therapists are following the rules, doing what many consider good psychotherapy. Where matters of dignity are concerned, at times the harder therapists endeavour to do the right thing, the more they may bring about situations that achieve the antithesis of an optimal outcome.

In considering the importance of dignity and dignity violations in a variety of contexts, meaningful discourse requires knowledge of their definitions and a capacity to perceive their presence and influence in clinical settings, topics addressed in other contributions. For the sake of consistency, I will rely on the definitions and approaches of Hicks (2011 and Chapter One, this volume) throughout. Once that knowledge and the skill sets relevant to recognising relevant phenomena are acquired, the presence of these phenomena is likely to be noted more frequently than might previously have been expected. For example, in 1975, Henderson (1975) reported that father-daughter incest occurred in one out of a million American families. Then, the scholarship of Herman (1981) and Russell (1986), among others, caused this estimate to be revised upward. Considering the wide range of incestuous boundary violations, some regrettable transgression occurs in one out of twenty biological father/daughter dyads and one in seven step-father/step-daughter pairs (Russell, 1986). A commensurate consciousness-raising for dignity violations is long overdue.

Dignity and indignity in scholarship and its clinical consequences

Why should clinicians concern themselves about dignity and indignity in scholarship? In exploring dignity violations in clinical practice, it is helpful to consider whether forces from beyond the consulting room have contributed to their occurrence, and may foment their recurrence. Caring and compassionate clinicians, determined to provide the best care possible, may remain blind to the dignity violations inflicted by what they believe to be optimal approaches to practicing their professions. At times, business as usual in the mental health professions generates dignity violations capable of taking on lives of their own, with far-ranging consequences, including hypocrisy.

What contributes to clinicians' concepts of what constitutes good care? What influences inform their determining the right thing to do? Their training, supervision, and study of the professional literature are likely to be major factors. If these sources promote ideas and practices that threaten the dignity of the therapeutic enterprise, hurtful attitudes may become ingrained within the professional identity of therapists, but remain so ego-syntonic that it will be difficult for those who hold them to consider their potentially problematic implications. Instead, because they contribute to therapists' security and comfort, the idea of re-evaluating them may threaten therapists' identities and their internalised stances and representations of valued mentors and schools of thought (Tessman, 2003). Their reassuring and self-validating qualities become part of a self-protective posture that Hirsch (2008) describes as "coasting in the countertransference". When therapists inform their therapeutic efforts with what they have been taught and seen modelled, there is an ongoing risk that they may behave dismissively to patients who are unfortunate enough to fail to conform to, or respond to, those teachings and examples. This dismissiveness may extend to colleagues whose ideas fail to mirror their own (Kris, 2005). It is hard to improve on Rogers and Hammerstein's poignant expression of the banal origins and the terrible impact of prejudiced thinking in a song from *South Pacific* entitled "You Have to Be Carefully Taught".

Years ago another analytic candidate and I covered each other's practice over vacations. My colleague noticed that one of my patients, a terribly abused incest survivor, seemed to have developed a sexualised transference to him. He interpreted her feelings as oedipal and truly erotic. Within hours she hung herself, nearly ending her life.

That same year a patient of mine expressed fears that her traumatic sexual experiences would be re-enacted between us. Treatment came to a stalemate. Cornelia B. Wilbur, MD, saw her in consultation, later becoming her therapist. Dr. Wilbur chided me for missing and mismanaging a florid erotic transference.

My colleague and I both had allowed our preferred models of understanding to define the reality of our patients' circumstances, and both of us proved terribly wrong. My colleague's attribution of erotic desire to this horribly abused woman resonated with the taunts of her abusers as they stimulated her against her will and humiliated her when her body reacted—"See, you want it, you little slut! Your body doesn't lie. You love it!" The apparent confirmation of their attributions by a competent and respected professional inappropriately validated her worst fears, that she actually was the sexually driven tramp her abusers insisted she was. Mortified beyond words, she nearly destroyed herself.

I had been researching re-victimisation and dysfunctional sexualisation (Kluft, 1989). My focus led me to misunderstand and mismanage my second patient's discovery of the normal sexuality she had somehow preserved. My errors overlooked, stifled, and undermined one of the most significant achievements of our work together. Dr. Wilbur proved better able to hear, validate, and address her concerns with compassion. Invalidations and dignity violations tend to generate a shame-saturated atmosphere in which the subtle enactment of pathological shame scripts is encouraged and treatment deteriorates. This profoundly important topic is beyond the scope of this contribution (see Nathanson, 1992).

Dignity issues in psychotherapy and trauma treatment

A particularly egregious pathway toward dignity violation is generated whenever patients become caught between conflicting professional opinions or paradigms of understanding. Regrettably, the following account is not fictional.

A therapist listened for years to a woman's accounts of horrible childhood mistreatment, all the while completely convinced that the patient's memories, most of which had emerged during their work together, were inaccurate confabulations. Since she believed that such "false memories" were created in the practices of unskilled and misguided therapists, she was displeased and resentful to find such material emerging in a treatment she was conducting. She had not shared this attitude with the patient, or with me when the patient came to me as a new psychopharmacology patient.

Two days after her first appointment with me, she was kidnapped, raped repeatedly, beaten, and left unconscious. After emergency treatment and being interviewed by the police, she identified her assailant in a book of mug shots. When she called her therapist and told her what had occurred, her therapist confronted her immediately with "That's just another false memory", and hung up. I became her psychotherapist. My predecessor took pains to inform me that although she might have been mistaken in this instance, she had patiently endured years of lurid but transparently untrue tales of childhood sexual exploitation. She warned me against encouraging further confabulations.

I supported my patient through the trial and conviction and imprisonment of her assailant. Indeed, her accounts of her past were horrible and difficult to believe. I treated her for years without concerning myself about the historical reality of her accounts.

Genealogy became her hobby. She found that many family members had extensive criminal backgrounds. Some had been convictions for child pornography. Aged distant relatives confirmed that she had been abused. Her deceased favourite uncle had written her a forgotten letter describing his preventing her father from murdering her. She reconnected with her estranged older sister, who confirmed her incest memories and accusations against other abusers.

Fifteen years after I met her, a niece revisited what had been my patient's childhood home. The current occupants presented her with a box stenciled with her grandfather's name, found when they converted the attic into a bedroom. Within were pornographic pictures involving my patient and her sister (the niece's mother) as children and teens. Only months later, a former neighbour forwarded to my patient the obituary of a doctor my patient alleged had been among her abusers. Six months later, a newspaper article reported that the new owners of the decedent's house had broken down a wall while doing renovations and discovered a hidden cache of pornographic materials. She later learned that some further documented her abuse.

My predecessor had listened to this woman's accounts of mistreatment for over seven years without dignifying her as a genuinely suffering human being or considering her accounts might constitute legitimate clinical material. Her preferred theory dictated that recovered memories were false unless proven otherwise. Overvaluing this model cheated the patient out of effective treatment for years and set her up for an absolutely devastating invalidation, a dignity violation that drove her to chronic suicidality and several serious suicide attempts.

Thinking about paradigms and myopia

The core psychoanalytic literature rarely addresses dignity. However, the literatures of applied psychoanalysis (e.g., international relations and conflict resolution), medical ethics, gender studies, recovery and patient advocacy, nursing, quality of life, end of life care, assisted suicide, and quality of care have accorded greater importance to dignity.

The study of dignity is most thoughtfully embraced by fields that share in common a concern for those perceived, acknowledged, or self-defined as less advantaged, less empowered, less privileged, and less intact, more needful of support and protection; that is, those who must struggle to find their own voices or their supporters. These disciplines are not ambivalent in their efforts to validate the difficulties of these populations and advocate for the correction of the dignity violations they endure. They acknowledge the endless cycles of insult following upon injury that are the natural consequences of indifference and/or hostility to the dignity concerns of others.

We in the mental health professions often embrace paradigms and models that are flawed and incomplete. They often were developed at levels of thinking remote from the reality of many clinical and human acts. Colleagues are all too often prepared to spend endless hours in arguing issues best classified as expressions of the narcissism of small differences (Freud, 1914c; Volkan, 1986). Proponents of many schools of thought are prepared to "go to war", and often do "go to war", about matters remote from clinical observations, but in which their narcissism and identities are deeply invested. Others, who do not share their investments, might wonder whether such convictions on the part of their colleagues are more a tribute to the intensity of their investments than to the essential merit of the ideas in which their investments have been made. When investment trumps merit, substantial risk arises that both professionals and patients will suffer dignity violations. The vilification and ostracism of Sandor Ferenczi by Freud and mainstream analysts is a heartbreaking case in point.

In *The Structure of Scientific Revolutions*, Thomas Kuhn (2012) demonstrates that the progress of scientific knowledge is neither smooth nor cumulative. It is characterised by a series of leaps called paradigm shifts. When prevailing theories and/or models fail to address some matter of importance, or prove to be flawed, a new paradigm, a driving idea or a model, will arise. This model will offer a different way, perhaps a more successful way, of understanding and exploring some problems of concern less well or differently addressed by its predecessor. New paradigms that both attract adherents and offer research possibilities may rise to challenge, compete with, and replace a previously ascendant paradigm entirely or in part.

Such transitions far transcend the acquisition of new models and new ways of thought. Adherents of different paradigms often come to organise the same data in very different ways. What seems self-evident to the followers of one may appear absurd or incomprehensible to the followers of another. Followers of a new paradigm may disregard data acquired under the aegis of the previous paradigm, the phenomenon of secondary loss (Laor, 1985). The followers of divergent schools of thought may come to perceive things so differently that, in effect, they live in different worlds. The advocates of the ascendant paradigm often behave as if they were entitled to decree the previous paradigm inferior, wrong, and unscientific, and to declare its followers intellectual primitives. Further, the secondary loss phenomenon may eclipse attention to and regard for legitimate scientific findings made under the earlier model. Since the adherents of the superseded paradigm find their work and contributions relegated to a diminished status, neglected, refuted, or all of the above, they are likely to fight tenaciously as best they can, to prove that their paradigm in fact embraces what is represented as new. The advocates of different weak paradigms often have not defeated their opponents, but they conduct themselves as if they had achieved glorious victories and deserve to be tendered unconditional surrenders.

That previous knowledge deemed important knowledge may be put aside, even forgotten may seem puzzling unless observations in Waelder's (1962) report of a meeting of philosophers and psychoanalysts are considered. Waelder described six levels of information and conceptualisations.

The level of observation refers to what is seen, heard, and can be inferred from derivatives of conflicts. The connectedness of observations with one another and with other mental contents and behaviours is the level of interpretation. From the aggregate of such observations and interpretations comes a level of clinical generalisations, allowing us to make statements about types of situations, symptoms, and groups of patients; that is, obsessives have issues with order and control. Above this is the level of clinical theory, ideas that are implicit in interpretations, or to which interpretations may lead, such as repression, defence, and the like. Next is the level of metapsychology, a more abstract level not implicit in the above but closely connected, involving concepts like cathexis and psychic energy. Finally, above this is the level of the theorist's philosophy. In the case of Freud, that meant positivism and the hope of human betterment through reason, tempered with increasing pessimism as he grew older.

These levels are not equally necessary and useful. Waelder considered observation and interpretation indispensible, generalisation and clinical theory following close behind. Noting similar remarks by Freud (1914c), Waelder observed that metapsychology and philosophy were usually irrelevant, and actually unnecessary.

Yet when academic battles rage in the mental health professions, the most basic and crucial levels are most vulnerable to being disregarded. Although an ascending paradigm may generate data of its own, the systematic disregard of data and observations developed under other paradigms may be considered by adherents of an ascending paradigm as a demonstration of correctness and scientific rigour rather than as a repulsive instance of intellectual exceptionalism.

Kuriloff (2013), whose work is discussed elsewhere in this volume as well, explores the impact upon American psychoanalysis of immigrant Jewish analysts who escaped the Holocaust and immigrated to North America. Shorn from their countries, cultures, homes, belongings, and often from family members unable to escape the Nazi menace, these men and women were abruptly deprived of these major aspects of their identities and the lives they had known. They clung to the one thing they could carry with them, their analytic identities. In focusing on what they valued and wished to preserve, they often turned away from what they had just left behind, the unspeakable horror of the Holocaust. As they averted their attention from their own traumata and the horrors endured by those who could not escape Hitler's diabolical ravages, they crafted an elegant but often reality-avoidant model of the mind and the treatment process, an ironic avoidance by highly traumatised individuals that took psychoanalysis out of the mainstream of the study of the traumatised for decades. This avoidance naturally brings a hermeneutic stance into analytic treatment. The therapist is enjoined to regard matters of external reality unreliable and unhelpful distractions from the business of addressing psychic reality (e.g., Fonagy & Target, 1996).

This sequence of events bears striking analogies to a statement repeated in many Jewish ceremonies. It alludes to the destruction of the Second Temple and the Diaspora. It asserts that the Jewish people did not preserve their holiest book, the Torah—the Torah preserved the Jewish people. Survival through adherence to a treasured and venerated source of knowledge and wisdom is embedded within the consciousness of Jews, even highly assimilated Jews.

The tenacious dedication of these individuals to the protection of what they preserved and of what they built upon the foundation of what they preserved begot a new orthodoxy in American psychoanalysis, an orthodoxy that most would agree became overly codified and rigid, and stifling of dissent. During my early years of analytic training, and beyond, I witnessed many unfortunate attempts to disparage dissenters and innovators.

We might ask, was such bellicose posturing and argumentation necessary? Children learn whom to dislike. As noted above, no scholarly formulation can surpass the poignant lyrics of Rogers and Hammerstein's "You've Got to Be Carefully Taught," from *South Pacific*. Parens (1979, 2014) described a basic fear/negativity of different others as normal paranoia. Schools of therapy as well as peoples and nations distinguish themselves, and declare their difference from others, on the basis of distinctions, however trivial, that they regard as crucial to their identities—the narcissism of small differences (Volkan, 1986).

How does the above impact upon the subject of dignity in the study of scholarship and patient care? To the extent that the ideas, values, and practices of any school of therapy are passed from one generation to the next with an eye toward prioritising preservation of a cherished and honoured perspective rather than embracing exploration and openness to innovation, that school of thought is positioned to generate therapists whose primary identities and allegiances are linked to privileging the levels of thinking quite distant from clinical observation, interpretation, and generalisation. These are the very levels that both Freud (1914c) and Waelder (1962) agreed were not firmly established, most likely to change, and unnecessary for doing good clinical work. Waelder (1962) bluntly stated that some of the best clinical analysts were relatively ignorant of metapsychology.

Establishing as a standard or ideal an idea that may bear only a tentative connection to a given clinical situation is fraught with potential difficulties. Three brief illustrations follow, one from hypnosis, one from the study of dissociation, and one from psychoanalysis.

Around 2000 I encountered three instances in which health professionals suffered severe unwanted symptoms in connection with trances they experienced while learning hypnosis. No previous publications suggested that adverse experiences might be prevalent in such settings. My concerns and recommendations were received with scepticism. I remained worried enough to begin what became a decade-long research project. I identified thirty workshop casualties and suggested steps to reduce such incidents. Four major publications (Kluft 2012a, b, c, & d) emerged from this project, three of which were acclaimed best paper of the year by a major scientific journal. One year, two tied for first place. However, the organisation that presented me with these awards did not implement my package of recommended changes. It ran contrary to prevailing and beloved paradigms of instruction which research (summarised in Gruzelier, 2000; Kluft, 2012a) has shown are associated with a significant incidence of unwanted complications. The dignity implications for students, patients, and science are clear.

Several years ago, I was asked to contribute a case study identifying and illustrating the core phenomena of dissociative identity disorder (DID) to a textbook. After reviewing the literature I compiled and depicted thirteen core phenomena (Kluft, 2009). Then, for my own curiosity, I (2013b) reviewed over twenty theoretical models of dissociation, trying to discern how many of these thirteen core phenomena were encompassed in each. The average was four point nine, or thirty-eight per cent. Ergo, training and research in this field are often being linked to incomplete and/or flawed models, raising serious issues.

At a panel at a psychoanalytic meeting, a speaker proposed a model of DID that was not well correlated with clinical reality. When I raised a question concerning this discrepancy the panel's chair insisted that I did not understand dissociation, a perspective rapidly echoed by three of the four others. One was non-committal. They challenged my understanding of the condition's DSM-IV criteria and description, and held their ground, dismissing my subsequent remarks as well. I found this rather surrealistic. I had participated in writing the criteria and description they maintained I did not understand. After the panel, the fourth panelist, who knew my work, apologised.

In the eyes of four of the five panel participants, my failure to embrace their chosen models, however problematic they might be, relegated me to the realm of the uncomprehending and unscientific. My inconvenient disagreement seems to have served as both rationale and justification for their actions. The majority of Donna Hicks' (2011) ten principles for treating a person with dignity had not been followed. Most of the ten pathways toward the violation of dignity had been pursued energetically. They need not have respected what I said in order to have respected me as a person; that is, to have accorded me dignity.

I invite the reader to imagine a situation in which someone close to the reader suffers DID. That person enters treatment, but when the reader informs himself about the therapist's approach to practice, the reader discovers that the therapist's model of treatment fail to address the actual nature of the condition, in whole or in part. What feelings and concerns would be invoked in the reader?

Dignity issues in the treatment of the traumatised

Our models are imperfect little creatures, short-lived presences on the stage of the history of knowledge and science. While they should be treated with respect, like a favourite pet, they are as unworthy of deification and worship as the golden calf of Biblical lore. We look to models and theories to be our useful servants (Levine, 1996), but we must be vigilant lest they become our imperious masters without our ever noticing that this malignant transformation has occurred.

When we knowingly or unknowingly accord theories or models more merit than is their due, we compromise our ability to accord our patients the dignity of being encountered as the unique individuals that they are. Perception will never be immaculate. It will always be both assisted and compromised by the tools of thought with which we approach our patients. But if we patiently build up our understanding from elements that are experience-near, we will have a much better chance of coming much closer to the mark even when we fall short of scoring a bull's eye. We will be more likely to encounter, address, and accord dignity to the unique suffering individuals whom we endeavour to treat.

Talya Lewis (personal communications and unpublished untitled manuscript) speaks of the need to validate the patient's experience, to create a door of communication that allows the patient to express and be understood, assured that sharing can be done without fear of hurt or having personal meanings distorted to the point that personal meaning is no longer conveyed. This is akin to Kohut's (1977, 1984) approach to empathic attunement, and his concept of leading edge interpretations.

Violations of dignity, failures to open Lewis' communicative door, are routinely encountered in the treatment of the traumatised (e.g., the egregious instance reported above).

The world of psychoanalysis continues to struggle with the subjects of external reality and the treatment of trauma, topics considerations of space preclude addressing here. Significant strides have been made, but one need only attend the discussion groups and panels of psycho-analytic organisations to appreciate how poorly contributions made by modern psychoanalytic explorers of trauma have become integrated into the thinking and practice of so many of their colleagues.

What hope is there for dignity in the treatment of trauma victims whose therapists fail to develop a degree of sensitivity to trauma and expertise in trauma treatment? Salient concerns are raised by a recent series of publications.

Israeli psychoanalyst Ilany Kogan (2003a) described her analysis of a woman who, like Kogan herself, was a second-generation Holocaust survivor. The shadow of the Holocaust affected every aspect of their work together. Kogan described how her patient, born to concentra-tion camp survivors who had lost the children of their first marriages in actions or the camps, often was not appreciated for herself. Instead, she often was perceived as an inadequate replacement for an idealised "beloved dead child" who had not survived, and also became the hap-less recipient of negative projections, both the parents' negative images of themselves and their representations of their Nazi tormentors. She was not treated well.

Three distinguished colleagues discussed Kogan's paper. Charles Brenner (2003) insisted Kogan had effected the patient's cure with her analytic explorations of oedipal material alluded to but not reviewed in her article. In his eyes, the importance of the Holocaust and Kogan's work with its impact was incidental. Ferro (2003) felt Kogan should not have emphasised work with external reality. Instead, she should have focused upon psychic reality, on aspects of the patient's fantasies and associations. Kogan, Ferro opined, should have soared above reality, like a little bird, flying on the wings of metaphor and poetry. Herzog (2003) concurred with Kogan. He agreed that addressing the Holocaust was a matter of grave importance in the treatment. Kogan's (2003b) astonishingly restrained response stated simply that reality actually matters.

The colleague who immediately confronted the woman who had been raped with an erroneous theory-driven and humiliating confrontation; the hypnosis teachers who pushed aside research findings not to their liking; the analysts on a panel who tried to browbeat and embarrass a colleague whose observations they found embarrassing; the analyst on that panel who knew his colleagues were wrong but kept his silence; and two of Kogan's discussants, so wedded to their paradigms that they trivialised the impact of the Holocaust: every single one was invested in a model of treatment or advocating for a paradigm of understanding that he or she believed was appropriate, accurate, and useful; every single one was positioned to pass along ideas and approaches that disempower and/or at times disrespect and/or dismiss the valid concerns of suffering individuals. This sanctions and perpetuates both disrespecting the dignity of those with whom one disagrees and violating of the dignity of patients whose circumstances and needs do not conform with the therapist's preferred approach, both under the aegis of "good thinking" and "good treatment".

Most disputes between schools of thought, most of what the members of our professions debate most strenuously, concern abstract ideas that, however beloved and revered, are of minor significance. They belong to the "dispensible" levels of discourse (Freud, 1914c; Waelder, 1962). We must wonder whether succumbing to the narcissism of small differences is defensible when it risks impacting the quality of care that we deliver. How can we validate and empathise with any degree of effectiveness if we approach our patients deliberately or unwittingly seeking to reconfirm our ideas in the process of our work with them, and privilege the reality of those ideas over the significance of our patients' autobiographical memories and subjective experiences, however fallible they may be? In doing so we forget that we are empowered to heal, not to promote paradigms, not to sit in judgment, and certainly not to serve as arbiters of historical reality.

My stance may appear so critical of theory that I have little confidence in the possibility of creative conceptualisation and model-building. To the contrary, my criticism is directed against attempts to build massive edifices without laying solid foundations, efforts that ask our clinical endeavours and our patients to dwell under the roofs of such dubious constructions. We must demand to be provided with arguments that are based upon the less abstract rather than the most abstract of Waelder's levels, ideas that can stand up to challenges because what they state and how they were derived can be explicated clearly, and consequently are empirically grounded. I strongly favour arguments rooted in observable phenomena rather than mythic fantasies or poetic metaphors. I am not advocating the simplistic approaches amenable to rapid measurement and statistical manipulation inherent in the "evidence-based treatment" models.

The contributions below were derived from clinical observation in a manner that permits the reader to have a reasonable degree of confidence in their theoretical components.

1. Luborsky's (Luborsky & Luborsky, 1993) CCRT research, demonstrating the validity of the concepts of transference and unconscious fantasy, and the importance of the therapeutic and helping alliance. It is derived from what patients actually say.
2. Faimberg's (2005) concept of listening to the patient's listening teaches us to study how a patient is actually making meaning out of what we say, allowing us to address potential difficulties and hurtful misunderstandings more adroitly.
3. Howard's (2008, in preparation; quoted with permission in Kluft, 2013a) pragmatic approach to documenting baseline qualities of alertness prior to hypnosis and again after trance is thought to have been terminated replaces traditional impressionistic ideas proven to be inaccurate (Kluft, 2012a). This enables clinicians using hypnosis to make a reasonable determination as to whether de-hypnosis has in fact been successful, and to recognise and interrupt many types of adverse sequelae.
4. Kohut and Wolfe's (1978) summary of the psychological and behavioural correlates of narcissistic disorders links them with therapeutic approaches. Once anchored to clinical manifestations, notwithstanding Kohut's apologies for identifying clinical rather than theoretical patters, Kohut's often-challenging ideas become far more accessible.
5. Coen's (2005) article on how to engage the withdrawn schizoid patient in a playful manner draws direct connections among theory, clinical phenomena, and clinical practice, making his ideas readily amenable to clinical application.

Conclusion

Influences upon academic discourse or clinical practice that directly or indirectly dissuade clinicians from meeting their patients in genuine and open-minded problem-solving clinical encounters, or communicate that attitude to others, risk generating therapeutic processes that fail to recognise and involve the unique subjectivities and perspectives of our patients, and may unwittingly introduce elements of depersonalisation and derealisation into therapeutic dyads. Such difficulties undermine the optimal potential of the patient, the therapist, and the therapy itself. By declining to engage patients in a manner respectful of how patients might be experiencing themselves and their worlds, they generate and inflict unnecessary dignity violations upon patients who do not deserve such mistreatment. Further, those who advocate stances driven by overvalued abstractions will find it easy to inflict similar dignity violations upon colleagues with whom they disagree, and pass on potentially harmful precepts to the next generation of therapists, who can then them impose them on the next generation of patients and upon those colleagues with whom they disagree.

By encouraging a firm grounding in the observation and study of clinical phenomena, an understanding of the importance of dignity, and an appreciation of the importance of avoiding unnecessary dignity violations, we can do better.

References

Brenner, C. (2003). Commentary on Ilany Kogan's "On being a dead, beloved child." *Psychoanalytic Quarterly*, 72: 769–776.

Coen, S. J. (2005). How to play with patients who would rather remain remote. *Journal of the American Psychoanalytic Association*, 53: 811–834.

Faimberg, H. (2005). *The Telescoping of generations: Listening to the narcissistic links between generations*. New York: Routledge.

Ferro, A. (2003). Commentary on Ilany Kogan's "On being a dead, beloved child." *Psychoanalytic Quarterly*, 72: 777–783.

Fonagy, P., & Target, M. (1996). Playing with reality: theory of mind and the normal development of psychic reality. *International Journal of Psychoanalysis*, 77: 217–233.

Freud, S. (1914c). On narcissism: an introduction. *S. E.*, 14: 67–102. London: Hogarth.

Gruzelier, J. (2000). Unwanted effects of hypnosis: A review of the evidence and its implications. *Contemporary Hypnosis, 17*: 163–193.

Henderson, D. (1975). Incest. In: A. Freedman, H. Kaplan & B. Sadock (Eds.), *Comprehensive Textbook of Psychiatry, Second Edition* (pp. 1532–1538). Baltimore: Williams and Wilkins.

Herman, J. (1981). *Father-daughter Incest*. Cambridge: Harvard.

Herzog, J. M. (2003). Commentary on Ilany Kogan's "On being a dead, beloved child". *Psychoanalytic Quarterly, 72*: 785–796.

Hicks, D. (2011). *Dignity*. New Haven: Yale University Press.

Hirsch, I. (2008). *Coasting in the Countertransference: Conflicts of Self Interest between Analyst and Patient*. New York: Routledge.

Howard, H. (2008). The Howard Alertness Scale. *Focus, 50*: 3–4.

Howard, H. (manuscript in preparation). *Clinical applications of the Howard Alertness Scale (HAS)*.

Kluft, R. P. (1989). Treating the patient who has been sexually exploited by a prior therapist. *Psychiatric Clinics of North America, 12*: 483–500.

Kluft, R. P. (2009). A clinician's understanding of dissociation: Fragments of an acquaintance. In: P. Dell & J. O'Neill (Eds.), *Dissociation and the Dissociative Disorders: DSM-V and Beyond* (pp. 599–623). New York: Taylor & Francis.

Kluft, R. P. (2012a): Issues in the detection of those suffering adverse effects in hypnosis training workshops. *American Journal of Clinical Hypnosis, 54*: 213–232.

Kluft, R. P. (2012b): Enhancing workshop safety: Learning from colleagues' adverse experiences (Part I—Structure/Content). *American Journal of Clinical Hypnosis, 55*: 85–103.

Kluft, R. P. (2012c). Enhancing workshop safety: Learning from colleagues' adverse experiences (Part II—Structure/Policy). *American Journal of Clinical Hypnosis, 55*: 104–122.

Kluft, R. P. (2012d): Approaches to difficulties in realerting subjects from hypnosis. *American Journal of Clinical Hypnosis, 55*: 140–159.

Kluft, R. P. (2013a). *Shelter From the Storm*. North Charleston, SC: CreateSpace Independent Production Platform.

Kluft, R. P. (2013b). *"That's why they're called lessons," said the Gryphon. "Because they lessen day by day." Reflections on the treatment of DID 1970–2013*. Lecture presented at Sheppard Pratt Hospital, Baltimore, MD, 27 April.

Kohut, H. (1977). *The Restoration of the Self*. New York: International Universities Press.

Kohut, H. (1984). *How Does Analysis Cure?* New York: International Universities Press.

Kohut, H., & Wolfe, E. (1978). The disorders of the self and their treatment: An outline. *International Journal of Psychoanalysis, 59*: 413–425.

Kogan, I. (2003a). On being a dead, beloved child. *Psychoanalytic Quarterly*, 72: 727–804.

Kogan, I. (2003b). Response to commentaries. *Psychoanalytic Quarterly*, 72: 797–803.

Kris, A. O. (2005). The lure of hypocrisy. *Journal of the American Psychoanalytic Association*, 53: 7–22.

Kuhn, T. (2012). *The Structure of Scientific Revolutions* (50th anniversary edition, with an introduction by Ian Hacking). Chicago: University of Chicago Press.

Kuriloff, E. (2013). *Contemporary Psychoanalysis and the Legacy of the Third Reich: History, Memory, Tradition*. New York: Routledge.

Laor, N. (1985). Prometheus the impostor. *British Medical Journal*, 290: 681–684.

Levine, S. (1996). *Useful Servants*. Northvale, NJ: Aronson.

Lewis, J. (1981). *Father-daughter Incest*. Cambridge: Harvard University Press.

Luborsky, L., & Luborsky, E. (1993). The era of measures of transference: The CCRT and other measures. *Journal of the American Psychoanalytic Association*, 41: 329–351.

Nathanson, D. (1992). *Shame and Pride*. New York: Norton.

Parens, H. (1979). *The Development of Aggression in Early Childhood*. Northvale, NJ: Aronson.

Parens, H. (2014). *War Is Not Inevitable: On the Psychology of War and Aggression*. New York: Lexington.

Russell, D. (1986). *The Ssecret Trauma: Incest in the Lives of Girls and Women*. New York: Basic Books.

Tessman, L. (2003). *The Analyst's Analyst Within*. New York: Routledge.

Volkan, V. (1986). The narcissism of minor differences in the psychological gap between opposing nations. *Psychoanalytic Inquiry*, 45: 255–273.

Volkan, V. (1997). Chosen trauma: unresolved mourning. In: V. Volkan, *Bloodlines: From Ethnic Pride to Ethnic Terrorism* (pp. 36–49). New York: Farrar, Straus, & Giroux.

Waelder, R. (1962). Psychoanalysis, scientific method, and philosophy. *Journal of the American Psychoanalytic Association*, 10: 617–637.

CHAPTER TEN

Kant you see? Viewing Hitchcock's *Vertigo* through the lens of dignity*

Susan S. Levine

Title sequence

I confess to having been spellbound by *Vertigo* since first seeing it in 1984 after its re-release—and I am not alone. Hitchcock's towering masterwork, which opened to mixed reviews, has gradually made its way to the top of *Sight & Sound*'s list of the greatest films (Christie, 2012). Many years ago I discovered something new about *Vertigo*, something about Madeleine/Judy that had been right under our noses. By linking these discoveries to the leitmotif of dignity, I hope to add to our understanding of *Vertigo*, a film that seems to be reborn on each viewing.

I predicate my reading on the auteur theory of film interpretation, that is, that the director be considered the author of the work, an especially valid methodology regarding Hitchcock (Lee, 1986, p. 226). The reading

---

*This essay is dedicated to beautiful elusive Madeleine.

I am offering here is the reading of a psychoanalyst rather than a particularly psychoanalytic reading. Berman (2001) provides an excellent summary of the psychoanalytic writings on *Vertigo*; most recently, Sanchez-Cardenas (2013) offers a reading using Matte-Blanco's theories. In my treatment of the film I am simply doing what a psychoanalyst does: listening to words and wondering about what they may mean; thinking about new frameworks through which to understand; and paying attention to my own countertransference. The analyst/viewer is always the detective, trying to put together the clues. My interpretation is informed by the French novel on which *Vertigo* was based, Boileau and Narcejac's (1958) *D'Entre les Morts*.[1] Like both the film and the book, my essay will be in two parts that become linked at the end. If you are a *Vertigo* virgin, I urge you to see the film before reading further; however, short plot summaries may be found at sites such as Sparknotes[2] or Wikipedia[3] and in books, such as in Truffaut (1969, p. 303). I also predicate my argument on the old psychoanalytic saw, that everything one needs to know about a patient is there in the first session if one only knows how to look for it. I will largely avoid psychoanalytic and theoretical terminology—not because it is not useful but because I want to apply the experience-near common sense framework of dignity.

The first part of *Vertigo* tells the story of crimes, a conspiracy to commit murder and a murder. The real Madeleine Elster is almost the MacGuffin of the film. (The MacGuffin is the essential but often unseen plot "gimmick" that drives the movie (Truffaut, 1969, p. 157). For instance, in *Notorious* (1946) we never find out a thing about why the ore from the mountains near Rio is important; however, we've been thrilled to see Cary Grant and Ingrid Bergman discover it in the wine bottles, terrified that they will be discovered by Claude Rains.) We catch a glimpse of Mrs. Elster only as she is thrown off the tower, just as we only hear a few seconds of the unintelligible state secrets in *The 39 Steps*. What we actually witness in the film are the accompanying and subsequent psychological crimes. Knowing that this is only one of many angles possible, I would like to recast *Vertigo* as a story of serial dignity violations (Hicks, 2011) and dignity abdications. *Vertigo* can be seen as a parable of means and ends. First, the means and ends of the Kantian categorical imperative; second, of the "means" (the mean people: Gavin, Madeleine/Judy, and Scottie) and of the ends (the endings of the two segments of the film); and third, about how all these function as Hitchcock's means of achieving his ends in this work of art.

Although "dignity" does not appear in the screenplay, and has not been emphasised in the *Vertigo* literature, it maps well on to the subject. While I have not been able to familiarise myself entirely with the vast *Vertigo* literature, the substantial materials I have surveyed address neither of my two intertwined subjects: first, dignity as a theme[4] and second, the significance of the names, Madeleine and Judy.

Part one: means and ends

My reading of *Vertigo* will use the tradition of dignity deriving from Immanuel Kant's (1724–1804) categorical imperative: "treat humanity, whether in ourselves or in others, always as an end in itself and never only as a means." "Dignity" has a complex history (Rosen, 2012). I am not utilising the term in its senses of elegance/gravitas/comportment or prestige/lordliness/status; each category has its own tradition. Scholars also disagree about whether "dignity" is, or should be, primarily a legal or a moral term. I am obviously using it as the latter. Akhtar (Chapter Two, this volume) proposes a psychoanalytic taxonomy of dignity and Richman (Chapter Three, this volume) a new philosophical one. Some philosophers actually refer to this formulation of the categorical imperative as "the principle of dignity" (Richman, p. 52). Kant explains further: "In the kingdom of ends, everything has either a price or a dignity. What has a price can be replaced by something else as its equivalent; what, on the other hand, is raised above all price and therefore admits of no equivalent has a dignity. Now, morality is the condition under which alone a rational being can be an end in itself. Morality, and humanity, insofar as it is capable of morality, is that which alone has dignity" (cited in Rosen, 2012, p. 24). The categorical nature of a moral obligation refers to the question of universality. That is, an action should be judged immoral if we would not wish that action to be adopted by everybody.

Dignity, as I will use the term, comprises states of mind, rights, and responsibilities. Human beings have an inherent worth that deserves to be acknowledged. They have the right to have their physical and psychological needs respected. A self-state of dignity is comprised of a non-hubristic pride in oneself and a realistic pleasure in one's capacities. Maintaining one's dignity requires living by moral standards, treating others as dignified beings, and living with authenticity and integrity. Dignity violations occur in the treatment of others as though they do not possess inherent worth. Not living up to one's obligation to oneself I will term a dignity abdication.

Let us begin this brief dignity inventory with the very first series of images: the title sequence itself conveys not only a mood but also a message from Hitchcock. The image of the eye, the entry into the pupil from which emerges the spellbinding, hypnotic swirling animation signals that the key to this film—and indeed to all film—is looking. The Saul Bass title sequence itself puts us on notice that this film will be about a pupil and that we must be apt pupils. As Judy chides Scottie, toward the end, "Can't you see?" We will be well served if we keep this question in mind.

The initial indignity of the film, though not a dignity violation, belongs to Scottie in his discovery of his acrophobia, the sudden onset of vertigo and his inability to do his job and rescue his colleague in the initial chase across the rooftops to catch a thief. As he convalesces in Midge's apartment looking out her front (or rear) window we watch his further humiliation as he realises he cannot cure himself by what we would now term exposure therapy, and that he remains vulnerable. From this point on, however, *Vertigo* can be regarded as a virtual catalogue of ways to violate the categorical imperative. How does everyone in this story abdicate their own dignity and violate the dignity of everyone else? Let us count the ways.

Preying on Scottie's weakness is at the centre of Gavin Elster's notorious family plot. Elster tells a far-fetched story about his wife, Madeleine, who is rich and strange: he tells Scottie that she has been acting as though she is possessed by her great-grandmother, Carlotta Valdes, who had committed suicide. Scottie's initial reaction is not to dignify the tale at all, to say, essentially, "That's for the birds." Elster and Judy violate Scottie's dignity by conspiring to put Scottie in a situation in which they know he will be unable to do what is necessary—to follow Madeleine up the tower in order to prevent her from committing suicide. Scottie should have learned from *Dial M for Murder* to beware of phone calls from old college classmates.

How does Gavin Elster manage to rope Scottie in? I believe that, in part, it is due to Scottie's inability to mourn the loss of a sense of himself as a competent cop. He scoffs at the request, relegating it to the profession whose name he cannot utter completely—psychoanalysis. Yet, he must also recognise it as an opportunity to regain his footing by doing what he does best, detecting, to restore his lost self-esteem and dignity. Scottie is more vulnerable than he consciously knows, because of his ennui, the loss of his profession and competence, the blow to his masculinity, and because of his curiosity—previously a strength. Scottie must have been in need of being swept away by romance, a bit like Emma Bovary. His ennui and naïveté are also reminiscent of the empty-headedness, or air-headedness that Bollas (1995, p. 197) describes in the victim to be of the serial killer, a certain quality of being primed to collude and to be helpless or perhaps pseudo-dumb. But most of all, Scottie is gullible, susceptible to the hoax, because of the beauty and mystery of Madeleine when he first lays eyes on her at Ernie's restaurant. Boileau and Narcejac (1997, p. 53, 1958, p. 62) describe the Scottie character as feeling not like a blood donor but like a soul donor to Madeleine ("donneur d'âme"). We know from the initial scene with Midge, that Scottie had some difficulty with intimacy; clearly he is drawn more to a fantasy woman than to the attractive and kind Midge.

Elster's use of Scottie is precisely as a means rather than an end; it is because of Scottie's objective attributes as a former detective, whose presence on the case will provide cover for Elster's crime and a ready scapegoat, a seemingly negligent babysitter, who cannot be found guilty in the eyes of the law—but is so in his own eyes. Elster not only does not take Scottie's personhood, his dignity, into account, but he puts a price on it. Elster was calculating, literally: what was Scottie's value as a pawn in the plot to kill his wife and possess her wealth. Scottie's loss of dignity is indeed showcased at the inquest. Elster and Judy have abdicated their own dignity as well, by acting without morality. They have lied to Scottie and manipulated his reality. Although we have some sympathy for Judy as a second victim (and we may even root for her a bit later on), she was apparently an "apt pupil" of Gavin Elster, willing to do anything to be able to win him. As Madeleine, whom we at first take to be suffering from some fugue or dissociative state, she is playing Scottie and us. We could term this "gaslighting", but that would only be Hitchcockian.

Not that Elster deserved fidelity from anyone, but Judy fell in love with Scottie while she was supposed to be working with and for Elster. Why was Scottie not suspicious of Madeleine's infidelity, by the way? Why did it not occur to Scottie that it was the detective's equivalent of a sexual boundary violation for him to have acted as he did with Madeleine, in addition to being what he must have known was a dignity violation to Gavin Elster? Judy was not supposed to care about how he will feel after he thinks she is dead, but she comes to regard Scottie as an end in himself, as being more than a means. Playing the role of Madeleine, she torments herself and him at the foot of the tower; in a voice we will on repeated viewings recognise as Judy's, she says, it is "not fair", it should not have "happened this way", and that if he loses her he'll know she loved him and wanted to "go on" loving him.

And so the lady vanishes. The movie comes to what feels like an abrupt and premature ending, a bit like when Janet Leigh is killed off so early in *Psycho*. Gavin Elster's end has been achieved, though we are not aware of this yet. Hitchcock's end of making us feel unsettled and confused and stunned has been achieved. We identify with Scottie's loss and his re-traumatisation that his vertigo prevented him from saving a life for the second time.

After the inquest, Scottie tortures himself into a sanitarium. He has the conviction that "the wrong man" (Boileau & Narcejac, 1997, p. 79) had been chosen to protect Madeleine. Scottie's dreams not only reflect his intrapsychic attempt to deal with trauma; they also reveal, I think, his attempt to master and understand the dignity violation he has been dealt, that is, the blow to his psychological integrity and his identity as a detective and a person with an essentially intact relationship with reality. He was been so swept off his feet by Madeleine, who appeared so young and innocent, that he had consciously forgotten his scepticism about the entire Carlotta story. Scottie also did not want to solve this mystery, because it would have led him to the unsavoury knowledge that Madeleine was not who she seemed to be. Simultaneously, he is trying to avoid certain unsavoury self-knowledge. When Madeleine is gone, he is left just with himself and with the mystery, so solving it represents both his connection to her and his defensive process. The dream sequence can be understood as Scottie's attempt to return to reality and to reawaken his unconscious suspicion that there is a puzzle here. He seems to be trying to put the images together in a way that makes sense, but he can only end with his falling. This was a staged mystery, and he doesn't have enough facts to figure out whodunit or why. We, too, allowed our reason to be overwhelmed by the compelling quality of the love story between the two stars. But, unlike Scottie, we are certain that something fishy must have gone on—after all, this is a Hitchcock film.

Scottie revisits all the Madeleine sites, in a camouflaged frenzy to sight Madeleine. The novel explains his logic: if Madeleine had been reincarnated once, this might well happen a second time. He finds several wrong women on several occasions until he spots Judy Barton leaving the department store where she works. He follows her home, and the pas-de-deux of dignity violations and abdications resumes. We learn the back story from Judy's to-be-torn-up letter, discovering that Elster further violated Judy's dignity by leaving her after the murder, running away with all the money and leaving her to live in a seedy hotel. (The room, however, was not seedy enough to have featured a torn curtain.) Even criminal conspirators care about their dignity, however. When Judy persuades Scottie that she is not Madeleine Elster, we hear this concern immediately: are you interested in me—or in ... her?

But, can't h/we see? Even as we see the actress we know to be Kim Novak on the streets of San Francisco, we are yet unsure that this is Madeleine. Hitchcock creates in us the same vertiginous "absolute certainty of recognition" and "equal certainty that Madeleine [is] dead" (Boileau & Narcejac, 1997, p. 115) that Scottie must feel. We can see in Judy simultaneously her accurate empathy and ultimate narcissism, "great tenderness and great cruelty" (Boileau & Narcejac, 1997, p. 152) as she writes to Scottie and then tears up the letter. She tells him he should not hold himself responsible, that he was the "victim" and the "witness" and that she was the "tool". Her instinct toward morality and dignity, to go away, having satisfied her wish to see him once again, is overridden by her love for him.

We have been manipulated into the position of imagining that this love story might conceivably work, albeit involving the original criminality and the ongoing violations of Scottie's dignity and abdication by Judy of hers. However, as analysts know and Woody Allen famously said, "the heart wants what it wants" (Allen, 2001). Each time I watch the film I find myself hoping that Scottie and Judy can find a way to be together. As Jaeger (2012, p. 325) notes, "The romanticism of *Vertigo* is so intense that it generates a nostalgia for what is lost in the rejection of an enchanting illusion." And then when Scottie discovers the truth, we are simultaneously anxious for Judy, and rooting for Scottie to achieve his revenge. We thus experience vicariously both sides of the dignity exchange. Hitchcock guides us to a place where we want incompatible things, like the unconscious that knows no "no"s. By watching a Hitchcock film, we consent to being taken to delicious and repulsive places in our thoughts and feelings—to places of immorality and indignity we hope we would not go in reality.

To include the letter from Judy and the sequence showing the murder on the tower created much disagreement between Hitchcock and his studio. It is fundamental to understanding *Vertigo* as a story of suspense, and not as a mystery (Spoto, 1983). The master of suspense maintains control of the viewer's emotions, just as Elster and Madeleine have controlled Scottie's. However—and this is key—it was never a suspense story for Scottie. He did not know the truth until he saw the necklace, so he does not get to enjoy the sadomasochistic pleasure of suspense, which carries the confident expectation of closure, even if not a happy ending. He is still suffering from the sadism of the first half of the film.

Scottie appears to violate Judy's dignity by progressively pressuring her to dress and groom herself like Madeleine. Could there be a clearer depiction of a man treating a woman as a means to the end of satisfying his fantasy (Gabbard, 1998)? These scenes are difficult to watch, so acutely do they depict the compromises of self and dignity in both characters. Some years ago, I watched *Vertigo* with a group of psychiatry residents; one of the young men expostulated during this scene, "Stop being such a dick!" (This comment actually helped me focus on the detective component of Scottie's identity!) Our horror at this "monstrous, inhuman" (Rothman, 2004, p. 231) process is mitigated by our knowledge that Scottie is, in fact, only making her into what she was; her protestations are not what he thinks them to be. As he re-dresses her, however, he actually begins the process of redressing the wrongs. Judy begs to be loved for herself (whoever that is), but she submits even to his beyond-the-pale insistence that she change her hair colour—which, he says, couldn't mean anything to her. Is Judy manning up in accepting this punishment, this violation of her dignity as the just desert for continuing to violate his?

Finally, in the hotel room after Judy twists her hair into the knot, the renaissance of Madeleine is complete. Judy's acceptance of Scottie's adoration and choosing to wear Carlotta's necklace confirms that she has become as deluded as he is. Perhaps she feels that she can live in the Madeleine persona that she had previously inhabited and that he would not find anything wrong with that ideal image. Does this represent a grandiose, contemptuous sort of dignity (Marcovitz, 1970)? We want to say to her, can't you see—that you are being foolish (not to mention undignified)? That this will sabotage the relationship?

Judy asks Scottie, "Can't you see?" as he helps her fasten Carlotta's necklace. He then knows, beyond a shadow of a doubt. She, too, must have something of the airhead about her, she, too, must want to co-operate in her own fall. And Scottie's sadistic partner to his masochism emerges as he instantaneously hatches the plan to take Judy back to the tower. Scottie becomes the ultimate dignity violator, completing the transformation before our eyes from victim-tool to villain (San Juan & McDevitt, 2013, p. 102). Although aiming to achieve what he feels is justice, Scottie is dominated by vengefulness. He terrifies Judy and humbles her in the forced re-enactment of the trip up the bell tower. At this point, Judy is deserving of being treated with dignity in the sense that a criminal retains basic human rights including not to be humiliated.

We, too, become perpetrators, if we identify with Scottie and root for him as he successfully climbs the tower stairs. In a tour de force ending, he reclaims his sense of reality, but also abdicates his dignity, and he loses his twice-fallen woman. The nun, whose presence startles Judy off the tower, says, "I heard voices"—in other less extraordinary contexts, a symptom of psychosis.

In the novel, the Gavin Elster character was actually punished for his evil—killed as he fled Paris from the investigation of his wife's death. Hitchcock resisted pressure from the Hollywood studio censor to include in the movie a final scene in which Scottie and Midge sit in her apartment listening to a radio report of Gavin Elster being caught by the police. In the film, everybody except the most responsible party is punished. Hitchcock doesn't offer us any balm to soothe the shock of this tragedy. In the novel, however, the Scottie character's moral responsibility for Judy's death is absolute: he strangles her.

Part two: "Can't you see?"

Art allows one to experience vicariously emotions and thoughts we would not wish to experience in reality. After reading Poe's "The Murders in the Rue Morgue", Hitchcock came to a realisation: "… fear, you see, is an emotion people like to feel when they know they're safe. When a person is sitting at home reading a tale of terror, one still feels secure. Naturally you shiver, but since you're in familiar surroundings and you know it's only your imagination that responds to the reading, you then feel a great relief and happiness—like someone who has a cold drink after being very thirsty. And then you appreciate the gentle lamp and the comfortable armchair you're sitting in …." (Spoto, 1983, p. 13) We seek to and consent to suffer these dignity violations, as we seek thrills and the possibility of danger when we get on a roller coaster. As Hitchcock told Truffaut (Truffaut, 1969, p. 397), "the stronger the evil, the stronger the film."

Hitchcock knew how to take his viewers to the cultural-intermediate-play space (Winnicott, 1971) of forbidden thoughts and wishes. And he took pleasure in their terror. Just a few years after the release of *Vertigo*, Higham (1962, p. 3) wrote: "At heart, Hitchcock has remained a practical joker, a cunning and sophisticated cynic amused at the French critical vogue for his work, contemptuous of the audience which he treats as the collective victim of a Pavlovian experiment, perennially fascinated by his own ability to exploit the cinema's resources." Indeed, Hitchcock even said his actors should be "treated like cattle"—denying that he had ever said that actors *were* cattle (Wood, 2009, p. 40). While there is a dignity to art as a cultural function and sublimation, Hitchcock may have used this as cover for his own instinctual satisfactions. Ultimately, we are the means to Hitchcock's end of visiting his sadistic fantasies upon us, especially in this most personal of all his films.

Hitchcock evokes in *Vertigo* the fear of the loss of dignity and of the integrity of the self (illusory as that might be). Gavin and Judy attacked the sanctity of Scottie's mind, the dignity of knowing what he knows. Indeed, one of the most harmful things a parent can do to a child is to undermine his or her sense of reality. Knowing that one's relationship with reality is adequately intact is an essential component of our humanness, of our basic sense of self. As we identify with Scottie, then, the fear that we get to experience and then dismiss, is of having our dignity violated, of having that capacity of our minds and our professionalism undermined. Becoming competent is, in great part, to know that we know what we know. Hitchcock has made Scottie into the man who did not know enough, even as he thought he knew too much.

In *Vertigo*, the clues for Scottie and us are embedded in the language, images, and sounds in ways that we can only understand in retrospect and after multiple viewings. And like the proverbial gun on the table in the Chekov play, we must assume that Hitchcock, with his exacting standards, deep involvement with screenwriters, and precisely planned storyboards, intended (consciously or unconsciously) everything he said and showed to bear meaning. As in psychoanalysis, we assume there to be meaning in just about everything (except, perhaps, the occasional cigar) even if we do not or cannot grasp it. Truffaut (1969, p. 401) comments to Hitchcock, "Emptiness has a magnetic appeal for you;

you see it as a challenge …. You see the film as a receptacle to be filled to the brim with cinematic ideas …." And Hitchcock assents.

And now I have kept you in suspense long enough. About thirty years ago, I had occasion to discover that the name "Madeleine" derived from the Hebrew, *migdal*, for tower. On one of my many re-viewings of *Vertigo* some fifteen years later, it suddenly clicked for me: Madeleine … tower! From the first scene of the film Hitchcock has inserted the signifier "tower" right under Scottie's nose, and ours. In the opening rooftop sequence itself we see Coit Tower in the night skyline of San Francisco, and it is later Madeleine's landmark to find Scottie's apartment. (Coit Tower was named after Lillie Hitchcock Coit, no relation. Hitchcock referred to it as a phallic symbol in his interview with Truffaut (Truffaut, 1969)). Hitchcock shows us Scottie and Madeleine alongside towers in the first half hour of the film, at the cemetery and at the McKittrick Hotel. The importance of "Madeleine" is clear in the novel, too; a tower appears there early on—the Eiffel Tower. And in Catholic France, readers of the original novel would likely have associated "Madeleine" with La Madeleine, Mary Magdalene. The French reader, and many viewers of the film, might also have thought of Proust's madeleine, signifying the powerful presence of the past in a present moment. Perhaps even Mel Brooks can be said to have appreciated the importance of the name, having cast Madeline Kahn as the leading lady in *High Anxiety*!

I remain puzzled about how what I discovered about the name "Madeleine" remained unseen for so many decades. Indeed, I only saw the name for what it was because I have my own beloved Madeleine (about whom I will say no more, thus further enacting my identification with Hitchcock in his love of teasing his audience). As I noted earlier, I examined an extensive sample of the Hitchcock scholarship in order to verify that my observations were, indeed, original. I read with bated breath and heightening anxiety, lest I discover that I was only rediscovering (like Scottie). I observed my repeated pattern of relieved disbelief and mild contempt as I went through paper after paper by distinguished analysts, philosophers, and film scholars. One scholar described which version of the script contained the alterations in the characters' names (Krohn, 2000). Another was so sensitive to language as to note the wit of Midge's cantilever/can't-I-leave-her bra design (Gordon, 2008, p. 29). And *they* had not seen the significance of the "Madeleine" name choice. (Pomerance, 2004). It then occurred to me that my cycle of anxiety and smugness might represent my own symptomatic identification with Judy.

And I identified with Scottie, as well. I attempted to find Kim Novak herself to see if she might have knowledge about the names; I called and emailed her agent, who only happened to be the chairman of William Morris Entertainment. I think this qualifies as obsessional (re)search!

Further reflections on "Madeleine" lead, of course, to Mary Magdalene, Mary of the tower, or of the village of Magdala. She was the redeemed sinner who became devoted to Jesus. I then became curious about any biblical possibilities of the name "Judy", and, aside from Judith and Holofernes, didn't come up with any. What meaning this may have is unknowable, but "Judy" is also of Hebrew origin, "Judith" meaning "of Judea" or "praised". Judith charms Holofernes, and then beheads this enemy of Israel. She is a heroine, and also a widow—a woman who has lost her man. So both "Madeleine" and "Judy" were women who sinned but were in the end regarded with great esteem. Hitchcock with his Roman Catholic upbringing would likely have had great familiarity with biblical figures.

I then became more curious about names in the novel and discovered that the name "Madeleine" was the only one of the original four main characters that had been retained. I concluded that Hitchcock indeed must have found that specific name important. "Roger" had been changed to "John/Scottie", "Paul" to "Gavin", and "Renée" to "Judy".[5] Note, too, the name "Midge" (a gnat, an annoyance), for the character created specifically for the film by the screenwriter Samuel Taylor (Barr, 2002, p. 29) as further evidence that there is indeed something in the choice of names worth our attention. "Elster" carries a meaning as well: it is German for "magpie", a bird that is known to eat the eggs and young of other birds. Hitchcock even draws attention to the name "Madeleine" by not having anyone utter it until about thirty-eight minutes into the film, on page fifty-six of the 190 page screenplay; this recalls the unspoken first name of the second Mrs. De Winter in *Rebecca*. As I contemplated the names, it struck me that "Madeleine" was not the only name with a meaning: there was also "Renée". It was suddenly obvious, to my eye: re-née—reborn. "Can't you see?" Did Hitchcock not see this, or did he choose not to use it? He could have teased us further by putting the truth right under our noses, like the necklace, just as I teased you earlier with my use of "renaissance" and "reborn"? And let us not forget to take our chapeaux off to Boileau and Narcejac for their original wit in using both evocative names!

Why might Hitchcock have discarded "Renée" when it would have been so slyly witty and so apt? One Hitchcock scholar (Poague, 2002, p. 273) described *Vertigo* as "a parable of birth-giving and separation". Sabbadini aptly uses the term "resurrect" in reference to Judy (2014, p. 98). What did Hitchcock gain from "Judy"? What's in a name? More properly, what was thought to be in a name in 1957, when the screen-play was being written? "Judy" was number thirty-eight on the list of the top forty baby names in that year (babycenter website.)[6] "Renée" and "Madeleine" do not appear on the list. The Social Security Admin-istration's list of the 200 most popular names of the 1950s reveals that "Judy" came in at twenty-seven, "Judith" at thirty-four, and "Renee" at 128; "Madeleine" is not on the list (Social Security Administration website.)[7] In the end, who made the decision to discard Renée is unim-portant, for Hitchcock accepted it.

What meanings did the choice of "Judy" bring to the film? "Judy" is a common name, literally and symbolically, for a common girl, unlike the refined and rare "Madeleine". "Judy" also includes the ironic sense of "praised". And perhaps there was a punch line for Hitchcock in "Judy", after all. "Judy" was the shrewish wife from the popular British Punch and Judy puppet tradition. Indeed, Hitchcock considered and rejected making a film from Arnold Bennett's story, "Punch and Judy", written for Hitchcock in 1929 (*The Sentinel*, 2012). Apparently, one of the central themes of the Bennett story was that, just like the puppets Punch and Judy, people *can* be manipulated. And, as we know, puppets can neither be killed nor brought back to life; Gavin Elster threw a puppet-like prop or stuntwoman off the tower. "Prof." Glyn Edwards, of punchandjudy.com wrote to me: "To my knowledge Judy has never been thrown anywhere (other than the fact that all traditional glove puppets exit as if through a trap door). It is the Baby who is thrown about in the traditional scripts—a piece of slapstick carried on into pantomime, early film, and vaudeville. A 3 year old Buster Keaton was physically thrown about in the act by his vaudeville father. Mostly a prop baby would be substituted for a live infant before the sight gags escalated. As all the cast of P&J are wooden there was no need for this substitution in the puppet show. Mr. Punch blames Judy for the mishap to the baby in the Victorian script by claiming he assumed she'd be there to catch it. The current version of this gag is for Mr. Punch to sit on the baby having misinterpreted Judy's instruction to do the babysitting" (personal communication,

3 June 2014). It should be noted, too, that Alfred Hitchcock was a great admirer of Buster Keaton.

Indeed, one can think of the entire narrative of *Vertigo* as a Punch-and-Judy-like exchange of blows to dignity. Thus "Judy" carries the additional meaning of a puppet worked by the puppeteer. The shrewish "Judy" puppet character is also mean to Punch and the baby. *Vertigo's* "Judy" was certainly mean as "Madeleine", even when she was at least partially manipulated by the puppeteer Gavin Elster. Yet she was an evil Galatea too, as an active participant in the deliberate violation of Scottie, even before Scottie became an evil Pygmalion (Levine, 2001; Stoichita, 2008), trying to make a marble statue come alive.

The end

"Judy" or "Renée"? *Vertigo* is suspense rather than mystery because we know the ending when Judy reads her letter and Hitchcock shows us what happened on the bell tower. But for Scottie, it is a mystery; he has to find the clues to figure out what's going on. To the extent that we identify with Scottie, then, the film must also be a mystery for us. So why did Hitchcock not plant the additional "Renée" clue to tease us more? "Judy" fits the story in all the various meanings; "Renée" would have served to intensify the "I can't believe I didn't see it" feeling, the identification with the detective who has missed a clue, like Scottie. It would thus have served to intensify our vicarious experience of being manipulated, being treated as means, not ends. All told, we are still trying to be apt pupils of *Vertigo*.

No matter how much Hitchcock may have used the viewer as the means to the end of his amusement, there is nonetheless a morality and a worth in the artistic endeavour of portraying the human condition. Language, fantasies, and the capacity to reason symbolically are essential to an understanding of what we value about being human. The capacity to play, to imagine, to have intermediate spaces between the real and the imaginary, signify the achievement of culture. In respecting the importance of words and symbolic representations—and indeed by playing with them—a filmmaker or a writer affirms the dignity of human culture and of this aspect of human identity. Thus Freud acknowledged the dignity of humour (1927d, p. 163).

Many critics have noted a dreamlike quality to *Vertigo* (for instance, Perry, 2003, p. 178). As Freud commented in discussing his dream of

Irma's injection, "There is at least one spot in every dream at which it is unplumbable—a navel, as it were, that is its point of contact with the unknown" (1900a, p. 111, footnote 1). A navel, like Madeleine's chignon, can be seen as drain-like, with vertiginous vortices. At the end of his analysis of his dream, Freud acknowledges that he knows more but is choosing to withhold that knowledge from us. Likewise, perhaps, with Hitchcock.

> This is the dream's navel, the spot where it reaches down into the unknown ... The dream-thoughts to which we are led by interpretation cannot, from the nature of things, have any definite endings; they are bound to branch out in every direction into the intricate network of our world of thought. It is at some point where this meshwork is particularly close that the dream-wish grows up, like a mushroom out of its mycelium (Freud, 1900a, p. 525).

Is Madeleine the fallen woman—and are we not fallen, too, for having used Scottie's travails as a means to our stimulation and pleasure? Are we not implicated in the dignity violation in so far as we have suspended our disbelief and enjoyed our identification with immorality? Or does the dignity of cultural discourse trump this? Did Hitchcock achieve his end by keeping me—and now you—in suspense in perpetuity, with the unanswerable mystery of "Judy" or "Renée"? Have we discovered that he made a choice or missed an opportunity? Did he have the last laugh by forcing us to continue the conversation with him from his place among the dead—making us enact the dreaded and wished for possibility that the dead remain present among us? The *Psycho*-analysis of *Vertigo* may remain interminable.

Notes

1. *D'Entre les Morts* was the title of the original novel. The film was released in France as *Sueurs Froides* (Cold Sweat), and the novel was later reprinted under this name. The title of the English translation was *Vertigo*.
2. http://www.sparknotes.com/film/vertigo/summary.html.
3. https://en.wikipedia.org/wiki/Vertigo_(film).
4. Žižek (1990, pp. 6, 7, 14; cited in Ravetto-Biagioli, 2011, pp. 84, 120) does bring up dignity in the Kantian sense in his discussion of *Vertigo*.

Citing Lacan's formula that sublimation raises the object to the dignity of the ideal Thing, Žižek compares the ordinary Judy to the sublime Madeleine. This rests on the assumption that without the defence of sublimation, our desires and drives would result in unrestrained acting on our impulses. To do so would be to treat others as means to the end of our satisfactions—not as entities with personal dignity. The golden rule of universality and our capacity for sublimation are what permit the acknowledgement of dignity and human rights following Kant. Dignity in its conventional moral sense does entail idealisations, and it leaves us the challenge of understanding consensual sadomasochistic relationships.

5. I thank Mariann Smith, (Consultant, Center for Humanities in Medicine, University of Buffalo Medical School) for pointing out to me that "Roger" derives from the Germanic "hrod" (fame) and "ger" (spear)—thus, a famous spear. "Roger" also is British slang for "penis" or "to have sex with" (personal communication, 25 September 2014). If we consider this more closely, it is clear that Scottie is, in fact, no Roger. In the second scene in Midge's apartment, Hitchcock shows Scottie as a man who wears a corset, who needs to use a cane, and who is apparently unable to identify the object Midge is designing as a brassiere. Let us note, too, that the film that Hitchcock turned his attention to even before finishing *Vertigo*, was *North by Northwest*. The lead character, played by Cary Grant, is named Roger Thornhill (Penis Penispenis!). The opening credits appear on a skyscraper, and the famous final image of the film is of a train speeding into a tunnel as Roger proceeds to roger the new Mrs. Thornhill, Eva Marie-Saint. I think it is fair to say that this is a phallic film, in contrast to *Vertigo*, about a de-manning. And I believe this bolsters my argument that Hitchcock selected character names with care.

6. http://www.babycenter.com/popularBabyNames.htm?year=1957. Date accessed: 22 May 2014.

7. http://www.ssa.gov/OACT/babynames/decades/names1950s.html. Date accessed: 22 May 2014.

References

Allen, W. (2001). Walter Isaacson interviews Woody Allen. *Time*, 24 June 2001. http://content.time.com/time/magazine/article/0,9171,160439,00.html. Date accessed: 7 July 2014.

Barr, C. (2002). *Vertigo*. London: BFI Publishing.

Berman, E. (2001). Hitchcock's *Vertigo*: the collapse of a rescue fantasy. In: G. O. Gabbard, (Ed.), *Psychoanalysis and Film*. London: Karnac.

Boileau, P., & Narcejac, N. (1958). *Sueurs Froides (D'Entres les Morts)*. Paris: Editions Denoël.

Boileau, P., & Narcejac, N. (1997). *Vertigo* (G. Sainsbury, Trans.). London: Bloomsbury Film Classics.

Bollas, C. (1995). The structure of evil. In: *Cracking Up: The Work of Unconscious Experience*. New York, NY: Hill and Wang.

Christie, I. (2012). The 50 greatest films of all time. *Sight & Sound*, September 2012. http://www.bfi.org.uk/news/50-greatest-films-all-time. Date accessed: 28 May 2015.

Freud, S. (1900a). *The Interpretation of Dreams. S. E., 4–5*. London: Hogarth.

Freud, S. (1927d). Humour. *S. E., 21*: 159–166. London: Hogarth.

Gabbard, G. O. (1998). *Vertigo*: Female objectification, male desire, and object loss. *Psychoanalytic Inquiry, 18*: 161–167.

Gordon, P. (2008). *Dial M for Mother: A Freudian Hitchcock*. Madison and Teaneck, NJ: Fairleigh Dickinson University Press.

Hicks, D. (2011). *Dignity: Its Essential Role in Resolving Conflict*. New Haven, CT: Yale.

Higham, C. (1962). Hitchcock's World. *Film Quarterly, 16*: 3–16.

Jaeger, C. S. (2012). *Enchantment*. Philadelphia, PA: University of Pennsylvania Press.

Krohn, B. (2000). *Hitchcock at Work*. London: Phaidon.

Lee, S. H. (1986). Existential themes in the films of Alfred Hitchcock. *Philosophy Research Archives, 11*: 225–244.

Levine, S. S. (2001). On the mirror stage with Henry and Eliza, or Play-ing with *Pygmalion* in Five Acts. In: Levine, S. S. (2009). *Loving Psychoanalysis: Technique and Theory in the Therapeutic Relationship*. Lanham, MD: Aronson.

Marcovitz, E. (1970). Dignity. *Bulletin of the Philadelphia Association for Psychoanalysis, 20*: 105–116.

Perry, D. R. (2003). *Hitchcock and Poe: The Legacy of Delight and Terror*. Lanham, MD: Scarecrow Press.

Poague, L. (2002). Engendering *Vertigo*. In: S. Gottlieb & C. Brookhouse (Eds.), *Framing Hitchcock: Selected Essays from the Hitchcock Annual*. Detroit, MI: Wayne State University Press.

Pomerance, M. (2004). *An Eye for Hitchcock*. New Brunswick, NJ: Rutgers University Press.

Ravetto-Biagioli, K. (2011). *Vertigo* and the vertiginous history of film theory. *Camera Obscura, 75*: 100–142.

Rosen, M. (2012). *Dignity: Its History and Meaning*. Cambridge, MA: Harvard University Press.

Rothman, W. (2004). *The "I" of the Camera: Essays in Film Criticism, History, and Aesthetics*. Cambridge: Cambridge University Press.

Sabbadini, A. (2014). *Moving Images: Psychoanalytic Reflections on Film*. East Sussex: Routledge.

Sanchez-Cardenas, M. (2013). Matte Blanco and narrativity: Hitchcock's *Vertigo. International Journal of Psychoanalysis, 94*: 825–840.

San Juan, E., & McDevitt, J. (2013). *Hitchcock's Villains: Murderers, Maniacs, and Mother Issues*. Lanham, MD: Scarecrow Press.

The Sentinel (2012). The amazing tale of Arnold Bennett, Alfred Hitchcock and the corrupt bankers ... *The Sentinel*, 6 July 2012. http://www.stokesentinel.co.uk/amazing-tale-Arnold-Bennett-Alfred-Hitchcock/story-16494970-detail/story.html. Date accessed: 22 May 2014. Spoto, D. (1983). *The Dark Side of Genius: The Life of Alfred Hitchcock*. New York, NY: Ballantine.

Stoichita, V. I. (2008). *The Pygmalion Effect: From Ovid to Hitchcock* (A. Anderson, Trans.). Chicago, IL: University of Chicago Press.

Truffaut, F. (1969). *Hitchcock*. London: Panther.

Winnicott, D. W. (1971). *Playing and Reality*. Harmondsworth: Penguin.

Wood, R. (2009). Retrospective. In: M. Deutelbaum & L. Poague (Eds.), *A Hitchcock Reader* (2nd ed). Oxford: Wiley-Blackwell.

Žižek, S. (1990). How the non-duped err. *Qui Parle, 4*: 1–20.

The dignity of persons needs to be affirmed, consistently, heartily

Stanley Coen

Having read these essays eagerly, I want to vigorously proclaim that we all need our personal dignity affirmed, consistently, heartily. Human dignity is a basic right, a vital need, to which every human being is entitled. Many have been robbed of such personal affirmation. In this epilogue to these key essays on the matter of dignity, I need to respond, exuberantly and personally.

Many times have I retold Donna Hicks' (Hicks, 2011) account of her held-back young Palestinian woman student telling her story to a dialogue workshop of Middle Eastern students living in the Boston area. Each time I cry. I can imagine myself as the grandfather, a revered grandfather indeed, humiliated by a very young Israeli soldier. The six-year-old granddaughter (I can easily imagine my own grand-daughters), enraged, runs to the soldier, shouting at him, "He's my grandfather! You can't yell at him!" A six-year-old needs to revere her grandfather. No one should interfere with that, certainly not a very young Israeli soldier. And the grandfather needs to be accorded respect and dignity. We all do. It is tragic that Israelis and Palestinians, filled with terror, rage, and hopelessness, have had such difficulty according each other respect and dignity.

And then we read about people like Donna Hicks who travel around the world attempting to get warring peoples to try, just a little bit, to feel empathy for the other's position. What a difference that makes. Remember the Israeli student's pain-filled response to the Palestinian student's story. Despite all the explanations in defence of intense border security, his people had harmed the Palestinian woman and her grandfather. Acknowledging this was brand new for him. What a difference it was to balance his country's need for protection and security against such injuries to the other's self-esteem. The young Israeli soldier could think only of terrorism and destruction. The six-year-old Palestinian girl imagined her grandfather, believing he would soon die, wanted to say goodbye to a very old, dear friend in East Jerusalem. That would be dignified.

I love that this account, and the others in Northern Ireland and elsewhere, do not founder on who is to blame for what has occurred. How moving it is to be able to accept that one has hurt another person, to empathise with that person's hurt, and to be able to apologise for having inflicted it. How wonderful it is that there are people like Donna Hicks who have learned how to facilitate such dialogue between embittered parties. She and Desmond Tutu, working together in Northern Ireland, helped to enable former members of the Irish Republican Army and British soldiers speak to each other. Spirituality, acceptance, compassion, dignity were required. I don't think we need to memorise Donna Hick's list of dignity factors but we can be inspired by her very moving accounts.

Desmond Tutu leads me to Pumla Gobodo-Madikizela, who served with him on the Truth and Reconciliation Commission in South Africa. Her book, *A Human Being Died That Night* (2003), recounts her extensive interviews with Eugene de Kock, the most infamous white brutaliser and torturer of black South Africans during apartheid. A dramatic version of her book is about to be performed on stage at the Brooklyn Academy of Music, as it has been in London's West End. In her interviews, she hoped to touch a bit of de Kock's humanity, to tap something of compassion, guilt, caring about others in him. What courage and dignity is required for Desmond Tutu, Pumla Gobodo-Madikizela, Nelson Mandela to forego revenge for their abuse. Instead, they have sought to heal themselves and their oppressors. The centrepiece of the book is the emotional reactions of the white torturer, shackled in irons, to this black woman psychologist empathically touching his hand. The many, diverse reactions—by both of them—to this hand-touching make the book fascinating. So is the attempt to restore dignity to someone who has relinquished it.

Jessica Stern (2014) reports her interview of a terrorist condemned for his crimes in Sweden to life imprisonment. She describes her own attempts, heavily endorsed by the Swedish government, to probe the humanity of this seemingly evil man, very much like Pumla Gobodo-Madikizela did. Here too, "boundary crossing" occurs between prisoner and interviewer. High security Swedish prisons require that no food or drink be brought into the prison by interviewers. Instead, for prolonged interviews, the prisoner brings food and drink from the prison commissary. On the table before them were two ham sandwiches. The sandwich nearest Jessica Stern had a bite taken out of it. She took the other sandwich. I immediately imagine the prisoner sadistically attacking Jessica Stern, wanting to bite, humiliate, degrade her by taking a bite out of her sandwich. I would expect addressing this "terrorist" behaviour would be the most effective immediate way of assessing the terrorist prisoner's current violence as well as his capacity for rehabilitation. At least, a psychoanalyst might assume that we could learn most from what transpires between prisoner and interviewer, if that could be confronted. Not being a clinically trained psychoanalyst, she did not make this the focal point of her interview. When I asked her about it,[1] her dignified response was that her terror kept her partly dissociated so that she could not use her mind fully. The Swedish government seeks to rehabilitate young imprisoned terrorists, to help them identify with and rejoin Swedish society rather than to continue to remain estranged, isolated, and violent.

José Mujica was President of Uruguay between 2010 and 2015. Because of his role as a leader of the Tupamaros, urban guerilla fighters, he was imprisoned for fourteen years. For a decade, Mujica was kept in solitary confinement, most of the time in a hole in the ground. He befriended a small frog and fed scraps of bread to the rats.[2] He too overcame his rage at his horrible treatment. He sought to help his country move forward. But it was clear how his abuse and isolation had led to his emotional constriction. That is how he survived. Even as President of Uruguay, he continued to live very simply, without any luxury. He donated most of his salary to the poor. He preserved his dignity. So too did the two lesbian women in Susan Vaughan's account who were chased and heckled by a group of young men. How wonderful that they could stop running away and instead shock the young men chasing them by affirming that they were lesbian and loved each other. They hugged and kissed each other. That's dignity. So is Dorothy Holmes's acknowledgment, so rare for an analyst of any race, that in her countertransference with a white patient, she did not want to feel like a poor degraded black servant. That had to be much too painful to bear. Her forthright rendering encourages her reader to have compassion for her need to avoid such pain. That's dignity. So too is beginning her chapter by acknowledging Ruth Simmons, the child of poor sharecroppers in East Texas, who overcame the strong odds that she would never escape the poverty of her beginnings. Ruth Simmons became president of Smith College, and then president of Brown University, the first African-American president of an Ivy League university. She believed that her mind had the power to transcend poverty and racial bias. She was right. That's dignity.

There is dignity in highlighting Eli Marcovitz's 1966 address on dignity. As far as his son Robert knows,[3] dignity had not been a special focus of Marcovitz. We don't know what led the Mental Health Association of Southeastern Pennsylvania to ask Marcovitz to talk about dignity. Marcovitz speaks wisely about how the "culture of poverty" impairs the dignity of children. I assume, just as I felt in Baltimore in 1966, Philadelphia was then beginning to resonate with the indignity of poverty, bias, racism, and the hopelessness of ever being able to join the American mainstream. Many of the contributors to this book come from the Philadelphia area. They should esteem their forbears, as they do Marcovitz, and, of course, Robert Waelder. It is dignified to be able to admire and respect our predecessors—as well as to be able to disagree with them and to follow our own newer paths. Historically, Marcovitz begins the discussion of dignity, which his colleagues then amplify much more fully in the light of the cultural changes of the past forty-five years. That's as it should be.

Salman Akhtar ends his chapter, seemingly about to shock us, by telling us that Sigmund Freud committed suicide. Yes, Freud did so with the help of his friend, colleague, physician, Max Schur. A few days before I write this, we had just celebrated Sigmund Freud's 159th birthday. Rather than shock us, Akhtar ends his chapter with Sigmund Freud's dignity in deciding that his life was over, that he had lived it fully and well, and was now ready to end it. That his beloved dog could not tolerate the stench from Freud's cancerous mouth had become unbearable. That's dignity.

A week before I write this, Marilyn Mosby, Maryland State Attorney for Baltimore City indicted six police officers in the death of Freddie Gray. Although her father and grandfather had been police officers, she was the *only black* student in her school in a wealthy white Boston suburb, to which she had to travel one hour from her home in Dorchester. Whatever the outcome of her rapid indictment, which my Federal prosecutor son-in-law says has to be too rushed, I am impressed by her courage and dignity. She did what Baltimore needed just then to help calm the rage and violence, especially among poor blacks who feel hopeless about ever entering the American mainstream. Baltimore has just been declared the worst city in America for poor black people. Of course, they feel hopeless. This too moves me. When I arrived in Baltimore in 1961 for an interview for an internship at The Johns Hopkins Hospital, I asked a woman which bus to take. She scolded me, "Young man, in Baltimore, only the blacks take the bus. Take a cab, and, mind you, only a Sun cab!" Of course, I took a bus. But in those days Hopkins Hospital had separate black and white newborn nurseries and surgical floors. I left Baltimore in 1966 just as it seemed to be headed towards conflagration, as did Detroit. I feel sad that such a large part of Baltimore has remained so trapped in bias and poverty. That's not dignity. I remember as a paediatric intern at Hopkins Hospital, caring for the young children of poor whites, mostly from Appalachia. Their parents felt just as hopeless and defeated, unable to provide much for their children, other than to stuff a bottle of milk into their mouths. This led to iron deficiency anemia. I went on to Appalachia—Lexington, Kentucky—with the U.S. Public Health Service[4] during the Vietnam War. In part-time community mental health work, we tried to help the poor whites and poor blacks trapped in a cul-de-sac in Paris, Kentucky to organise themselves, à la Saul Alinsky. The group, from the white and black churches of this cul-de-sac wanted to elect a man to serve as treasurer. He protested that he couldn't read or write. The group chanted their support for him. They and the Lord would help him. They sang a hymn. I cried then too.

Gerard Fromm opens his chapter wonderfully with Auden's elegy, "In Memory of Sigmund Freud" (1940). Indeed, Auden pays dignified tribute to Sigmund Freud. Quoting Auden, Fromm dignifies psychoanalysis. We sound really good! "Of whom shall we speak" and "to be enthusiastic over the night" are both so moving. So many have just died and need to be mourned but Sigmund Freud should not be lost among them. I encourage you to reread Auden's poem, again and again. Telling the unhappy present to recite the past like a poetry lesson until it falters is such a wonderful description of psychoanalytic process. So too is enthusiastically welcoming the horrors of the night, exiles, delectable creatures, who long to escape into the future. Long ago, I loved hearing Anne-Marie Sandler describe helping her child patient make friends with the angry part of himself. That is the path toward integration and healing.

Fromm writes that "psychoanalysis dignifies both the recital and the faltering." Auden's lines could replace the informational booklet about what psychoanalysis is offered by the American Psychoanalytic Association. Auden says it so much better. Fromm is convincing that the daily patient/staff community meetings at the Austen Riggs Center in Stockbridge, MA emphasise the dignity of each participant. Trying to grasp the other's position, despite one's own bias, is a wonderful psychoanalytic approach. From one's own constricted position, it is so easy to dismiss the other's contention. It is so much better to stay open to trying to learn something new from this other person. That patients, as well as staff, have something to contribute, that each one may be carrying something that the whole group needs to understand, opens up wonderful possibilities. And it dignifies each person, patient or staff. That is impressive about Austen Riggs. Their community helps to preserve this generous attitude towards the other, so easily lost outside a community, in private practice. The binary opposition between insider and outsider begins to collapse.

Like Fromm, Akhtar, a poet himself, descended from poets, shows us dignity in even a single line of poetry: Pablo Neruda's "What is sadder than a train stopped in rain?" or Jorge Luis Borges's "there is a door that I have closed until the end of the world." I love what Akhtar has written about preserving the dignity of the consulting room and preserving the analyst's respectful attitude toward the analytic space and his work. I don't recall another analyst saying so clearly why the analytic space needs to be protected from desecration. Yes, indeed, the dignity and sanctity of the analytic space needs to be preserved. Alcohol, condoms, sex, pornography, marijuana defile the consulting room. From this perspective of always guarding the sacredness of the analytic space, analysts must remain aware of their need to manage and master their temptations to cross or violate their patients' boundaries. Making the analytic space holy may help us do so, if we can resonate with what we have cherished about our own received traditions. Akhtar here, and elsewhere, has written well about the emotional value of inanimate objects, including those in the consulting room—for the patient and for the analyst. This may especially apply for immigrant patients and immigrant analysts but it also does for everyone else. Akhtar helps us preserve our dignity as psychoanalysts, advising us not to allow patient behaviours that impugn the dignity of the analytic process. Here are connections to Auden, to Fromm, to Holmes, to Vaughan, to Kluft, to Kravis, to Richman, to Levine. Yes, indeed, dignity is what this book is about!

Akhtar has helped me to grasp some of the difficulty of being an analytic patient when there is sharp cultural difference between patient and analyst. When I organised a panel and wrote about Masud Khan's reception today (Coen, 2010), Akhtar helped me put some of this in a cultural perspective. Masud Khan rose rapidly to psychoanalytic eminence as a writer, editor, lecturer, especially about perverse and schizoid states. Because of his misuse of patients and colleagues, he later just as rapidly crashed and burned. Many were highly critical that he hadn't allowed himself to take much psychoanalytic help. His close friend, Robert Stoller, desperately tried to help Khan manage himself via a series of therapeutic interventions. Akhtar suggested that I try to imagine how difficult, perhaps impossible, it would have been for a British psychoanalyst to treat Masud Khan just after the partition of India and Pakistan, with all the tensions then extant between them and Britain. Masud Khan was then only one of two Muslim Pakistani analysts in the world. To help me try to appreciate how extraordinarily difficult that must have been, Akhtar invited me to imagine my being the only Jewish analyst in the world. I felt horrified. I grasped that he wanted me to appreciate how extraordinarily difficult it can be to be an outsider. Although I know this well, I needed his reminder.

Susan Vaughan, drawing on Foucault, emphasises the danger in any binary construction that one pole will be esteemed, the other degraded. She shows us—and we need to see this again and again—how our constricted views of what is possible heaps indignity on others, here in relation to expressions of gender. Psychoanalysts should listen, witness, affirm, not judge their patients. Vaughan gives us the moving example of the child of a gay couple surprising his parents by imagining transgender possibilities, which the parents had not imagined. Wonderful that a child can see further than his parents! How awful that once upon a time, say in the 1970s, most, if not all of us, were so intent on interpreting heterosexual conflict in our gay and lesbian patients. Ralph Roughton, at a faculty retreat of the Columbia University Center for Psychoanalytic Training and Research in the early 1990s, had many of us in tears as he told about his own mistreatment of gay men, before he could more fully accept that men could, should, love each other. I recall with horror from the 1970s that I would not accept my gay patient's (now dead from HIV-AIDS) report that his sharing a bed with his woman friend felt good because he could feel close with her. I, of course, had to press for sexual feelings. Nor could I then grasp that he needed me to appreciate quietly, without any interpretation, that he was also reporting his feeling close with me. I was touched recently that an interview of the graphic memoirist, Alison Bechdel, in the *New York Times* magazine (17 May 2015) comfortably went beyond her being lesbian to inquire about her transgender possibilities, her actually wanting to be a man. While she could acknowledge that she has always wanted to be a man, she could also say that she was glad to be a woman who wanted to be a man. Alison Bechdel[5] is our poster girl/boy for the value of psychoanalytic treatment.

I love Dorothy Holmes's quote from Muriel Barbery, "Poverty is a reaper. It harvests everything inside us that might have made us capable of social intercourse with others, and leaves us empty, purged of feeling, so that we endure all the darkness of the present day" (Barbery, 2008). And Holmes is certainly correct that until quite recently psychoanalysis has rejected social science perspectives, or considered them to dilute the essence of psychoanalysis. Freud and his early followers were so intent on preserving and protecting their young science, so afraid of it being usurped by others. And Holmes is correct that Freud would not really consider his own background, especially his being a Jew. Praising Emily Kuriloff's (2014) book on the effects of the Holocaust on Jewish psychoanalysts—what has been unspoken—is appropriate. I wholeheartedly concur. Years ago at the American Psychoanalytic Association, Harold Blum stood up from the audience at a panel, astounding everyone present by telling about re-analyses in which the first analysis by a Holocaust survivor analyst had totally omitted the patient's own Holocaust trauma. We know that trauma can become buried, secreted, unavailable, yet continue to have profound effects on a person and on those around him.

But we need to acknowledge that psychoanalysis and psychoanalysts lag behind the times. At least, we follow the times. We generally are not tradition breakers. Once a major change has occurred in our culture, we adapt ourselves to it: the sexual revolution, feminism, acceptance of LGBTQ, racial bias and bias against otherness because of the colour of one's skin, poverty, foreignness, difference in religion, culture, customs, and so on. At a University Forum of the American Psychoanalytic Association in 2012 on immigration, Richard Shweder,[6] a distinguished cultural anthropologist, regarded female circumcision, especially in Sierra Leone, as women desiring to share their views of women's genital beauty with their female ancestors. Wasn't this a cultural anthropologist trying to show westerners our bias against cultural diversity? Adrienne Harris, as discussant, objected most vigorously that this was genital mutilation—not female circumcision—being hidden behind the pretence of aesthetic preference. She insisted that we needed to stop it, not to tolerate and accept it. Shweder thoroughly disagreed, insisting that Harris and others needed to view this through the eyes of women in Sierra Leone: having smooth, rounded genitalia allowed these young women to bond with their maternal ancestors. Couldn't this be similar to ritual circumcision of males, linking them to their circumcised forefathers, all the way back to Abraham? Although Abraham was the name of my father, most of the audience sided with Harris that this was destructive to women and needed to be stopped. Could Donna Hicks have helped them feel some empathy for the other's position? Not likely! Indeed, there is a group of psychoanalysts working with the United Nations in the attempt to stop mistreatment of women worldwide: genital mutilation, human trafficking. This helps to affirm the dignity of women. And that affirms the dignity of all people!

On the other hand, Holmes is correct that, on our own, we will tend to avoid our difficulties rather than seek to grasp and manage them, especially about difference. We need to have this pushed right up in our faces. I took delight at a 2012 panel of the American Psychoanalytic Association, "Analyzing the children of immigrants", in describing how I had told my Persian patient that she had not as yet acknowledged the major difference between us, that she was Arab and I was Jewish. Of course, I must have said this when I was annoyed at this patient whom I usually enjoyed so very much. She shrieked at me about my ignorance, my stupidity. I was wrong, she wasn't an Arab, she was Persian, she had many Jewish friends, she supported Israel. I wanted to tell this then and want to retell it now so as to help others be prepared for the problems that difference has to cause, at least *some* of the time.

I have especially valued Aisha Abbasi's clinical presentations in which she uses her Pakistani Muslim background in her work with patients with similar as well as with different backgrounds.

A very long time ago, my training analyst told me that I needed to acknowledge how very different I was from the other candidates and graduate analysts at Columbia who did not share my roots. He meant my being the child of Eastern European immigrants who spoke Yiddish, Russian, Polish, who huddled together in a Jewish ghetto in New York City. He meant that my father was a garment worker with a Cheder education, that my mother hadn't continued her education beyond high school in Russia, and so on. But my training analyst, I discovered, also had working class parents, a Germanic name, was Christian, and had married a very wealthy woman. I was to find some others, teachers, supervisors, colleagues, with backgrounds like mine. On a Monday morning early in the analysis he spoke about having read of a new Yiddish-English dictionary in the *New York Times* book review. I sobbed, touched that my analyst, with me in mind, had read this review. Only later, *not then*, did I feel demeaned by his having made a big deal of this. Only later did I feel that he was sequestering my foreignness rather than sharing it with me. When I felt envious of his lovely office in an elegant home, he said that as a psychoanalyst I would not earn the money I imagined. We did not analyse sufficiently how much I wanted to become an insider like him, nor did he invite me to imagine his path. When I felt angry that getting paid for a consultation was difficult, he suggested I donate the money to charity. Charitableness would temper my feelings of emotional deprivation; then we wouldn't have to confront them—in me or, I assume, in him. Did he need to dissociate himself from his own outsider feelings? Mine remained, requiring more analysis.

Salman Akhtar, Kenneth Richman, and Susan Levine basically agree, despite each one's idiosyncratic attempt to characterise a basic human dignity as well as a dignity based on achievement. Basic human dignity is intrinsic to human life; Akhtar might say dignity is intrinsic to all life or perhaps even to inanimate objects, which can have their own profound value. How people lead their lives, what they accomplish, how they behave towards themselves and others determines this second form of dignity, which has to be earned, not merely inherited. Richman clarifies that basic human dignity can never be abrogated. But committing violations of others' dignity does violate the perpetrator's own dignity. Pumla Gobodo-Madikizela and Jessica Stern, in part, sought to restore dignity to their perpetrator interviewees by helping them to acknowledge, with a bit of care and compassion, the violent harm they had caused to others—as well as to themselves.

I'm not sure, however, that it's been made clear how dignified behaviour differs from the dignity of one's achievements, one's position in the world. In a book on dignity, I think we need to differentiate between our narcissistic enhancement because of our accomplishments, and the dignity of using what we have accomplished, learned, achieved so as to really behave with dignity toward ourselves as well as toward others. Indeed, accomplishment can make it more difficult to resist the pressure for even more accomplishment, so that one can be satisfied, content with what one has already done. The pressure to accomplish even more can interfere with one's pleasure in oneself and in others. I am aware of such pressure in myself even as I write this. I accepted this writing assignment just after I had already accepted another one as well as a major reading task. Yes, indeed, writing this epilogue on dignity was not an invitation I wanted to turn down, especially from Susan Levine and the contributors to this volume, all of whom I like and admire greatly. But I've gotten much better at being able to say "no" to myself, to keep myself in balance about writing and speaking tasks, so that I don't feel overly pressured by them. Yes, it was worth my accepting this task but I want to use my own struggle to acknowledge, for myself and for our readers, that I too have to manage that part of me that wants to take on more than I can comfortably do. I feel dignified, I respect myself, when I can keep myself in balance, allow others to take on what I can't do, especially when I want to be generative and nurturing with other younger, aspiring writers and speakers. When I can balance—manage, contain—my own narcissistic neediness as against my loving, generative feelings for others, I feel dignified. When I surrender to my drivenness to accomplish, I do not feel dignified. I feel ashamed of myself.

Kenneth Richman uses *A Little Princess* (Burnett, 2000) well to show us her dignified behaviour and attitude towards herself and others, separate and apart from her being a princess. What a lovely story for children to read and for readers to grasp that a regal attitude toward oneself and others cannot be taken away from us. If you have not yet seen the First Lady's commencement speech at Tuskegee University (9 May 2015), watch it on YouTube. Michelle Obama was wonderful showing young graduates of what had begun as the Tuskegee Normal School for Colored Teachers, then Tuskegee Institute, how she preserves her dignity in the face of contemptuous racist attacks. She insists this is just *noise*, not to be listened to, not to distract or trap one in its hatred. She encourages the graduates to follow her example. Her speech is a testament to human dignity. Cable news slandered her by calling her Obama's "baby mamma", a vile racist epithet. Her forceful counter was to knock aside this *noise* and proceed.

Tuskegee University has a National Center for Bioethics in Research and Health Care, which was founded two years after President Clinton apologised for the Tuskegee Syphilis Experiment. Three hundred and ninety-nine black sharecroppers with syphilis, mostly illiterate, were left untreated for forty years. The study was conducted by the U.S. Public Health Service which told them that they were receiving free health care from the U.S. government. I am appalled by this. Remember, I served in the U.S. Public Health Service. Once upon a time, gross mistreatment of patients could be justified as necessary for medical research. But then it was not considered as a violation of dignity. It was simply not considered. What a fitting setting for Michelle Obama to help to restore dignity that had been abused.

I'm reminded of Dorothy Holmes's emphasis that Ruth Simmons persisted and proceeded, believing in herself and in the power of her mind, to transcend the poverty and bias against her as the daughter of poor sharecroppers in East Texas. Michelle Obama, fortunately, had a very different upbringing. But she shows us her dignity, helping all the rest of us, black, white, and every other colour, ethnicity, gender, to affirm our own. I was so inspired watching the First Lady, and reading these chapters on dignity, to envision inviting Michelle Obama to participate in a University Forum on dignity at the American Psychoanalytic Association. Bringing dignity to psychoanalysts and to psychoanalysis can involve bringing dignified people to us from whom we can learn and who can inspire us. A number of friends spoke reverently about Pumla Gobodo-Madikizela, whom they had met at a conference in South Africa last summer. I am proud to bring her to our group. The same goes for Homi Bhaba, Raka Ray, Zadie Smith, and Chris Abani. I was proud that the cast of our panel, "Analysing the children of immigrants", included analysts born in India, Pakistan, Iran, and Lithuania. Kimberlyn Leary, then the Chair of the Program Committee at APsaA, asked me why I had not included an American-born white analyst. I, of course, responded that we've had enough of them. True to her dignity, she persuaded me to balance our presenters with an "insider".

My insider friend, Peggy Hutson, presented the child of Holocaust survivors. It was fascinating to see analyst and patient become caught up in each one's previously foreclosed trauma, to the benefit of both patient and analyst. Dignity, of course, involves inclusion rather than exclusion. I didn't get that at first.

All the authors of this book emphasise violations of dignity. That is a central focus of this book. Violations of dignity make people feel bad about themselves. It is a major premise of this book that people's dignity needs to be affirmed. Akhtar makes this explicit. He refers to Killingmo's concept that analysts need to present an affirmative attitude towards their patients before they try to interpret conflict. Some time ago I learned about Killingmo from Akhtar (Coen, 2005). Especially the schizoid patient needs to feel the analyst's matching, attunement, holding, affirmation sufficiently—now regarded as legitimate analytic functions—before the analyst can interpret (Akhtar, 1995; Ghent, 1992, 1993; Killingmo, 1989, 1995; Meares, 1993; Meares & Anderson, 1993; Rayner, 1992; Sanville, 1991; Rustin unpublished; Teicholz, 1995). The patient's core self and sense of togetherness are to be enhanced by the analyst's matching and attunement (Rayner, 1992). This work precedes interpretation which leads instead to differentiation. "Empathic withholding of interpretive interruption", as Stone put it (1981), allows the patient to use the analyst and the treatment as he needs without premature disruptive challenge from the analyst (Balint, 1968; Bromberg, 1983; Khan, 1974; Kohut, 1971; Slochower, 1991, 1992, 1996; Steingart, 1983, 1995). The analyst begins by accepting the assigned role he is forced to play in enactments with borderline or narcissistic analysands (Steingart, 1983, 1995). They struggle for control over what is to be regarded as real and unreal about the analytic relationship, sadistically coercing the analyst to their view.

This holds not only for the withdrawn but for all of us. Each author shows us in his or her examples the destructive effects on self-esteem of dignity violations. Robert Kravis shows us this in child development, how parents must be with their children, as well as how analysts in child treatment must be with their child patients. Kravis, like Akhtar, emphasises the reversals. Patients violate the dignity of their analysts, as they repeat in treatment how their own dignity has been violated. It is clinically valuable to emphasise such repetition of dignity violations in treatment rather than to merely object to the intensity of a patient's angry behaviour with the analyst, so easy to do in the treatment of angry, cruel patients.

Richard Kluft shows us violations of a psychoanalyst's dignity by other psychoanalysts. A candidate patient once objected about an eminent teacher's sadistic behaviour toward him, "But she's a psychoanalyst, she's been analysed." Yes, this man was someone who needed to deny his mistreatment by others, who would not *see* the violations of his dignity. Kluft may be giving us too much credit when he describes analysts' sadism in terms of the rigidity of their theories and their unwillingness to learn something new. Indeed, Kluft has made major contributions about traumatised patients and how to help them. Colleagues' envy of Kluft's contributions on trauma can lead them to want to dismiss Kluft and his work. This has to be—unless, of course, we/they can grasp and manage that Kluft is enviable and that we have to contain our envy so that we can instead learn from him. Just this past week, Edgar Levenson, a very accomplished, distinguished psychoanalyst, said at his ninetieth birthday party at the Wm. A. White Institute in New York City, that the good part of his having turned ninety is that colleagues admire him but don't envy him. Kluft warns us that we can cling to constricted versions of our theories so as not to have to see our patients' painful trauma. Analysts' defensive focus on fantasy, wish, conflict, and patients' defensive activity can protect analysts from traumatic external reality. Kluft, like Holmes, cites Kuriloff (2014) about Holocaust-survivor psychoanalysts' extreme clinging to theory so as to protect themselves from their own and their patients' Holocaust trauma.

Susan Levine reads Hitchcock's *Vertigo* via the infliction of dignity violations. She does so skillfully and playfully. The reader has fun following her detective work with the film and the novel on which it was based. She opens her mind to the reader so we can *see*, along with her, and the film's characters, what they, she, and we have not seen before. In this otherwise, very *serious* book on dignity, it is a pleasure to conclude with a highly imaginative essay. And, yes indeed, heed Levine's recommendation to watch *Vertigo* again. This is a dignified way to conclude, showcasing an analyst/writer at her best, showing us how well she opens up her mind to her imagination, which she allows to lead her forward, before she then, again, thinks seriously about where she's gone. That's dignity.

Homi Bhabha[7] seeks to give the different other a voice as he deconstructs the binary positions of insider/outsider. Note how the authors in this volume have done the same, trying to help the outsider each is considering feel like an insider. The "outsider" needs to create his own names, names that soar above those imposed upon him by others. This bestows agency and authority on him. Bhabha emphasises "the discourse of the enslaved or the indentured" (1994, p. 334), using Derek Walcott's poem "Names"[8] to do so. Here is another fine poem for you to read. Walcott opens with: "My race began as the sea began, with no nouns, and with no horizon, with pebbles under my tongue—I began with no memory … no future." He ends triumphantly with: "These palms are greater than Versailles, for no man made them, their fallen columns greater than Castille, no man unmade them" (Walcott, 1986, pp. 305–308).

Notes

1. University Forum, January, 2015, Meeting of the American Psychoanalytic Association, N.Y.C., "How do we negotiate our relationships to terror in political, cultural, and clinical life?" with Jessica Stern, PhD, Brig. Gen. U.S. Army (Ret.), Stephen Xenakis, MD, M. Gerard Fromm PhD, and Jane Tillman, PhD.
2. *New York Times*, 4 January 2013, The Saturday Profile, by Simon Romero, p. 1.
3. Personal communication to Susan Levine, 26 May 2015.
4. At this federal prison, prisoners, like the Swedish terrorist with Jessica Stern, enjoyed sadistically taunting the guards and staff about how they could contaminate the food they prepared with human waste.
5. Author of *Fun Home, Are You My Mother?* and lesbian comic strips, who has spoken at the American Psychoanalytic Association and the Association for Psychoanalytic Medicine.
6. William Claude Reavis Distinguished Service Professor of Human Development at the University of Chicago.
7. Anne F. Rothenberg Professor of the Humanities in the Department of English and Director of the Humanities Center at Harvard University.
8. "Names" was originally published in *Sea Grapes* (1976).

References

Akhtar, S. (1995). Review of *Losing and Fusing: Borderline Transitional Object and Sself Relations* by R. H. Lewin & C. G. Schulz. *Psychoanalytic. Quarterly, 64*: 583–588.
Bhabha, H. K. (1994). *The Location of Culture*. London: Routledge.

Balint, M. (1968). *The Basic Fault: Therapeutic Aspects of Regression*. London: Tavistock.

Barbery, M. (2008). *The Elegance of the Hedgehog*. New York: Europa.

Bromberg, P. (1983). The mirror and the mask—on narcissism and psychoanalytic growth. *Contemporary Psychoanalysis, 19*: 359–387.

Burnett, F. H. (2000). *A Little Princess*. New York: Scholastic.

Coen, S. J. (2005). How to play with patients who would rather remain remote. *Journal of the American Psychoanalytic. Association, 53*: 811–834.

Coen, S. J. (2010). Book review essay: Rereading Masud Khan today: Have his writings fallen with him? *Journal of the American Psychoanalytic Association, 58*: 1005–1020.

Ghent, E. (1992). Paradox and process. *Psychoanalytic Dialogues, 2*: 135–159.

Ghent, E. (1993). Wish, need, and neediness: Commentary on Shabad's "Resentment, indignation, entitlement". *Psychoanalytic Dialogues, 3*: 495–507.

Gobodo-Madikizela, P. (2003). *A Human Being Died That Night: A South African Woman Confronts The Legacy of Apartheid*. Boston, MA: Houghton Mifflin.

Hicks, D. (2011). *Dignity: Its Essential Role in Resolving Conflict*. New Haven: Yale University Press.

Khan, M. M. R. (1974). Vicissitudes of being, knowing, and experiencing in the therapeutic situation. In: *The Privacy of the Self* (pp. 203–218). New York: International Universities Press.

Killingmo, B. (1989). Conflict and deficit: Implications for technique. *International Journal of Psychoanalysis, 70*: 65–79.

Killingmo, B. (1995). Affirmation in psychoanalysis. *International Journal of Psychoanalysis, 76*: 503–518.

Kohut, H. (1971). *The Analysis of the Self*. New York: International Universities Press.

Kuriloff, E. (2014). *Contemporary Psychoanalysis and the Legacy of the Third Reich: History, Memory, Tradition*. New York: Routledge.

Meares, R. (1993). *The Metaphor of Play: Disruption and Restoration in the Borderline Experience*. Northvale, N J: Jason Aronson.

Meares, R., & Anderson, J. (1993). Intimate space—on the developmental significance of exchange. *Contemporary Psychoanalysis, 29*: 595–612.

Rayner, E. (1992). Matching, attunement and the psychoanalytic dialogue. *International Journal of Psychoanalysis, 73*: 39–54.

Rustin, J. (unpublished). The bond of love: bi-directional transformation for patient and analyst.

Sanville, J. (1991). *The Playground of Psychoanalytic Therapy*. Hillsdale, NJ: Analytic Press.

Slochower, J. (1991). Variations in the analytic holding environment. *International Journal of Psychoanalysis, 72*: 709–717.

Slochower, J. (1992). A hateful borderline patient and the holding environment. *Contemporary Psychoanalysis, 28*: 72–88.

Slochower, J. (1996). Holding and the fate of the analyst's subjectivity. *Psychoanalytic Dialogues, 6*: 323–353.

Steingart, I. (1983). *Pathological Play in Borderline and Narcissistic Personalities: Patterns of Real and Not-Real Meaning in Splitting and Denial, Love, Hate, and Ambivalence, and Social Ideology*. New York: SP Medical and Scientific Books.

Steingart, I. (1995). *A Thing Apart: Love and Reality in the Therapeutic Relationship*. Northvale, NJ: Jason Aronson.

Stern, J. (2014). A case study of a Neo-Nazi and his reintegration into Swedish society. *Behavioral Sciences and the Law*. Wiley Online Library DOL 10.10021bal.2119.

Stone, L. (1981). Notes on the noninterpretive elements in the psychoanalytic situation and process. *Journal of the American Psychoanalytic Association, 29*: 89–118.

Teicholz, J. (1995). Loewald's "positive neutrality" and the affirmative potential of psychoanalytic interpretations. *Psychoanalytic Study of the Child, 50*: 048–075.

Walcott, D. (1986). *Collected Poems 1948–1984*. New York: Farrar, Straus & Giroux.

For Product Safety Concerns and Information please contact our EU
representative GPSR@taylorandfrancis.com
Taylor & Francis Verlag GmbH, Kaufingerstraße 24, 80331 München, Germany

www.ingramcontent.com/pod-product-compliance
Lightning Source LLC
Chambersburg PA
CBHW070323270326
41926CB00017B/3732